Cram101 Textbook Outlines to accompany:

Organizational Behavior

Moorhead and Griffin, 7th Edition

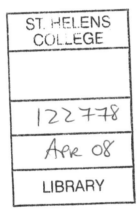
An Academic Internet Publishers (AIPI) publication (c) 2007.

You have a discounted membership at www.Cram101.com with this book.

Get all of the practice tests for the chapters of this textbook, and access in-depth reference material for writing essays and papers. Here is an example from a Cram101 Biology text:

When you need problem solving help with math, stats, and other disciplines, www.Cram101.com will walk through the formulas and solutions step by step.

With Cram101.com online, you also have access to extensive reference material.

You will nail those essays and papers. Here is an example from a Cram101 Biology text:

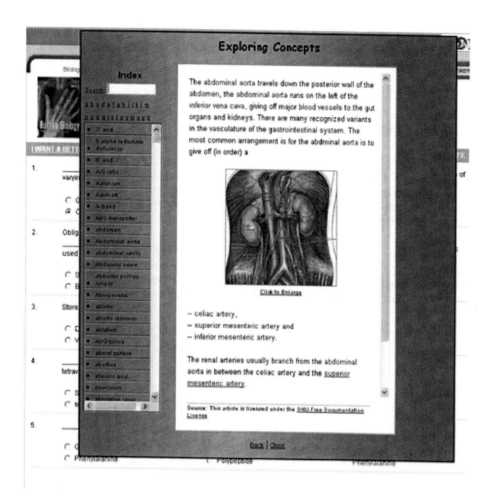

Visit **www.Cram101.com**, click Sign Up at the top of the screen, and enter DK73DW in the promo code box on the registration screen. Access to www.Cram101.com is normally $9.95, but because you have purchased this book, your access fee is only $4.95. Sign up and stop highlighting textbooks forever.

Learning System

Cram101 Textbook Outlines is a learning system. The notes in this book are the highlights of your textbook, you will never have to highlight a book again.

How to use this book. Take this book to class, it is your notebook for the lecture. The notes and highlights on the left hand side of the pages follow the outline and order of the textbook. All you have to do is follow along while your intructor presents the lecture. Circle the items emphasized in class and add other important information on the right side. With Cram101 Textbook Outlines you'll spend less time writing and more time listening. Learning becomes more efficient.

Cram101.com Online

Increase your studying efficiency by using Cram101.com's practice tests and online reference material. It is the perfect complement to Cram101 Textbook Outlines. Use self-teaching matching tests or simulate in-class testing with comprehensive multiple choice tests, or simply use Cram's true and false tests for quick review. Cram101.com even allows you to enter your in-class notes for an integrated studying format combining the textbook notes with your class notes.

Visit **www.Cram101.com**, click Sign Up at the top of the screen, and enter **DK73DW1776** in the promo code box on the registration screen. Access to www.Cram101.com is normally $9.95, but because you have purchased this book, your access fee is only $4.95. Sign up and stop highlighting textbooks forever.

Organizational Behavior
Moorhead and Griffin, 7th

CONTENTS

Management	Management characterizes the process of leading and directing all or part of an organization, often a business, through the deployment and manipulation of resources. Early twentieth-century management writer Mary Parker Follett defined management as "the art of getting things done through people."
Corporation	A legal entity chartered by a state or the Federal government that is distinct and separate from the individuals who own it is a corporation. This separation gives the corporation unique powers which other legal entities lack.
Warehouse	Warehouse refers to a location, often decentralized, that a firm uses to store, consolidate, age, or mix stock; house product-recall programs; or ease tax burdens.
Industry	A group of firms that produce identical or similar products is an industry. It is also used specifically to refer to an area of economic production focused on manufacturing which involves large amounts of capital investment before any profit can be realized, also called "heavy industry".
Firm	An organization that employs resources to produce a good or service for profit and owns and operates one or more plants is referred to as a firm.
Premium	Premium refers to the fee charged by an insurance company for an insurance policy. The rate of losses must be relatively predictable: In order to set the premium (prices) insurers must be able to estimate them accurately.
Service	Service refers to a "non tangible product" that is not embodied in a physical good and that typically effects some change in another product, person, or institution. Contrasts with good.
Chief operating officer	A chief operating officer is a corporate officer responsible for managing the day-to-day activities of the corporation. The chief operating officer is one of the highest ranking members of an organization, monitoring the daily operations of the company and reporting to the chief executive officer directly.
Chief executive officer	A chief executive officer is the highest-ranking corporate officer or executive officer of a corporation, or agency. In closely held corporations, it is general business culture that the office chief executive officer is also the chairman of the board.
Freight in	Freight in refers to a part of the cost of inventory. It is the transportation cost of the goods purchased.
Organizational Behavior	The study of human behavior in organizational settings, the interface between human behavior and the organization, and the organization itself is called organizational behavior.
Customer satisfaction	Customer satisfaction is a business term which is used to capture the idea of measuring how satisfied an enterprise's customers are with the organization's efforts in a marketplace.
Leadership	Management merely consists of leadership applied to business situations; or in other words: management forms a sub-set of the broader process of leadership.
Productivity	Productivity refers to the total output of goods and services in a given period of time divided by work hours.
Technology	The body of knowledge and techniques that can be used to combine economic resources to produce goods and services is called technology.
Customer service	The ability of logistics management to satisfy users in terms of time, dependability, communication, and convenience is called the customer service.
Customer database	Customer database refers to a computer database specifically designed for storage, retrieval, and analysis of customer data by marketers.
Annual report	An annual report is prepared by corporate management that presents financial information including financial statements, footnotes, and the management discussion and analysis.
Trust	An arrangement in which shareholders of independent firms agree to give up their stock in exchange for trust certificates that entitle them to a share of the trust's common profits.

Foundation	A Foundation is a type of philanthropic organization set up by either individuals or institutions as a legal entity (either as a corporation or trust) with the purpose of distributing grants to support causes in line with the goals of the foundation.
Comprehensive	A comprehensive refers to a layout accurate in size, color, scheme, and other necessary details to show how a final ad will look. For presentation only, never for reproduction.
Consultant	A professional that provides expert advice in a particular field or area in which customers occasionaly require this type of knowledge is a consultant.
Policy	Similar to a script in that a policy can be a less than completely rational decision-making method. Involves the use of a pre-existing set of decision steps for any problem that presents itself.
Points	Loan origination fees that may be deductible as interest by a buyer of property. A seller of property who pays points reduces the selling price by the amount of the points paid for the buyer.
Logo	Logo refers to device or other brand name that cannot be spoken.
Corporate Strategy	Corporate strategy is concerned with the firm's choice of business, markets and activities and thus it defines the overall scope and direction of the business.
Hosting	Internet hosting service is a service that runs Internet servers, allowing organizations and individuals to serve content on the Internet.
Context	The effect of the background under which a message often takes on more and richer meaning is a context. Context is especially important in cross-cultural interactions because some cultures are said to be high context or low context.
Evaluation	The consumer's appraisal of the product or brand on important attributes is called evaluation.
Variable	A variable is something measured by a number; it is used to analyze what happens to other things when the size of that number changes.
Possession	Possession refers to respecting real property, exclusive dominion and control such as owners of like property usually exercise over it. Manual control of personal property either as owner or as one having a qualified right in it.
Empowerment	Giving employees the authority and responsibility to respond quickly to customer requests is called empowerment.
Interest	In finance and economics, interest is the price paid by a borrower for the use of a lender's money. In other words, interest is the amount of paid to "rent" money for a period of time.
Wage	The payment for the service of a unit of labor, per unit time. In trade theory, it is the only payment to labor, usually unskilled labor. In empirical work, wage data may exclude other compenzation, which must be added to get the total cost of employment.
Forbes	David Churbuck founded online Forbes in 1996. The site drew attention when it uncovered Stephen Glass' journalistic fraud in The New Republic in 1998, a scoop that gave credibility to internet journalism.
Collaboration	Collaboration occurs when the interaction between groups is very important to goal attainment and the goals are compatible. Wherein people work together —applying both to the work of individuals as well as larger collectives and societies.
Allocate	Allocate refers to the assignment of income for various tax purposes. A multistate corporation's nonbusiness income usually is distributed to the state where the nonbusiness assets are located; it is not apportioned with the rest of the entity's income.
Economics	The social science dealing with the use of scarce resources to obtain the maximum satisfaction of society's virtually unlimited economic wants is an economics.
Human Relations	Human relations movement refers to the period following the Hawthorne Studies, that was based on the

Go to **Cram101.com** for the Practice Tests for this Chapter.

Movement	assumption that employee satisfaction is a key determinant of performance. It marked the beginning of organizational development.
Maslow	Maslow was an American psychologist. He is mostly noted today for his proposal of a hierarchy of human needs.
Human relations approach	Human relations approach refers the idea that the best way to improve production was to respect workers and show concern for their needs. Became popular in the 1920s and remained influential through the 1950s.
Enterprise	Enterprise refers to another name for a business organization. Other similar terms are business firm, sometimes simply business, sometimes simply firm, as well as company, and entity.
Scientific management	Studying workers to find the most efficient ways of doing things and then teaching people those techniques is scientific management.
Theory X	Theory X refers to concept described by Douglas McGregor indicating an approach to management that takes a negative and pessimistic view of workers.
Theory Y	Theory Y refers to concept described by Douglas McGregor reflecting an approach to management that takes a positive and optimistic perspective on workers.
Organizational goals	Objectives that management seeks to achieve in pursuing the firm's purpose are organizational goals.
Security	Security refers to a claim on the borrower future income that is sold by the borrower to the lender. A security is a type of transferable interest representing financial value.
Supply and demand	The partial equilibrium supply and demand economic model originally developed by Alfred Marshall attempts to describe, explain, and predict changes in the price and quantity of goods sold in competitive markets.
Supply	Supply is the aggregate amount of any material good that can be called into being at a certain price point; it comprises one half of the equation of supply and demand. In classical economic theory, a curve representing supply is one of the factors that produce price.
Bankruptcy	Bankruptcy is a legally declared inability or impairment of ability of an individual or organization to pay their creditors.
Personal finance	Personal finance is the application of the principles of financial economics to an individual's (or a family's) financial decisions.
Contribution	In business organization law, the cash or property contributed to a business by its owners is referred to as contribution.
Organization structure	The system of task, reporting, and authority relationships within which the organization does its work is referred to as the organization structure.
Labor	People's physical and mental talents and efforts that are used to help produce goods and services are called labor.
Human resource planning	Forecasting the organization's human resource needs, developing replacement charts for all levels of the organization, and preparing inventories of the skills and abilities individuals need to move within the organization is called human resource planning.
Labor market	Any arrangement that brings buyers and sellers of labor services together to agree on conditions of work and pay is called a labor market.
Market	A market is, as defined in economics, a social arrangement that allows buyers and sellers to discover information and carry out a voluntary exchange of goods or services.
Industrial	Industrial engineering is the engineering discipline that concerns the development, improvement,

engineering	implementation and evaluation of integrated systems of people, knowledge, equipment, energy, material and process.
Labor relations	The field of labor relations looks at the relationship between management and workers, particularly groups of workers represented by a labor union.
Controlling	A management function that involves determining whether or not an organization is progressing toward its goals and objectives, and taking corrective action if it is not is called controlling.
Complexity	The technical sophistication of the product and hence the amount of understanding required to use it is referred to as complexity. It is the opposite of simplicity.
Technological change	The introduction of new methods of production or new products intended to increase the productivity of existing inputs or to raise marginal products is a technological change.
Respondent	Respondent refers to a term often used to describe the party charged in an administrative proceeding. The party adverse to the appellant in a case appealed to a higher court.
Margin	A deposit by a buyer in stocks with a seller or a stockbroker, as security to cover fluctuations in the market in reference to stocks that the buyer has purchased but for which he has not paid is a margin. Commodities are also traded on margin.
Yield	The interest rate that equates a future value or an annuity to a given present value is a yield.
Contingency perspective	Contingency perspective suggests that, in most organizations, situations and outcomes are contingent on, or influenced by, other variables.
Manufacturing	Production of goods primarily by the application of labor and capital to raw materials and other intermediate inputs, in contrast to agriculture, mining, forestry, fishing, and services a manufacturing.
Operation	A standardized method or technique that is performed repetitively, often on different materials resulting in different finished goods is called an operation.
Inputs	The inputs used by a firm or an economy are the labor, raw materials, electricity and other resources it uses to produce its outputs.
Profit	Profit refers to the return to the resource entrepreneurial ability; total revenue minus total cost.
Stockholder	A stockholder is an individual or company (including a corporation) that legally owns one or more shares of stock in a joined stock company. The shareholders are the owners of a corporation. Companies listed at the stock market strive to enhance shareholder value.
Investment	Investment refers to spending for the production and accumulation of capital and additions to inventories. In a financial sense, buying an asset with the expectation of making a return.
Dividend	Amount of corporate profits paid out for each share of stock is referred to as dividend.
Shell	One of the original Seven Sisters, Royal Dutch/Shell is the world's third-largest oil company by revenue, and a major player in the petrochemical industry and the solar energy business. Shell has six core businesses: Exploration and Production, Gas and Power, Downstream, Chemicals, Renewables, and Trading/Shipping, and operates in more than 140 countries.
Contingency approach	Contingency approach refers to the dominant perspective in organizational behavior, it argues that there's no single best way to manage behavior. What 'works' in any given context depends on the complex interplay between a variety of person and situational factors.
Universal approach	An approach to organization design where prescriptions or propositions are designed to work in any circumstance is called universal approach.
Direct relationship	Direct relationship refers to the relationship between two variables that change in the same direction, for example, product price and quantity supplied.

Go to **Cram101.com** for the Practice Tests for this Chapter.

Compaq	Compaq was founded in February 1982 by Rod Canion, Jim Harris and Bill Murto, three senior managers from semiconductor manufacturer Texas Instruments. Each invested $1,000 to form the company. Their first venture capital came from Ben Rosen and Sevin-Rosen partners. It is often told that the architecture of the original PC was first sketched out on a placemat by the founders while dining in the Houston restaurant, House of Pies.
Marketing	Promoting and selling products or services to customers, or prospective customers, is referred to as marketing.
Board of directors	The group of individuals elected by the stockholders of a corporation to oversee its operations is a board of directors.
Specialist	A specialist is a trader who makes a market in one or several stocks and holds the limit order book for those stocks.
Bill Gates	Bill Gates is the co-founder, chairman, former chief software architect, and former CEO of Microsoft Corporation. He is one of the best-known entrepreneurs of the personal computer revolution and he is widely respected for his foresight and ambition.
Jack Welch	In 1986, GE acquired NBC. During the 90s, Jack Welch helped to modernize GE by emphasizing a shift from manufacturing to services. He also made hundreds of acquisitions and made a push to dominate markets abroad. Welch adopted the Six Sigma quality program in late 1995.
Classical organization theory	An early approach to management that focused on how organizations can be structured most effectively to meet their goals is a classical organization theory.
Weber	Weber was a German political economist and sociologist who is considered one of the founders of the modern study of sociology and public administration. His major works deal with rationalization in sociology of religion and government, but he also wrote much in the field of economics. His most popular work is his essay The Protestant Ethic and the Spirit of Capitalism.
Interpersonal skills	Interpersonal skills are used to communicate with, understand, and motivate individuals and groups.
Business Week	Business Week is a business magazine published by McGraw-Hill. It was first published in 1929 under the direction of Malcolm Muir, who was serving as president of the McGraw-Hill Publishing company at the time. It is considered to be the standard both in industry and among students.
Financial statement	Financial statement refers to a summary of all the transactions that have occurred over a particular period.
Revenue	Revenue is a U.S. business term for the amount of money that a company receives from its activities, mostly from sales of products and/or services to customers.
Appeal	Appeal refers to the act of asking an appellate court to overturn a decision after the trial court's final judgment has been entered.
Loyalty	Marketers tend to define customer loyalty as making repeat purchases. Some argue that it should be defined attitudinally as a strongly positive feeling about the brand.
Assessment	Collecting information and providing feedback to employees about their behavior, communication style, or skills is an assessment.
Balance	In banking and accountancy, the outstanding balance is the amount of money owned, (or due), that remains in a deposit account (or a loan account) at a given date, after all past remittances, payments and withdrawal have been accounted for. It can be positive (then, in the balance sheet of a firm, it is an asset) or negative (a liability).
Brand	A name, symbol, or design that identifies the goods or services of one seller or group of sellers and distinguishes them from the goods and services of competitors is a brand.

Go to **Cram101.com** for the Practice Tests for this Chapter.

Licensing	Licensing is a form of strategic alliance which involves the sale of a right to use certain proprietary knowledge (so called intellectual property) in a defined way.
Extrinsic reward	Extrinsic reward refers to something given to you by someone else as recognition for good work; extrinsic rewards include pay increases, praise, and promotions.
Welfare	Welfare refers to the economic well being of an individual, group, or economy. For individuals, it is conceptualized by a utility function. For groups, including countries and the world, it is a tricky philosophical concept, since individuals fare differently.
Instrument	Instrument refers to an economic variable that is controlled by policy makers and can be used to influence other variables, called targets. Examples are monetary and fiscal policies used to achieve external and internal balance.
Brief	Brief refers to a statement of a party's case or legal arguments, usually prepared by an attorney. Also used to make legal arguments before appellate courts.
Bureaucracy	Bureaucracy refers to an organization with many layers of managers who set rules and regulations and oversee all decisions.

Management	Management characterizes the process of leading and directing all or part of an organization, often a business, through the deployment and manipulation of resources. Early twentieth-century management writer Mary Parker Follett defined management as "the art of getting things done through people."
Industry	A group of firms that produce identical or similar products is an industry. It is also used specifically to refer to an area of economic production focused on manufacturing which involves large amounts of capital investment before any profit can be realized, also called "heavy industry".
Continental Airlines	Continental Airlines is an airline of the United States. Based in Houston, Texas, it is the 6th largest airline in the U.S. and the 8th largest in the world. Continental's tagline, since 1998, has been Work Hard, Fly Right.
Bankruptcy	Bankruptcy is a legally declared inability or impairment of ability of an individual or organization to pay their creditors.
Trust	An arrangement in which shareholders of independent firms agree to give up their stock in exchange for trust certificates that entitle them to a share of the trust's common profits.
Marketing	Promoting and selling products or services to customers, or prospective customers, is referred to as marketing.
Negligence	The omission to do something that a reasonable person, guided by those considerations that ordinarily regulate human affairs, would do, or doing something that a prudent and reasonable person would not do is negligence.
Organizational Behavior	The study of human behavior in organizational settings, the interface between human behavior and the organization, and the organization itself is called organizational behavior.
Layoff	A layoff is the termination of an employee or (more commonly) a group of employees for business reasons, such as the decision that certain positions are no longer necessary.
Downsizing	The process of eliminating managerial and non-managerial positions are called downsizing.
Security	Security refers to a claim on the borrower future income that is sold by the borrower to the lender. A security is a type of transferable interest representing financial value.
Firm	An organization that employs resources to produce a good or service for profit and owns and operates one or more plants is referred to as a firm.
Distribution	Distribution in economics, the manner in which total output and income is distributed among individuals or factors.
Downturn	A decline in a stock market or economic cycle is a downturn.
Aid	Assistance provided by countries and by international institutions such as the World Bank to developing countries in the form of monetary grants, loans at low interest rates, in kind, or a combination of these is called aid. Aid can also refer to assistance of any type rendered to benefit some group or individual.
Market	A market is, as defined in economics, a social arrangement that allows buyers and sellers to discover information and carry out a voluntary exchange of goods or services.
Recovery	Characterized by rizing output, falling unemployment, rizing profits, and increasing economic activity following a decline is a recovery.
Operation	A standardized method or technique that is performed repetitively, often on different materials resulting in different finished goods is called an operation.
Globalization	The increasing world-wide integration of markets for goods, services and capital that attracted special attention in the late 1990s is called globalization.

Technology	The body of knowledge and techniques that can be used to combine economic resources to produce goods and services is called technology.
Chief financial officer	Chief financial officer refers to executive responsible for overseeing the financial operations of an organization.
Public relations	Public relations refers to the management function that evaluates public attitudes, changes policies and procedures in response to the public's requests, and executes a program of action and information to earn public understanding and acceptance.
Human resources	Human resources refers to the individuals within the firm, and to the portion of the firm's organization that deals with hiring, firing, training, and other personnel issues.
Appreciation	Appreciation refers to a rise in the value of a country's currency on the exchange market, relative either to a particular other currency or to a weighted average of other currencies. The currency is said to appreciate. Opposite of 'depreciation.' Appreciation can also refer to the increase in value of any asset.
Contribution	In business organization law, the cash or property contributed to a business by its owners is referred to as contribution.
Screening	Screening in economics refers to a strategy of combating adverse selection, one of the potential decision-making complications in cases of asymmetric information.
Pfizer	Pfizer is the world's largest pharmaceutical company based in New York City. It produces the number-one selling drug Lipitor (atorvastatin, used to lower blood cholesterol).
Organization culture	The set of values that helps the organization's employees understand which actions are considered acceptable and which unacceptable is referred to as the organization culture.
Group dynamics	The term group dynamics implies that individual behaviors may differ depending on individuals' current or prospective connections to a sociological group. Group dynamics is the field of study within the social sciences that focuses on the nature of groups. Urges to belong or to identify may make for distinctly different attitudes (recognized or unrecognized), and the influence of a group may rapidly become strong, influencing or overwhelming individual proclivities and actions.
Joint venture	Joint venture refers to an undertaking by two parties for a specific purpose and duration, taking any of several legal forms.
Competitor	Other organizations in the same industry or type of business that provide a good or service to the same set of customers is referred to as a competitor.
Union	A worker association that bargains with employers over wages and working conditions is called a union.
General Electric	In 1876, Thomas Alva Edison opened a new laboratory in Menlo Park, New Jersey. Out of the laboratory was to come perhaps the most famous invention of all—a successful development of the incandescent electric lamp. By 1890, Edison had organized his various businesses into the Edison General Electric Company.
Domestic	From or in one's own country. A domestic producer is one that produces inside the home country. A domestic price is the price inside the home country. Opposite of 'foreign' or 'world.'.
Context	The effect of the background under which a message often takes on more and richer meaning is a context. Context is especially important in cross-cultural interactions because some cultures are said to be high context or low context.
Management functions	Management functions were set forth by Henri Fayol; they include planning, organizing, leading, and controling.

US airways	US Airways is an airline based in Tempe, Arizona, owned by US Airways Group, Inc.. As of May 2006, the combined airline is the fifth largest airline in the United States and has a fleet of 358 mainline jet aircraft and 295 express aircraft connecting 237 destinations in North America, Central America, the Caribbean, Hawaii, and Europe.
Sears	Before the Sears catalog, farmers typically bought supplies (often at very high prices) from local general stores. Sears took advantage of this by publishing his catalog with clearly stated prices, so that consumers could know what he was selling and at what price, and order and obtain them conveniently. The catalog business soon grew quickly.
Tactic	A short-term immediate decision that, in its totality, leads to the achievement of strategic goals is called a tactic.
Environmental scanning	The process of identifying the factors that can affect marketing success is environmental scanning.
Management team	A management team is directly responsible for managing the day-to-day operations (and profitability) of a company.
Corporation	A legal entity chartered by a state or the Federal government that is distinct and separate from the individuals who own it is a corporation. This separation gives the corporation unique powers which other legal entities lack.
Authority	Authority in agency law, refers to an agent's ability to affect his principal's legal relations with third parties. Also used to refer to an actor's legal power or ability to do something. In addition, sometimes used to refer to a statute, case, or other legal source that justifies a particular result.
Leadership	Management merely consists of leadership applied to business situations; or in other words: management forms a sub-set of the broader process of leadership.
Multinational corporation	An organization that manufactures and markets products in many different countries and has multinational stock ownership and multinational management is referred to as multinational corporation.
Inventory	Tangible property held for sale in the normal course of business or used in producing goods or services for sale is an inventory.
Evaluation	The consumer's appraisal of the product or brand on important attributes is called evaluation.
General Motors	General Motors is the world's largest automaker. Founded in 1908, today it employs about 327,000 people around the world. With global headquarters in Detroit, it manufactures its cars and trucks in 33 countries.
Controlling	A management function that involves determining whether or not an organization is progressing toward its goals and objectives, and taking corrective action if it is not is called controlling.
Figurehead role	In the figurehead role, the manager represents the organization in all matters of formality. The top level manager represents the company legally and socially to those outside of the organization. The supervisor represents the work group to higher management and higher management to the work group.
Informational roles	Informational roles in management refers to the monitor, the disseminator, and the spokesperson.
Dell Computer	Dell Computer, formerly PC's Limited, was founded on the principle that by selling personal computer systems directly to customers, PC's Limited could best understand their needs and provide the most effective computing solutions to meet those needs.

Microsoft	Microsoft is a multinational computer technology corporation with 2004 global annual sales of US$39.79 billion and 71,553 employees in 102 countries and regions as of July 2006. It develops, manufactures, licenses, and supports a wide range of software products for computing devices.
Entrepreneur	The owner/operator. The person who organizes, manages, and assumes the risks of a firm, taking a new idea or a new product and turning it into a successful business is an entrepreneur.
Innovation	Innovation refers to the first commercially successful introduction of a new product, the use of a new method of production, or the creation of a new form of business organization.
Labor	People's physical and mental talents and efforts that are used to help produce goods and services are called labor.
Labor union	A group of workers organized to advance the interests of the group is called a labor union.
Contract	A contract is a "promise" or an "agreement" that is enforced or recognized by the law. In the civil law, a contract is considered to be part of the general law of obligations.
Press release	A written public news announcement normally distributed to major news services is referred to as press release.
Exxon	Exxon formally replaced the Esso, Enco, and Humble brands on January 1, 1973, in the USA. The name Esso, pronounced S-O, attracted protests from other Standard Oil spinoffs because of its similarity to the name of the parent company, Standard Oil.
Interpersonal skills	Interpersonal skills are used to communicate with, understand, and motivate individuals and groups.
Conceptual skill	The ability to analyze and solve complex problems is called conceptual skill. Conceptual skill involves the formulation of ideas.
Basic research	Involves discovering new knowledge rather than solving specific problems is called basic research.
Customer satisfaction	Customer satisfaction is a business term which is used to capture the idea of measuring how satisfied an enterprise's customers are with the organization's efforts in a marketplace.
Service	Service refers to a "non tangible product" that is not embodied in a physical good and that typically effects some change in another product, person, or institution. Contrasts with good.
Information technology	Information technology refers to technology that helps companies change business by allowing them to use new methods.
Slowdown	A slowdown is an industrial action in which employees perform their duties but seek to reduce productivity or efficiency in their performance of these duties. A slowdown may be used as either a prelude or an alternative to a strike, as it is seen as less disruptive as well as less risky and costly for workers and their union.
Boot	Boot is any type of personal property received in a real property transaction that is not like kind, such as cash, mortgage notes, a boat or stock. The exchanger pays taxes on the boot to the extent of recognized capital gain. In an exchange if any funds are not used in purchasing the replacement property, that also will be called boot.
Workforce diversity	The similarities and differences in such characteristics as age, gender, ethnic heritage, physical abilities and disabilities, race, and sexual orientation among the employees of organizations is called workforce diversity.
Apple Computer	Apple Computer has been a major player in the evolution of personal computing since its

Go to **Cram101.com** for the Practice Tests for this Chapter.

founding in 1976. The Apple II microcomputer, introduced in 1977, was a hit with home users.

Assignment	A transfer of property or some right or interest is referred to as assignment.
Composition	An out-of-court settlement in which creditors agree to accept a fractional settlement on their original claim is referred to as composition.
Americans with Disabilities Act	The Americans with Disabilities Act of 1990 is a wide-ranging civil rights law that prohibits discrimination based on disability.
Equal employment opportunity	The government's attempt to ensure that all individuals have an equal opportunity for employment, regardless of race, color, religion, sex, age, disability, or national origin is equal employment opportunity.
Generation x	Generation x refers to the 15 percent of the U.S. population born between 1965 and 1976 a period also known as the baby bust.
Recession	A significant decline in economic activity. In the U.S., recession is approximately defined as two successive quarters of falling GDP, as judged by NBER.
Enron	Enron Corportaion's global reputation was undermined by persistent rumours of bribery and political pressure to secure contracts in Central America, South America, Africa, and the Philippines. Especially controversial was its $3 billion contract with the Maharashtra State Electricity Board in India, where it is alleged that Enron officials used political connections within the Clinton and Bush administrations to exert pressure on the board.
Profit	Profit refers to the return to the resource entrepreneurial ability; total revenue minus total cost.
Verizon	Verizon a Dow 30 company, is a broadband and telecommunications provider. The acquisition of GTE by Bell Atlantic, on June 30, 2000, which formed Verizon, was among the largest mergers in United States business history. Verizon, with MCI, is currently the second largest telecommunications company in the United States.
Investment	Investment refers to spending for the production and accumulation of capital and additions to inventories. In a financial sense, buying an asset with the expectation of making a return.
Motorola	The Six Sigma quality system was developed at Motorola even though it became most well known because of its use by General Electric. It was created by engineer Bill Smith, under the direction of Bob Galvin (son of founder Paul Galvin) when he was running the company.
Hilton Hotels	Since its founding in 1919, Hilton Hotels has grown to become the America's first coast-to-coast hotel chain, placing special emphasis on business travel, but owning and operating a number of resorts and leisure-oriented hotels as well. Hilton Hotels became the first international hotel chain with the opening of the Caribe Hilton in San Juan, Puerto Rico.
Change management	Change management is the process of developing a planned approach to change in an organization. Typically the objective is to maximize the collective benefits for all people involved in the change and minimize the risk of failure of implementing the change.
Information system	An information system is a system whether automated or manual, that comprises people, machines, and/or methods organized to collect, process, transmit, and disseminate data that represent user information.
Intranet	Intranet refers to a companywide network, closed to public access, that uses Internet-type technology. A set of communications links within one company that travel over the Internet but are closed to public access.
Flat structure	Flat structure refers to a management structure characterized by an overall broad span of control and relatively few hierarchical levels.

Social responsibility	Social responsibility is a doctrine that claims that an entity whether it is state, government, corporation, organization or individual has a responsibility to society.
Competitive Strategy	An outline of how a business intends to compete with other firms in the same industry is called competitive strategy.
Service technology	Technology characterized by intangible outputs and direct contact between employees and customers is called service technology.
Manufacturing	Production of goods primarily by the application of labor and capital to raw materials and other intermediate inputs, in contrast to agriculture, mining, forestry, fishing, and services a manufacturing.
Productivity	Productivity refers to the total output of goods and services in a given period of time divided by work hours.
Differentiation Strategy	Differentiation strategy requires innovation and significant points of difference in product offerings, brand image, higher quality, advanced technology, or superior service in a relatively broad array of market segments.
Cost leadership	Organization's ability to achieve lower costs relative to competitors through productivity and efficiency improvements, elimination of waste, and tight cost control is cost leadership.
Cost Leadership Strategy	Using a serious commitment to reducing expenses that, in turn, lowers the price of the items sold in a relatively broad array of market segments is called cost leadership strategy.
Instrument	Instrument refers to an economic variable that is controlled by policy makers and can be used to influence other variables, called targets. Examples are monetary and fiscal policies used to achieve external and internal balance.
Timex	Timex is the best-known American watch manufacturer, famous for half a century for durable low-cost timepieces. Timex headquarters are located in Middlebury, Connecticut.
Targeting	In advertizing, targeting is to select a demographic or other group of people to advertise to, and create advertisements appropriately.
Business strategy	Business strategy, which refers to the aggregated operational strategies of single business firm or that of an SBU in a diversified corporation refers to the way in which a firm competes in its chosen arenas.
Complexity	The technical sophistication of the product and hence the amount of understanding required to use it is referred to as complexity. It is the opposite of simplicity.
Economy	The income, expenditures, and resources that affect the cost of running a business and household are called an economy.
Trend	Trend refers to the long-term movement of an economic variable, such as its average rate of increase or decrease over enough years to encompass several business cycles.
Shell	One of the original Seven Sisters, Royal Dutch/Shell is the world's third-largest oil company by revenue, and a major player in the petrochemical industry and the solar energy business. Shell has six core businesses: Exploration and Production, Gas and Power, Downstream, Chemicals, Renewables, and Trading/Shipping, and operates in more than 140 countries.
Writing off	Writing off refers to the allocation of the cost of an asset over several accounting periods. Also, to expense a cost, that is, put it on the income statement as an expense.
Capitalism	Capitalism refers to an economic system in which capital is mostly owned by private individuals and corporations. Contrasts with communism.
Trading bloc	Trading bloc refers to a group of countries that are somehow closely associated in international trade, usually in some sort of PTA.

Fund	Independent accounting entity with a self-balancing set of accounts segregated for the purposes of carrying on specific activities is referred to as a fund.
Face value	The nominal or par value of an instrument as expressed on its face is referred to as the face value.
Accounting	A system that collects and processes financial information about an organization and reports that information to decision makers is referred to as accounting.
Stock option	A stock option is a specific type of option that uses the stock itself as an underlying instrument to determine the option's pay-off and therefore its value.
Option	A contract that gives the purchaser the option to buy or sell the underlying financial instrument at a specified price, called the exercise price or strike price, within a specific period of time.
Stock	In financial terminology, stock is the capital raized by a corporation, through the issuance and sale of shares.
Interest	In finance and economics, interest is the price paid by a borrower for the use of a lender's money. In other words, interest is the amount of paid to "rent" money for a period of time.
Corporate tax	Corporate tax refers to a direct tax levied by various jurisdictions on the profits made by companies or associations. As a general principle, this varies substantially between jurisdictions.
Policy	Similar to a script in that a policy can be a less than completely rational decision-making method. Involves the use of a pre-existing set of decision steps for any problem that presents itself.
Ethical dilemma	An ethical dilemma is a situation that often involves an apparent conflict between moral imperatives, in which to obey one would result in transgressing another.
Advertising campaign	A comprehensive advertising plan that consists of a series of messages in a variety of media that center on a single theme or idea is referred to as an advertising campaign.
Advertising	Advertising refers to paid, nonpersonal communication through various media by organizations and individuals who are in some way identified in the advertising message.
Inputs	The inputs used by a firm or an economy are the labor, raw materials, electricity and other resources it uses to produce its outputs.
Honda	With more than 14 million internal combustion engines built each year, Honda is the largest engine-maker in the world. In 2004, the company began to produce diesel motors, which were both very quiet whilst not requiring particulate filters to pass pollution standards. It is arguable, however, that the foundation of their success is the motorcycle division.
Quality improvement	Quality is inversely proportional to variability thus quality Improvement is the reduction of variability in products and processes.
Raw material	Raw material refers to a good that has not been transformed by production; a primary product.
Tangible	Having a physical existence is referred to as the tangible. Personal property other than real estate, such as cars, boats, stocks, or other assets.
Variable	A variable is something measured by a number; it is used to analyze what happens to other things when the size of that number changes.
Overtime	Overtime is the amount of time someone works beyond normal working hours.
Tradeoff	The sacrifice of some or all of one economic goal, good, or service to achieve some other goal, good, or service is a tradeoff.

Stakeholder	A stakeholder is an individual or group with a vested interest in or expectation for organizational performance. Usually stakeholders can either have an effect on or are affected by an organization.
Turnover	Turnover in a financial context refers to the rate at which a provider of goods cycles through its average inventory. Turnover in a human resources context refers to the characteristic of a given company or industry, relative to rate at which an employer gains and loses staff.
Job satisfaction	Job satisfaction describes how content an individual is with his or her job. It is a relatively recent term since in previous centuries the jobs available to a particular person were often predetermined by the occupation of that person's parent.
Organizational commitment	A person's identification with and attachment to an organization is called organizational commitment.
Return on investment	Return on investment refers to the return a businessperson gets on the money he and other owners invest in the firm; for example, a business that earned $100 on a $1,000 investment would have a ROI of 10 percent: 100 divided by 1000.
Balance	In banking and accountancy, the outstanding balance is the amount of money owned, (or due), that remains in a deposit account (or a loan account) at a given date, after all past remittances, payments and withdrawal have been accounted for. It can be positive (then, in the balance sheet of a firm, it is an asset) or negative (a liability).
Interpersonal roles	In management there are three important interpersonal roles: the figurehead, the leader, and the liaison.
Basic skills	Basic skills refer to reading, writing, and communication skills needed to understand the content of a training program.
Matching	Matching refers to an accounting concept that establishes when expenses are recognized. Expenses are matched with the revenues they helped to generate and are recognized when those revenues are recognized.
Global competition	Global competition exists when competitive conditions across national markets are linked strongly enough to form a true international market and when leading competitors compete head to head in many different countries.
Lockheed Martin	Lockheed Martin is the world's largest defense contractor (by defense revenue). As of 2005, 95% of revenues came from the U.S. Department of Defense, other U.S. federal government agencies, and foreign military customers.
Strike	The withholding of labor services by an organized group of workers is referred to as a strike.
Boeing	Boeing is the world's largest aircraft manufacturer by revenue. Headquartered in Chicago, Illinois, Boeing is the second-largest defense contractor in the world. In 2005, the company was the world's largest civil aircraft manufacturer in terms of value.
Acquisition	A company's purchase of the property and obligations of another company is an acquisition.
Credit	Credit refers to a recording as positive in the balance of payments, any transaction that gives rise to a payment into the country, such as an export, the sale of an asset, or borrowing from abroad.
Subcontractor	A subcontractor is an individual or in many cases a business that signs a contract to perform part or all of the obligations of another's contract. A subcontractor is hired by a general or prime contractor to perform a specific task as part of the overall project.
Grant	Grant refers to an intergovernmental transfer of funds . Since the New Deal, state and local

governments have become increasingly dependent upon federal grants for an almost infinite variety of programs.

Purchasing

Purchasing refers to the function in a firm that searches for quality material resources, finds the best suppliers, and negotiates the best price for goods and services.

Core

A core is the set of feasible allocations in an economy that cannot be improved upon by subset of the set of the economy's consumers (a coalition). In construction, when the force in an element is within a certain center section, the core, the element will only be under compression.

Points

Loan origination fees that may be deductible as interest by a buyer of property. A seller of property who pays points reduces the selling price by the amount of the points paid for the buyer.

Prototype

A prototype is built to test the function of a new design before starting production of a product.

Analyst

Analyst refers to a person or tool with a primary function of information analysis, generally with a more limited, practical and short term set of goals than a researcher.

Brief

Brief refers to a statement of a party's case or legal arguments, usually prepared by an attorney. Also used to make legal arguments before appellate courts.

30

Go to **Cram101.com** for the Practice Tests for this Chapter.

Globalization	The increasing world-wide integration of markets for goods, services and capital that attracted special attention in the late 1990s is called globalization.
Demographic	A demographic is a term used in marketing and broadcasting, to describe a demographic grouping or a market segment.
Service	Service refers to a "non tangible product" that is not embodied in a physical good and that typically effects some change in another product, person, or institution. Contrasts with good.
Management	Management characterizes the process of leading and directing all or part of an organization, often a business, through the deployment and manipulation of resources. Early twentieth-century management writer Mary Parker Follett defined management as "the art of getting things done through people."
Brand	A name, symbol, or design that identifies the goods or services of one seller or group of sellers and distinguishes them from the goods and services of competitors is a brand.
Purchasing	Purchasing refers to the function in a firm that searches for quality material resources, finds the best suppliers, and negotiates the best price for goods and services.
Human resources	Human resources refers to the individuals within the firm, and to the portion of the firm's organization that deals with hiring, firing, training, and other personnel issues.
Task force	A temporary team or committee formed to solve a specific short-term problem involving several departments is the task force.
Specialist	A specialist is a trader who makes a market in one or several stocks and holds the limit order book for those stocks.
Firm	An organization that employs resources to produce a good or service for profit and owns and operates one or more plants is referred to as a firm.
Board of directors	The group of individuals elected by the stockholders of a corporation to oversee its operations is a board of directors.
Gain	In finance, gain is a profit or an increase in value of an investment such as a stock or bond. Gain is calculated by fair market value or the proceeds from the sale of the investment minus the sum of the purchase price and all costs associated with it.
Promotion	Promotion refers to all the techniques sellers use to motivate people to buy products or services. An attempt by marketers to inform people about products and to persuade them to participate in an exchange.
Policy	Similar to a script in that a policy can be a less than completely rational decision-making method. Involves the use of a pre-existing set of decision steps for any problem that presents itself.
Business ethics	The study of what makes up good and bad conduct as related to business activities and values is business ethics.
Diversity marketing	Diversity marketing is a marketing paradigm which sees marketing as essentially an effort in communication with diverse publics. According to the paradigm, the main focus of marketing today should be to create effective communication methods and a communication mix appropriate to each of the diverse groups active in the market.
Bottom line	The bottom line is net income on the last line of a income statement.
Marketing	Promoting and selling products or services to customers, or prospective customers, is referred to as marketing.
Pfizer	Pfizer is the world's largest pharmaceutical company based in New York City. It produces the

Go to **Cram101.com** for the Practice Tests for this Chapter.

number-one selling drug Lipitor (atorvastatin, used to lower blood cholesterol).

Organizational Behavior	The study of human behavior in organizational settings, the interface between human behavior and the organization, and the organization itself is called organizational behavior.
Workforce diversity	The similarities and differences in such characteristics as age, gender, ethnic heritage, physical abilities and disabilities, race, and sexual orientation among the employees of organizations is called workforce diversity.
Multicultural organization	The multicultural organization has six characteristics: pluralism, full structural integration, full integration of informal networks, an absence of prejudice and discrimination, equal identification among employees with organizational goals for majority and minority groups, and low levels of intergroup conflict.
Trend	Trend refers to the long-term movement of an economic variable, such as its average rate of increase or decrease over enough years to encompass several business cycles.
Layoff	A layoff is the termination of an employee or (more commonly) a group of employees for business reasons, such as the decision that certain positions are no longer necessary.
Downturn	A decline in a stock market or economic cycle is a downturn.
Buying power	The dollar amount available to purchase securities on margin is buying power. The amount is calculated by adding the cash held in the brokerage accounts and the amount that could be spent if securities were fully margined to their limit. If an investor uses their buying power, they are purchasing securities on credit.
Market	A market is, as defined in economics, a social arrangement that allows buyers and sellers to discover information and carry out a voluntary exchange of goods or services.
Consolidation	The combination of two or more firms, generally of equal size and market power, to form an entirely new entity is a consolidation.
Prejudice	Prejudice is, as the name implies, the process of "pre-judging" something. It implies coming to a judgment on a subject before learning where the preponderance of evidence actually lies, or forming a judgment without direct experience.
Management system	A management system is the framework of processes and procedures used to ensure that an organization can fulfill all tasks required to achieve its objectives.
Incentive	An incentive is any factor (financial or non-financial) that provides a motive for a particular course of action, or counts as a reason for preferring one choice to the alternatives.
Incentive system	An incentive system refers to plans in which employees can earn additional compenzation in return for certain types of performance.
Evaluation	The consumer's appraisal of the product or brand on important attributes is called evaluation.
Job satisfaction	Job satisfaction describes how content an individual is with his or her job. It is a relatively recent term since in previous centuries the jobs available to a particular person were often predetermined by the occupation of that person's parent.
Bureau of Labor Statistics	The Bureau of Labor Statistics is a unit of the United States Department of Labor, is the principal fact-finding agency for the U.S. government in the field of labor economics and statistics.
Labor	People's physical and mental talents and efforts that are used to help produce goods and services are called labor.
Labor force	In economics the labor force is the group of people who have a potential for being employed.

Standing	Standing refers to the legal requirement that anyone seeking to challenge a particular action in court must demonstrate that such action substantially affects his legitimate interests before he will be entitled to bring suit.
Conference Board	The Conference Board is the world's preeminent business membership and research organization, best known for the Consumer Confidence Index and the index of leading indicators. For 90 years, The Conference Board has equipped the world's leading corporations with practical knowledge through issues-oriented research and senior executive peer-to-peer meetings.
Union	A worker association that bargains with employers over wages and working conditions is called a union.
Economy	The income, expenditures, and resources that affect the cost of running a business and household are called an economy.
Distribution	Distribution in economics, the manner in which total output and income is distributed among individuals or factors.
Industry	A group of firms that produce identical or similar products is an industry. It is also used specifically to refer to an area of economic production focused on manufacturing which involves large amounts of capital investment before any profit can be realized, also called "heavy industry".
British Petroleum	British Petroleum, is a British energy company with headquarters in London, one of four vertically integrated private sector oil, natural gas, and petrol (gasoline) "supermajors" in the world, along with Royal Dutch Shell, ExxonMobil and Total.
Gap	In December of 1995, Gap became the first major North American retailer to accept independent monitoring of the working conditions in a contract factory producing its garments. Gap is the largest specialty retailer in the United States.
Equal employment opportunity	The government's attempt to ensure that all individuals have an equal opportunity for employment, regardless of race, color, religion, sex, age, disability, or national origin is equal employment opportunity.
Affirmative action	Policies and programs that establish procedures for increasing employment and promotion for women and minorities are called affirmative action.
Integration	Economic integration refers to reducing barriers among countries to transactions and to movements of goods, capital, and labor, including harmonization of laws, regulations, and standards. Integrated markets theoretically function as a unified market.
Valuing diversity	Valuing diversity refers to putting an end to the assumption that everyone who is not a member of the dominant group must assimilate. The first step is to recognize that diversity exists in organizations so that we can begin to manage it.
Teamwork	That which occurs when group members work together in ways that utilize their skills well to accomplish a purpose is called teamwork.
Assimilation	Assimilation refers to the process through which a minority group learns the ways of the dominant group. In organizations, this means that when people of different types and backgrounds are hired, the organization attempts to mold them to fit the existing organizational culture.
Organizational culture	The mindset of employees, including their shared beliefs, values, and goals is called the organizational culture.
International management	International management refers to the management of business operations conducted in more than one country.
International	International business refers to any firm that engages in international trade or investment.

Go to **Cram101.com** for the Practice Tests for this Chapter.

Business	
International trade	The export of goods and services from a country and the import of goods and services into a country is referred to as the international trade.
Communication network	A communication network refer to networks that form spontaneously and naturally as the interactions among workers continue over time.
Developing country	Developing country refers to a country whose per capita income is low by world standards. Same as LDC. As usually used, it does not necessarily connote that the country's income is rising.
Technology	The body of knowledge and techniques that can be used to combine economic resources to produce goods and services is called technology.
Electronic mail	Electronic mail refers to electronic written communication between individuals using computers connected to the Internet.
Competitor	Other organizations in the same industry or type of business that provide a good or service to the same set of customers is referred to as a competitor.
Production	The creation of finished goods and services using the factors of production: land, labor, capital, entrepreneurship, and knowledge.
Domestic	From or in one's own country. A domestic producer is one that produces inside the home country. A domestic price is the price inside the home country. Opposite of 'foreign' or 'world.'.
Nestle	Nestle is the world's biggest food and beverage company. In the 1860s, a pharmacist, developed a food for babies who were unable to be breastfed. His first success was a premature infant who could not tolerate his own mother's milk nor any of the usual substitutes. The value of the new product was quickly recognized when his new formula saved the child's life.
Exchange rate	Exchange rate refers to the price at which one country's currency trades for another, typically on the exchange market.
Exchange	The trade of things of value between buyer and seller so that each is better off after the trade is called the exchange.
Customs	Customs is an authority or agency in a country responsible for collecting customs duties and for controlling the flow of people, animals and goods (including personal effects and hazardous items) in and out of the country.
Tariff	A tax imposed by a nation on an imported good is called a tariff.
Foreign Corrupt Practices Act	The Foreign Corrupt Practices Act of 1977 is a United States federal law requiring any company that has publicly-traded stock to maintain records that accurately and fairly represent the company's transactions; additionally, requires any publicly-traded company to have an adequate system of internal accounting controls.
Commerce	Commerce is the exchange of something of value between two entities. It is the central mechanism from which capitalism is derived.
Lease	A contract for the possession and use of land or other property, including goods, on one side, and a recompense of rent or other income on the other is the lease.
Bribery	When one person gives another person money, property, favors, or anything else of value for a favor in return, we have bribery. Often referred to as a payoff or 'kickback.'
Market share	That fraction of an industry's output accounted for by an individual firm or group of firms is called market share.

Go to **Cram101.com** for the Practice Tests for this Chapter.

Exxon Mobil	Exxon Mobil is the largest publicly traded integrated oil and gas company in the world, formed on November 30, 1999, by the merger of Exxon and Mobil. It is the sixth-largest company in the world as ranked by the Forbes Global 2000 and the largest company in the world (by revenue) as ranked by the Fortune Global 500.
Corporation	A legal entity chartered by a state or the Federal government that is distinct and separate from the individuals who own it is a corporation. This separation gives the corporation unique powers which other legal entities lack.
Texaco	Texaco is the name of an American oil company that was merged into Chevron Corporation in 2001. For many years, Texaco was the only company selling gasoline in all 50 states, but this is no longer true.
Mobil	Mobil is a major oil company which merged with the Exxon Corporation in 1999. Today Mobil continues as a major brand name within the combined company.
Exxon	Exxon formally replaced the Esso, Enco, and Humble brands on January 1, 1973, in the USA. The name Esso, pronounced S-O, attracted protests from other Standard Oil spinoffs because of its similarity to the name of the parent company, Standard Oil.
Amoco	Amoco was formed as Standard Oil (Indiana) in 1889 by John D. Rockefeller as part of the Standard Oil trust. In 1910, with the rise in popularity of the automobile, Amoco decided to specialize in providing gas to everyday families and their cars. In 1911, the year it became independent from the Standard Oil trust, the company sold 88% of the gasoline and kerosene sold in the midwest.
Ford	Ford is an American company that manufactures and sells automobiles worldwide. Ford introduced methods for large-scale manufacturing of cars, and large-scale management of an industrial workforce, especially elaborately engineered manufacturing sequences typified by the moving assembly lines.
General Motors	General Motors is the world's largest automaker. Founded in 1908, today it employs about 327,000 people around the world. With global headquarters in Detroit, it manufactures its cars and trucks in 33 countries.
Joint venture	Joint venture refers to an undertaking by two parties for a specific purpose and duration, taking any of several legal forms.
Volkswagen	Volkswagen or VW is an automobile manufacturer based in Wolfsburg, Germany in the state of Lower Saxony. It forms the core of this Group, one of the world's four largest car producers. Its German tagline is "Aus Liebe zum Automobil", which is translated as "For the love of the car" - or, For Love of the People's Cars,".
Toyota	Toyota is a Japanese multinational corporation that manufactures automobiles, trucks and buses. Toyota is the world's second largest automaker by sales. Toyota also provides financial services through its subsidiary, Toyota Financial Services, and participates in other lines of business.
Honda	With more than 14 million internal combustion engines built each year, Honda is the largest engine-maker in the world. In 2004, the company began to produce diesel motors, which were both very quiet whilst not requiring particulate filters to pass pollution standards. It is arguable, however, that the foundation of their success is the motorcycle division.
Manufacturing	Production of goods primarily by the application of labor and capital to raw materials and other intermediate inputs, in contrast to agriculture, mining, forestry, fishing, and services a manufacturing.
Investment	Investment refers to spending for the production and accumulation of capital and additions to inventories. In a financial sense, buying an asset with the expectation of making a return.

Go to **Cram101.com** for the Practice Tests for this Chapter.

41

Merger	Merger refers to the combination of two firms into a single firm.
Chrysler	The Chrysler Corporation was an American automobile manufacturer that existed independently from 1925–1998. The company was formed by Walter Percy Chrysler on June 6, 1925, with the remaining assets of Maxwell Motor Company.
BMW	BMW is an independent German company and manufacturer of automobiles and motorcycles. BMW is the world's largest premium carmaker and is the parent company of the BMW MINI and Rolls-Royce car brands, and, formerly, Rover.
Consideration	Consideration in contract law, a basic requirement for an enforceable agreement under traditional contract principles, defined in this text as legal value, bargained for and given in exchange for an act or promise. In corporation law, cash or property contributed to a corporation in exchange for shares, or a promise to contribute such cash or property.
Synergy	Corporate synergy occurs when corporations interact congruently. A corporate synergy refers to a financial benefit that a corporation expects to realize when it merges with or acquires another corporation.
Power distance	Power distance refers to the degree to which the less powerful members of society expect there to be differences in the levels of power. A high score suggests that there is an expectation that some individuals wield larger amounts of power than others. Countries with high power distance rating are often characterized by a high rate of political violence.
Collectivism	Collectivism is a term used to describe that things should be owned by the group and used for the benefit of all rather than being owned by individuals.
Authority	Authority in agency law, refers to an agent's ability to affect his principal's legal relations with third parties. Also used to refer to an actor's legal power or ability to do something. In addition, sometimes used to refer to a statute, case, or other legal source that justifies a particular result.
Economic growth	Economic growth refers to the increase over time in the capacity of an economy to produce goods and services and to improve the well-being of its citizens.
Bond	Bond refers to a debt instrument, issued by a borrower and promising a specified stream of payments to the purchaser, usually regular interest payments plus a final repayment of principal.
Uncertainty avoidance	The extent to which people prefer to be in clear and unambiguous situations is referred to as the uncertainty avoidance.
Preference	The act of a debtor in paying or securing one or more of his creditors in a manner more favorable to them than to other creditors or to the exclusion of such other creditors is a preference. In the absence of statute, a preference is perfectly good, but to be legal it must be bona fide, and not a mere subterfuge of the debtor to secure a future benefit to himself or to prevent the application of his property to his debts.
Materialism	Materialism refers to how a person or group chooses to spend their resources, particularly money and time. In common use, the word more specifically refers to a person who primarily pursues wealth and luxury. Sometimes such a person displays conspicuous consumption.
Acquisition	A company's purchase of the property and obligations of another company is an acquisition.
Categorizing	The act of placing strengths and weaknesses into categories in generic internal assessment is called categorizing.
Interest	In finance and economics, interest is the price paid by a borrower for the use of a lender's money. In other words, interest is the amount of paid to "rent" money for a period of time.
Socialization	Socialization is the process by which human beings or animals learn to adopt the behavior

patterns of the community in which they live. For both humans and animals, this is typically thought to occur during the early stages of life, during which individuals develop the skills and knowledge necessary to function within their culture and environment.

Labor productivity	In labor economics labor productivity is a measure of the efficiency of the labor force. It is usually measured as output per hour of all people. When comparing labor productivity one mostly looks at the change over time.
Productivity	Productivity refers to the total output of goods and services in a given period of time divided by work hours.
Labor force participation rate	Labor force participation rate refers to the percentage of the working -age population who are members of the labor force.
Hearing	A hearing is a proceeding before a court or other decision-making body or officer. A hearing is generally distinguished from a trial in that it is usually shorter and often less formal.
Allowance	Reduction in the selling price of goods extended to the buyer because the goods are defective or of lower quality than the buyer ordered and to encourage a buyer to keep merchandise that would otherwise be returned is the allowance.
Glass ceiling	Glass ceiling refers to a term that refers to the many barriers that can exist to thwart a woman's rise to the top of an organization; one that provides a view of the top, but a ceiling on how far a woman can go.
Attrition	The practice of not hiring new employees to replace older employees who either quit or retire is referred to as attrition.
Turnover	Turnover in a financial context refers to the rate at which a provider of goods cycles through its average inventory. Turnover in a human resources context refers to the characteristic of a given company or industry, relative to rate at which an employer gains and loses staff.
Xerox	Xerox was founded in 1906 as "The Haloid Company" manufacturing photographic paper and equipment. The company came to prominence in 1959 with the introduction of the first plain paper photocopier using the process of xerography (electrophotography) developed by Chester Carlson, the Xerox 914.
Hosting	Internet hosting service is a service that runs Internet servers, allowing organizations and individuals to serve content on the Internet.
Security	Security refers to a claim on the borrower future income that is sold by the borrower to the lender. A security is a type of transferable interest representing financial value.
Managing director	Managing director is the term used for the chief executive of many limited companies in the United Kingdom, Commonwealth and some other English speaking countries. The title reflects their role as both a member of the Board of Directors but also as the senior manager.
DuPont	DuPont was the inventor of CFCs (along with General Motors) and the largest producer of these ozone depleting chemicals (used primarily in aerosol sprays and refrigerants) in the world, with a 25% market share in the late 1980s.
Reverse discrimination	The view that the preferential treatment associated with affirmative action efforts constitutes discrimination against other groups is known as reverse discrimination.
Americans with Disabilities Act	The Americans with Disabilities Act of 1990 is a wide-ranging civil rights law that prohibits discrimination based on disability.
Accommodation	Accommodation is a term used to describe a delivery of nonconforming goods meant as a partial

Go to **Cram101.com** for the Practice Tests for this Chapter.

performance of a contract for the sale of goods, where a full performance is not possible.

Reasonable accommodation	Making facilities readily accessible to and usable by individuals with physical or mental limitations is referred to as reasonable accommodation.
Restructuring	Restructuring is the corporate management term for the act of partially dismantling and reorganizing a company for the purpose of making it more efficient and therefore more profitable.
Eastman Kodak	Eastman Kodak Company is an American multinational public company producing photographic materials and equipment. Long known for its wide range of photographic film products, it has focused in recent years on three main businesses: digital photography, health imaging, and printing. This company remains the largest supplier of films in the world, both for the amateur and professional markets.
Warehouse	Warehouse refers to a location, often decentralized, that a firm uses to store, consolidate, age, or mix stock; house product-recall programs; or ease tax burdens.
Insurance	Insurance refers to a system by which individuals can reduce their exposure to risk of large losses by spreading the risks among a large number of persons.
Subsidiary	A company that is controlled by another company or corporation is a subsidiary.
Damages	The sum of money recoverable by a plaintiff who has received a judgment in a civil case is called damages.
Shell	One of the original Seven Sisters, Royal Dutch/Shell is the world's third-largest oil company by revenue, and a major player in the petrochemical industry and the solar energy business. Shell has six core businesses: Exploration and Production, Gas and Power, Downstream, Chemicals, Renewables, and Trading/Shipping, and operates in more than 140 countries.
Digital Equipment Corporation	Digital Equipment Corporation was a pioneering company in the American computer industry. Its PDP and VAX products were arguably the most popular mini-computers for the scientific and engineering communities during the 70s and 80s.
Apple Computer	Apple Computer has been a major player in the evolution of personal computing since its founding in 1976. The Apple II microcomputer, introduced in 1977, was a hit with home users.
Holding	The holding is a court's determination of a matter of law based on the issue presented in the particular case. In other words: under this law, with these facts, this result.
Boeing	Boeing is the world's largest aircraft manufacturer by revenue. Headquartered in Chicago, Illinois, Boeing is the second-largest defense contractor in the world. In 2005, the company was the world's largest civil aircraft manufacturer in terms of value.
Organizational goals	Objectives that management seeks to achieve in pursuing the firm's purpose are organizational goals.
Convergence	The blending of various facets of marketing functions and communication technology to create more efficient and expanded synergies is a convergence.
Applicant	In many tribunal and administrative law suits, the person who initiates the claim is called the applicant.
Capitalism	Capitalism refers to an economic system in which capital is mostly owned by private individuals and corporations. Contrasts with communism.
Complexity	The technical sophistication of the product and hence the amount of understanding required to use it is referred to as complexity. It is the opposite of simplicity.
Organization structure	The system of task, reporting, and authority relationships within which the organization does its work is referred to as the organization structure.

Go to **Cram101.com** for the Practice Tests for this Chapter.

Product line	A group of products that are physically similar or are intended for a similar market are called the product line.
Leadership	Management merely consists of leadership applied to business situations; or in other words: management forms a sub-set of the broader process of leadership.
Avon	Avon is an American cosmetics, perfume and toy seller with markets in over 135 countries across the world and a sales of $7.74 billion worldwide.
Competitive advantage	A business is said to have a competitive advantage when its unique strengths, often based on cost, quality, time, and innovation, offer consumers a greater percieved value and there by differtiating it from its competitors.
Personnel	A collective term for all of the employees of an organization. Personnel is also commonly used to refer to the personnel management function or the organizational unit responsible for administering personnel programs.
Product development	In business and engineering, new product development is the complete process of bringing a new product to market. There are two parallel aspects to this process : one involves product engineering ; the other marketing analysis. Marketers see new product development as the first stage in product life cycle management, engineers as part of Product Lifecycle Management.
Pluralism	A theory of government that attempts to reaffirm the democratic character of society by asserting that open, multiple, competing, and responsive groups preserve traditional democratic values in a mass industrial state. Pluralism assumes that power will shift from group to group as elements in the mass public transfer their allegiance in response to their perceptions of their individual interests.
Motorola	The Six Sigma quality system was developed at Motorola even though it became most well known because of its use by General Electric. It was created by engineer Bill Smith, under the direction of Bob Galvin (son of founder Paul Galvin) when he was running the company.
Expense	In accounting, an expense represents an event in which an asset is used up or a liability is incurred. In terms of the accounting equation, expenses reduce owners' equity.
Mission statement	Mission statement refers to an outline of the fundamental purposes of an organization.
Mentoring	Mentoring refers to a developmental relationship between a more experienced mentor and a less experienced partner referred to as a mentee or protégé. Usually - but not necessarily - the mentor/protégé pair will be of the same sex.
Focus group	A small group of people who meet under the direction of a discussion leader to communicate their opinions about an organization, its products, or other given issues is a focus group.
Openness	Openness refers to the extent to which an economy is open, often measured by the ratio of its trade to GDP.
Conflict resolution	Conflict resolution is the process of resolving a dispute or a conflict. Successful conflict resolution occurs by providing each side's needs, and adequately addressing their interests so that they are each satisfied with the outcome. Conflict resolution aims to end conflicts before they start or lead to physical fighting.
Mediation	Mediation consists of a process of alternative dispute resolution in which a (generally) neutral third party using appropriate techniques, assists two or more parties to help them negotiate an agreement, with concrete effects, on a matter of common interest.
Internationa-ization	Internationalization refers to another term for fragmentation. Used by Grossman and Helpman.

Corporate citizenship	A theory of responsibility that says a business has a responsibility to do good is corporate citizenship. Terms used in the business sector to refer to business giving, ie. business relationships and partnerships with not-for-profit organizations.
Information technology	Information technology refers to technology that helps companies change business by allowing them to use new methods.
Welfare	Welfare refers to the economic well being of an individual, group, or economy. For individuals, it is conceptualized by a utility function. For groups, including countries and the world, it is a tricky philosophical concept, since individuals fare differently.
Contract	A contract is a "promise" or an "agreement" that is enforced or recognized by the law. In the civil law, a contract is considered to be part of the general law of obligations.
Fund	Independent accounting entity with a self-balancing set of accounts segregated for the purposes of carrying on specific activities is referred to as a fund.
Partnership	In the common law, a partnership is a type of business entity in which partners share with each other the profits or losses of the business undertaking in which they have all invested.
Business case	The business case addresses, at a high level, the business need that a project seeks to resolve. It includes the reasons for the project, the expected business benefits, the options considered (with reasons for rejecting or carrying forward each option), the expected costs of the project, a gap analysis and the expected risks.
Gross domestic product	Gross domestic product refers to the total value of new goods and services produced in a given year within the borders of a country, regardless of by whom.
Net worth	Net worth is the total assets minus total liabilities of an individual or company
Class action	In law, a class action is an equitable procedural device used in litigation to determine the rights of and remedies, if any, for large numbers of people whose cases involve common questions of law and fact. Traditionally, they have been used to litigate antitrust and securities lawsuits, as well as school desegregation cases, but more recently have been used for a wide range of legal disputes that involve a large number of injured parties.
Complaint	The pleading in a civil case in which the plaintiff states his claim and requests relief is called complaint. In the common law, it is a formal legal document that sets out the basic facts and legal reasons that the filing party (the plaintiffs) believes are sufficient to support a claim against another person, persons, entity or entities (the defendants) that entitles the plaintiff(s) to a remedy (either money damages or injunctive relief).
Operation	A standardized method or technique that is performed repetitively, often on different materials resulting in different finished goods is called an operation.
Supply	Supply is the aggregate amount of any material good that can be called into being at a certain price point; it comprises one half of the equation of supply and demand. In classical economic theory, a curve representing supply is one of the factors that produce price.
Keiretsu	Keiretsu is a set of companies with interlocking business relationships and shareholdings. It is a type of business group.
Enron	Enron Corportaion's global reputation was undermined by persistent rumours of bribery and political pressure to secure contracts in Central America, South America, Africa, and the Philippines. Especially controversial was its $3 billion contract with the Maharashtra State Electricity Board in India, where it is alleged that Enron officials used political connections within the Clinton and Bush administrations to exert pressure on the board.
Corpus	The body or principal of a trust. Suppose, for example, Grant transfers an apartment building into a trust, income payable to Ruth for life, with the remainder to Shawn upon Ruth's death.

	Corpus of the trust is the apartment building.
Utility	Utility refers to the want-satisfying power of a good or service; the satisfaction or pleasure a consumer obtains from the consumption of a good or service.
Commodity	Could refer to any good, but in trade a commodity is usually a raw material or primary product that enters into international trade, such as metals or basic agricultural products.
Market capitalization	Market capitalization is a business term that refers to the aggregate value of a firm's outstanding common shares. In essence, market capitalization reflects the total value of a firm's equity currently available on the market. This measure differs from equity value to the extent that a firm has outstanding stock options or other securities convertible to common shares. The size and growth of a firm's market capitalization is often one of the critical measurements of a public company's success or failure.
Forbes	David Churbuck founded online Forbes in 1996. The site drew attention when it uncovered Stephen Glass' journalistic fraud in The New Republic in 1998, a scoop that gave credibility to internet journalism.
Shares	Shares refer to an equity security, representing a shareholder's ownership of a corporation. Shares are one of a finite number of equal portions in the capital of a company, entitling the owner to a proportion of distributed, non-reinvested profits known as dividends and to a portion of the value of the company in case of liquidation.
Stock	In financial terminology, stock is the capital raized by a corporation, through the issuance and sale of shares.
Privilege	Generally, a legal right to engage in conduct that would otherwise result in legal liability is a privilege. Privileges are commonly classified as absolute or conditional. Occasionally, privilege is also used to denote a legal right to refrain from particular behavior.
Venue	A requirement distinct from jurisdiction that the court be geographically situated so that it is the most appropriate and convenient court to try the case is the venue.
Stockholder	A stockholder is an individual or company (including a corporation) that legally owns one or more shares of stock in a joined stock company. The shareholders are the owners of a corporation. Companies listed at the stock market strive to enhance shareholder value.
Bookkeeping	The recording of business transactions is called bookkeeping.
Allegation	An allegation is a statement of a fact by a party in a pleading, which the party claims it will prove. Allegations remain assertions without proof, only claims until they are proved.
Accounting	A system that collects and processes financial information about an organization and reports that information to decision makers is referred to as accounting.
Chief financial officer	Chief financial officer refers to executive responsible for overseeing the financial operations of an organization.
Negotiation	Negotiation is the process whereby interested parties resolve disputes, agree upon courses of action, bargain for individual or collective advantage, and/or attempt to craft outcomes which serve their mutual interests.
Profit	Profit refers to the return to the resource entrepreneurial ability; total revenue minus total cost.
Conflict of interest	A conflict that occurs when a corporate officer or director enters into a transaction with the corporation in which he or she has a personal interest is a conflict of interest.
License	A license in the sphere of Intellectual Property Rights (IPR) is a document, contract or agreement giving permission or the 'right' to a legally-definable entity to do something

(such as manufacture a product or to use a service), or to apply something (such as a trademark), with the objective of achieving commercial gain.

Broker	In commerce, a broker is a party that mediates between a buyer and a seller. A broker who also acts as a seller or as a buyer becomes a principal party to the deal.
Buyer	A buyer refers to a role in the buying center with formal authority and responsibility to select the supplier and negotiate the terms of the contract.
Creative accounting	Creative accounting refers to an accounting practice that may or may not follow the letter of the rules of standard accounting practices but certainly deviate from the spirit of those rules. They are characterized by excessive complication and the use of novel ways of characterizing income, assets or liabilities.
Asset	An item of property, such as land, capital, money, a share in ownership, or a claim on others for future payment, such as a bond or a bank deposit is an asset.
Financial statement	Financial statement refers to a summary of all the transactions that have occurred over a particular period.
Parent company	Parent company refers to the entity that has a controlling influence over another company. It may have its own operations, or it may have been set up solely for the purpose of owning the Subject Company.
Corporate finance	Corporate finance is a specific area of finance dealing with the financial decisions corporations make and the tools as well as analyses used to make these decisions. The discipline as a whole may be divided among long-term and short-term decisions and techniques with the primary goal being the enhancing of corporate value by ensuring that return on capital exceeds cost of capital, without taking excessive financial risks.
Analyst	Analyst refers to a person or tool with a primary function of information analysis, generally with a more limited, practical and short term set of goals than a researcher.
Arthur Andersen	Arthur Andersen was once one of the Big Five accounting firms, performing auditing, tax, and consulting services for large corporations. In 2002 the firm voluntarily surrendered its licenses to practice as Certified Public Accountants in the U.S. pending the result of prosecution by the U.S. Department of Justice over the firm's handling of the auditing of Enron.
Mistake	In contract law a mistake is incorrect understanding by one or more parties to a contract and may be used as grounds to invalidate the agreement. Common law has identified three different types of mistake in contract: unilateral mistake, mutual mistake, and common mistake.
Securities and exchange commission	Securities and exchange commission refers to U.S. government agency that determines the financial statements that public companies must provide to stockholders and the measurement rules that they must use in producing those statements.
Financial market	In economics, a financial market is a mechanism which allows people to trade money for securities or commodities such as gold or other precious metals. In general, any commodity market might be considered to be a financial market, if the usual purpose of traders is not the immediate consumption of the commodity, but rather as a means of delaying or accelerating consumption over time.
Federal Reserve	The Federal Reserve System was created via the Federal Reserve Act of December 23rd, 1913. All national banks were required to join the system and other banks could join. The Reserve Banks opened for business on November 16th, 1914. Federal Reserve Notes were created as part of the legislation, to provide an elastic supply of currency.
Disclosure	Disclosure means the giving out of information, either voluntarily or to be in compliance with legal regulations or workplace rules.

| Dynegy | Dynegy is a large operator of power plants and a player in the natural gas liquids business, based in Houston, Texas. Once known as The Natural Gas Clearinghouse, the company adopted the more vibrant New Economy branding in 1998. |

56

Go to **Cram101.com** for the Practice Tests for this Chapter.

Economy	The income, expenditures, and resources that affect the cost of running a business and household are called an economy.
Firm	An organization that employs resources to produce a good or service for profit and owns and operates one or more plants is referred to as a firm.
Advertising	Advertising refers to paid, nonpersonal communication through various media by organizations and individuals who are in some way identified in the advertising message.
Purchasing	Purchasing refers to the function in a firm that searches for quality material resources, finds the best suppliers, and negotiates the best price for goods and services.
Production	The creation of finished goods and services using the factors of production: land, labor, capital, entrepreneurship, and knowledge.
Corporation	A legal entity chartered by a state or the Federal government that is distinct and separate from the individuals who own it is a corporation. This separation gives the corporation unique powers which other legal entities lack.
Option	A contract that gives the purchaser the option to buy or sell the underlying financial instrument at a specified price, called the exercise price or strike price, within a specific period of time.
Closing	The finalization of a real estate sales transaction that passes title to the property from the seller to the buyer is referred to as a closing. Closing is a sales term which refers to the process of making a sale. It refers to reaching the final step, which may be an exchange of money or acquiring a signature.
Xerox	Xerox was founded in 1906 as "The Haloid Company" manufacturing photographic paper and equipment. The company came to prominence in 1959 with the introduction of the first plain paper photocopier using the process of xerography (electrophotography) developed by Chester Carlson, the Xerox 914.
Consultant	A professional that provides expert advice in a particular field or area in which customers occassionaly require this type of knowledge is a consultant.
Lucent Technologies	Lucent Technologies is a company composed of what was formerly AT&T Technologies, which included Western Electric and Bell Labs. It was spun-off from AT&T on September 30, 1996. On April 2, 2006, they announced a merger with its French competitor, Alcatel. The combined company has revenues of approximately $25 billion U.S. based on 2005 calendar results.
Health insurance	Health insurance is a type of insurance whereby the insurer pays the medical costs of the insured if the insured becomes sick due to covered causes, or due to accidents. The insurer may be a private organization or a government agency.
Technology	The body of knowledge and techniques that can be used to combine economic resources to produce goods and services is called technology.
Insurance	Insurance refers to a system by which individuals can reduce their exposure to risk of large losses by spreading the risks among a large number of persons.
Ford	Ford is an American company that manufactures and sells automobiles worldwide. Ford introduced methods for large-scale manufacturing of cars, and large-scale management of an industrial workforce, especially elaborately engineered manufacturing sequences typified by the moving assembly lines.
Disney	Disney is one of the largest media and entertainment corporations in the world. Founded on October 16, 1923 by brothers Walt and Roy Disney as a small animation studio, today it is one of the largest Hollywood studios and also owns nine theme parks and several television networks, including the American Broadcasting Company (ABC).

Incentive	An incentive is any factor (financial or non-financial) that provides a motive for a particular course of action, or counts as a reason for preferring one choice to the alternatives.
Productivity	Productivity refers to the total output of goods and services in a given period of time divided by work hours.
Service	Service refers to a "non tangible product" that is not embodied in a physical good and that typically effects some change in another product, person, or institution. Contrasts with good.
Welfare	Welfare refers to the economic well being of an individual, group, or economy. For individuals, it is conceptualized by a utility function. For groups, including countries and the world, it is a tricky philosophical concept, since individuals fare differently.
Fraud	Tax fraud falls into two categories: civil and criminal. Under civil fraud, the IRS may impose as a penalty of an amount equal to as much as 75 percent of the underpayment.
Profit	Profit refers to the return to the resource entrepreneurial ability; total revenue minus total cost.
Siemens	Siemens is the world's largest conglomerate company. Worldwide, Siemens and its subsidiaries employs 461,000 people (2005) in 190 countries and reported global sales of €75.4 billion in fiscal year 2005.
Contract	A contract is a "promise" or an "agreement" that is enforced or recognized by the law. In the civil law, a contract is considered to be part of the general law of obligations.
Buyer	A buyer refers to a role in the buying center with formal authority and responsibility to select the supplier and negotiate the terms of the contract.
Psychological contract	A person's set of expectations regarding what he or she will contribute to the organization and what the organization, in return, will provide to the individual is called psychological contract.
Contribution	In business organization law, the cash or property contributed to a business by its owners is referred to as contribution.
Loyalty	Marketers tend to define customer loyalty as making repeat purchases. Some argue that it should be defined attitudinally as a strongly positive feeling about the brand.
Financial market	In economics, a financial market is a mechanism which allows people to trade money for securities or commodities such as gold or other precious metals. In general, any commodity market might be considered to be a financial market, if the usual purpose of traders is not the immediate consumption of the commodity, but rather as a means of delaying or accelerating consumption over time.
Merrill Lynch	Merrill Lynch through its subsidiaries and affiliates, provides capital markets services, investment banking and advisory services, wealth management, asset management, insurance, banking and related products and services on a global basis. It is best known for its Global Private Client services and its strong sales force.
Investment	Investment refers to spending for the production and accumulation of capital and additions to inventories. In a financial sense, buying an asset with the expectation of making a return.
Market	A market is, as defined in economics, a social arrangement that allows buyers and sellers to discover information and carry out a voluntary exchange of goods or services.
Tangible	Having a physical existence is referred to as the tangible. Personal property other than real estate, such as cars, boats, stocks, or other assets.

Go to **Cram101.com** for the Practice Tests for this Chapter.

Promotion	Promotion refers to all the techniques sellers use to motivate people to buy products or services. An attempt by marketers to inform people about products and to persuade them to participate in an exchange.
Downsizing	The process of eliminating managerial and non-managerial positions are called downsizing.
Trend	Trend refers to the long-term movement of an economic variable, such as its average rate of increase or decrease over enough years to encompass several business cycles.
Globalization	The increasing world-wide integration of markets for goods, services and capital that attracted special attention in the late 1990s is called globalization.
Management	Management characterizes the process of leading and directing all or part of an organization, often a business, through the deployment and manipulation of resources. Early twentieth-century management writer Mary Parker Follett defined management as "the art of getting things done through people."
Premium	Premium refers to the fee charged by an insurance company for an insurance policy. The rate of losses must be relatively predictable: In order to set the premium (prices) insurers must be able to estimate them accurately.
Operation	A standardized method or technique that is performed repetitively, often on different materials resulting in different finished goods is called an operation.
Expatriate manager	A national of one country appointed to a management position in another country is an expatriate manager.
Expatriate	Employee sent by his or her company to live and manage operations in a different country is called an expatriate.
Formal contract	Formal contract refers to a contract that requires a special form or method of creation.
Compensation package	The total array of money, incentives, benefits, perquisites, and awards provided by the organization to an employee is the compensation package.
Assignment	A transfer of property or some right or interest is referred to as assignment.
Subsidy	Subsidy refers to government financial assistance to a domestic producer.
Expense	In accounting, an expense represents an event in which an asset is used up or a liability is incurred. In terms of the accounting equation, expenses reduce owners' equity.
Domestic	From or in one's own country. A domestic producer is one that produces inside the home country. A domestic price is the price inside the home country. Opposite of 'foreign' or 'world.'.
Innovation	Innovation refers to the first commercially successful introduction of a new product, the use of a new method of production, or the creation of a new form of business organization.
Human resources	Human resources refers to the individuals within the firm, and to the portion of the firm's organization that deals with hiring, firing, training, and other personnel issues.
Employment test	A written or computerbased test designed to measure a particular attribute such as intelligence or aptitude is an employment test.
Evaluation	The consumer's appraisal of the product or brand on important attributes is called evaluation.
Applicant	In many tribunal and administrative law suits, the person who initiates the claim is called the applicant.
Consideration	Consideration in contract law, a basic requirement for an enforceable agreement under traditional contract principles, defined in this text as legal value, bargained for and given

Go to **Cram101.com** for the Practice Tests for this Chapter.

in exchange for an act or promise. In corporation law, cash or property contributed to a corporation in exchange for shares, or a promise to contribute such cash or property.

Matching	Matching refers to an accounting concept that establishes when expenses are recognized. Expenses are matched with the revenues they helped to generate and are recognized when those revenues are recognized.
Leadership	Management merely consists of leadership applied to business situations; or in other words: management forms a sub-set of the broader process of leadership.
Context	The effect of the background under which a message often takes on more and richer meaning is a context. Context is especially important in cross-cultural interactions because some cultures are said to be high context or low context.
Argument	The discussion by counsel for the respective parties of their contentions on the law and the facts of the case being tried in order to aid the jury in arriving at a correct and just conclusion is called argument.
Scope	Scope of a project is the sum total of all projects products and their requirements or features.
Affective component	The component of an attitude that reflects the specific feelings regarding the personal impact of the antecedents is called the affective component.
Interest	In finance and economics, interest is the price paid by a borrower for the use of a lender's money. In other words, interest is the amount paid to "rent" money for a period of time.
Performance feedback	The process of providing employees with information regarding their performance effectiveness is referred to as performance feedback.
Workplace behavior	The pattern of action by the members of an organization that directly or indirectly influences organizational effectiveness is workplace behavior.
Receiver	A person that is appointed as a custodian of other people's property by a court of law or a creditor of the owner, pending a lawsuit or reorganization is called a receiver.
Screening	Screening in economics refers to a strategy of combating adverse selection, one of the potential decision-making complications in cases of asymmetric information.
Categorizing	The act of placing strengths and weaknesses into categories in generic internal assessment is called categorizing.
Attribution	Under certain circumstances, the tax law applies attribution rules to assign to one taxpayer the ownership interest of another taxpayer.
Attribution theory	Attribution theory suggests that we attribute causes to behavior based on observations of certain characteristics of that behavior. Employees observe their own behavior, determine whether it is a response to external or internal factors, and shape their future motivated behavior accordingly.
Thomas Edison	Thomas Edison was one of the first inventors to apply the principles of mass production to the process of invention, and can therefore be credited with the creation of the first industrial research laboratory. He developed many devices which greatly influenced life in the 20th century.
Emancipation	Emancipation is the act of freeing or being freed/the relinquishment of control; its meaning encompasses both being able to be as one is (or as a political group chooses to be) without having to adjust to another power, while simultaneously being a contributing part or party to the whole.
Complexity	The technical sophistication of the product and hence the amount of understanding required to

Go to **Cram101.com** for the Practice Tests for this Chapter.

use it is referred to as complexity. It is the opposite of simplicity.

Openness

Openness refers to the extent to which an economy is open, often measured by the ratio of its trade to GDP.

Foundation

A Foundation is a type of philanthropic organization set up by either individuals or institutions as a legal entity (either as a corporation or trust) with the purpose of distributing grants to support causes in line with the goals of the foundation.

Preparation

Preparation refers to usually the first stage in the creative process. It includes education and formal training.

Devise

In a will, a gift of real property is called a devise.

Restructuring

Restructuring is the corporate management term for the act of partially dismantling and reorganizing a company for the purpose of making it more efficient and therefore more profitable.

Citibank

In April of 2006, Citibank struck a deal with 7-Eleven to put its ATMs in over 5,500 convenience stores in the U.S. In the same month, it also announced it would sell all of its Buffalo and Rochester New York branches and accounts to M&T Bank.

Bank statement

Monthly report from a bank that shows deposits recorded, checks cleared, other debits and credits, and a running bank balance is referred to as a bank statement.

Manufacturing

Production of goods primarily by the application of labor and capital to raw materials and other intermediate inputs, in contrast to agriculture, mining, forestry, fishing, and services a manufacturing.

Verification

Verification refers to the final stage of the creative process where the validity or truthfulness of the insight is determined. The feedback portion of communication in which the receiver sends a message to the source indicating receipt of the message and the degree to which he or she understood the message.

Trial

An examination before a competent tribunal, according to the law of the land, of the facts or law put in issue in a cause, for the purpose of determining such issue is a trial. When the court hears and determines any issue of fact or law for the purpose of determining the rights of the parties, it may be considered a trial.

Prototype

A prototype is built to test the function of a new design before starting production of a product.

Product prototype

A representation of a proposed product that has at least some of the functionality of the final product; also a middle stage in the product development process in which a working product prototype has been constructed.

Revenue

Revenue is a U.S. business term for the amount of money that a company receives from its activities, mostly from sales of products and/or services to customers.

Turnover

Turnover in a financial context refers to the rate at which a provider of goods cycles through its average inventory. Turnover in a human resources context refers to the characteristic of a given company or industry, relative to rate at which an employer gains and loses staff.

Organizational citizenship

The extent to which a person's behavior makes a positive overall contribution to the organization is referred to as organizational citizenship.

Performance behaviors

The total set of work-related behaviors that the organization expects the individual to display are referred to as performance behaviors.

Jury

A body of lay persons, selected by lot, or by some other fair and impartial means, to

ascertain, under the guidance of the judge, the truth in questions of fact arising either in civil litigation or a criminal process is referred to as jury.

Labor
People's physical and mental talents and efforts that are used to help produce goods and services are called labor.

Labor market
Any arrangement that brings buyers and sellers of labor services together to agree on conditions of work and pay is called a labor market.

Balance
In banking and accountancy, the outstanding balance is the amount of money owned, (or due), that remains in a deposit account (or a loan account) at a given date, after all past remittances, payments and withdrawal have been accounted for. It can be positive (then, in the balance sheet of a firm, it is an asset) or negative (a liability).

Flexible work schedule
A flexible work schedule is a shedule in which an employee has a forty hour work week but can set their own schedule within the limits set by the employer.

Financial liability
A financial liability is something that is owed to another party. This is typically contrasted with an asset which is something of value that is owned.

Liability
A liability is a present obligation of the enterprise arizing from past events, the settlement of which is expected to result in an outflow from the enterprise of resources embodying economic benefits.

Organizational citizenship behaviors
Organizational citizenship behaviors refers to the voluntary, 'above the call of duty' behavior that are vitally important but often unrecognized sources of firm success.

Variable
A variable is something measured by a number; it is used to analyze what happens to other things when the size of that number changes.

Big five personality traits
A set of fundamental traits that are especially relevant to organizations are the big five personality traits.

Conscientiou-ness
Conscientiousness is the trait of being painstaking and careful, or the quality of being in accord with the dictates of one's conscience.Conscientiousness includes traits such as self-discipline, carefulness, thoroughness, orderedness, deliberation (the tendency to think carefully before acting) and need for achievement.

Cognitive dissonance
The anxiety a person experiences when he or she simultaneously possesses two sets of knowledge or perceptions that are contradictory or incongruent is referred to as the cognitive dissonance.

Job satisfaction
Job satisfaction describes how content an individual is with his or her job. It is a relatively recent term since in previous centuries the jobs available to a particular person were often predetermined by the occupation of that person's parent.

Organizational commitment
A person's identification with and attachment to an organization is called organizational commitment.

General Motors
General Motors is the world's largest automaker. Founded in 1908, today it employs about 327,000 people around the world. With global headquarters in Detroit, it manufactures its cars and trucks in 33 countries.

Exxon
Exxon formally replaced the Esso, Enco, and Humble brands on January 1, 1973, in the USA. The name Esso, pronounced S-O, attracted protests from other Standard Oil spinoffs because of its similarity to the name of the parent company, Standard Oil.

Competitor
Other organizations in the same industry or type of business that provide a good or service to the same set of customers is referred to as a competitor.

Go to **Cram101.com** for the Practice Tests for this Chapter.

Corporate culture	The whole collection of beliefs, values, and behaviors of a firm that send messages to those within and outside the company about how business is done is the corporate culture.
Sam Walton	I guess in all my years, what I heard more often than anything was: a town of less than 50,000 population cannot support a discount store for very long. Sam Walton was the founder of two American retailers, Wal-Mart and Sam's Club.
Minimum wage	The lowest wage employers may legally pay for an hour of work is the minimum wage.
Policy	Similar to a script in that a policy can be a less than completely rational decision-making method. Involves the use of a pre-existing set of decision steps for any problem that presents itself.
Stock	In financial terminology, stock is the capital raized by a corporation, through the issuance and sale of shares.
Wage	The payment for the service of a unit of labor, per unit time. In trade theory, it is the only payment to labor, usually unskilled labor. In empirical work, wage data may exclude other compenzation, which must be added to get the total cost of employment.
Union	A worker association that bargains with employers over wages and working conditions is called a union.
Retailing	All activities involved in selling, renting, and providing goods and services to ultimate consumers for personal, family, or household use is referred to as retailing.
Bankruptcy	Bankruptcy is a legally declared inability or impairment of ability of an individual or organization to pay their creditors.
Kmart	Kmart is an international chain of discount department stores in the United States, Australia, and New Zealand. Kmart merged with Sears in early 2005, creating the Sears Holdings Corporation.
Analyst	Analyst refers to a person or tool with a primary function of information analysis, generally with a more limited, practical and short term set of goals than a researcher.
Customer service	The ability of logistics management to satisfy users in terms of time, dependability, communication, and convenience is called the customer service.
Organizational Behavior	The study of human behavior in organizational settings, the interface between human behavior and the organization, and the organization itself is called organizational behavior.
Warehouse	Warehouse refers to a location, often decentralized, that a firm uses to store, consolidate, age, or mix stock; house product-recall programs; or ease tax burdens.
Correlation	A correlation is the measure of the extent to which two economic or statistical variables move together, normalized so that its values range from -1 to +1. It is defined as the covariance of the two variables divided by the square root of the product of their variances.

Security	Security refers to a claim on the borrower future income that is sold by the borrower to the lender. A security is a type of transferable interest representing financial value.
Teamwork	That which occurs when group members work together in ways that utilize their skills well to accomplish a purpose is called teamwork.
Team building	A term that describes the process of identifying roles for team members and helping the team members succeed in their roles is called team building.
Consultant	A professional that provides expert advice in a particular field or area in which customers occassionaly require this type of knowledge is a consultant.
Reorganization	Reorganization occurs, among other instances, when one corporation acquires another in a merger or acquisition, a single corporation divides into two or more entities, or a corporation makes a substantial change in its capital structure.
Downsizing	The process of eliminating managerial and non-managerial positions are called downsizing.
Interest	In finance and economics, interest is the price paid by a borrower for the use of a lender's money. In other words, interest is the amount of paid to "rent" money for a period of time.
Economy	The income, expenditures, and resources that affect the cost of running a business and household are called an economy.
Merger	Merger refers to the combination of two firms into a single firm.
Human resources	Human resources refers to the individuals within the firm, and to the portion of the firm's organization that deals with hiring, firing, training, and other personnel issues.
Firm	An organization that employs resources to produce a good or service for profit and owns and operates one or more plants is referred to as a firm.
Trust	An arrangement in which shareholders of independent firms agree to give up their stock in exchange for trust certificates that entitle them to a share of the trust's common profits.
Alienation	The voluntary act or acts by which one-person transfers his or her own property to another is referred to as alienation.
Depression	Depression refers to a prolonged period characterized by high unemployment, low output and investment, depressed business confidence, falling prices, and widespread business failures. A milder form of business downturn is a recession.
Productivity	Productivity refers to the total output of goods and services in a given period of time divided by work hours.
Gain	In finance, gain is a profit or an increase in value of an investment such as a stock or bond. Gain is calculated by fair market value or the proceeds from the sale of the investment minus the sum of the purchase price and all costs associated with it.
Openness	Openness refers to the extent to which an economy is open, often measured by the ratio of its trade to GDP.
Investment	Investment refers to spending for the production and accumulation of capital and additions to inventories. In a financial sense, buying an asset with the expectation of making a return.
Bottom line	The bottom line is net income on the last line of a income statement.
Fund	Independent accounting entity with a self-balancing set of accounts segregated for the purposes of carrying on specific activities is referred to as a fund.
Customer service	The ability of logistics management to satisfy users in terms of time, dependability, communication, and convenience is called the customer service.

Go to **Cram101.com** for the Practice Tests for this Chapter.

Turnover	Turnover in a financial context refers to the rate at which a provider of goods cycles through its average inventory. Turnover in a human resources context refers to the characteristic of a given company or industry, relative to rate at which an employer gains and loses staff.
Service	Service refers to a "non tangible product" that is not embodied in a physical good and that typically effects some change in another product, person, or institution. Contrasts with good.
Sticky	Sticky is a term used in economics used to describe a situation in which a variable is resistant to change. For example, nominal wages are often said to be sticky.
Industry	A group of firms that produce identical or similar products is an industry. It is also used specifically to refer to an area of economic production focused on manufacturing which involves large amounts of capital investment before any profit can be realized, also called "heavy industry".
Jack Welch	In 1986, GE acquired NBC. During the 90s, Jack Welch helped to modernize GE by emphasizing a shift from manufacturing to services. He also made hundreds of acquisitions and made a push to dominate markets abroad. Welch adopted the Six Sigma quality program in late 1995.
Standard of living	Standard of living refers to the level of consumption that people enjoy, on the average, and is measured by average income per person.
Option	A contract that gives the purchaser the option to buy or sell the underlying financial instrument at a specified price, called the exercise price or strike price, within a specific period of time.
Promotion	Promotion refers to all the techniques sellers use to motivate people to buy products or services. An attempt by marketers to inform people about products and to persuade them to participate in an exchange.
Affiliation	A relationship with other websites in which a company can cross-promote and is credited for sales that accrue through their site is an affiliation.
Channel	Channel, in communications (sometimes called communications channel), refers to the medium used to convey information from a sender (or transmitter) to a receiver.
Consideration	Consideration in contract law, a basic requirement for an enforceable agreement under traditional contract principles, defined in this text as legal value, bargained for and given in exchange for an act or promise. In corporation law, cash or property contributed to a corporation in exchange for shares, or a promise to contribute such cash or property.
Management	Management characterizes the process of leading and directing all or part of an organization, often a business, through the deployment and manipulation of resources. Early twentieth-century management writer Mary Parker Follett defined management as "the art of getting things done through people."
Tradeoff	The sacrifice of some or all of one economic goal, good, or service to achieve some other goal, good, or service is a tradeoff.
Trend	Trend refers to the long-term movement of an economic variable, such as its average rate of increase or decrease over enough years to encompass several business cycles.
Machiavellianism	Machiavellianism refers to a personality trait. People who possess this trait behave to gain power and to control the behavior of others.
Human relations approach	Human relations approach refers the idea that the best way to improve production was to respect workers and show concern for their needs. Became popular in the 1920s and remained influential through the 1950s.

Go to **Cram101.com** for the Practice Tests for this Chapter.

Job satisfaction	Job satisfaction describes how content an individual is with his or her job. It is a relatively recent term since in previous centuries the jobs available to a particular person were often predetermined by the occupation of that person's parent.
Hierarchy of needs	Hierarchy of needs refers to Maslow's theory that human needs are arranged in an order or hierarchy based on their importance. The need hierarchy includes physiological, safety, social-love and belonging, esteem, and self-actualization needs.
ERG theory	Alderfer expanded Maslow's hierarchy of needs by categorizing the hierarchy into his ERG theory. Alderfer categorized the lower order needs (Physiological and Safety) into the Existence category. He fit Maslow's interpersonal love and esteem needs into the relatedness category. The growth category contained the Self Actualization and self esteem needs.
Hierarchy	A system of grouping people in an organization according to rank from the top down in which all subordinate managers must report to one person is called a hierarchy.
Maslow	Maslow was an American psychologist. He is mostly noted today for his proposal of a hierarchy of human needs.
Wage	The payment for the service of a unit of labor, per unit time. In trade theory, it is the only payment to labor, usually unskilled labor. In empirical work, wage data may exclude other compenzation, which must be added to get the total cost of employment.
Merit pay	A compenzation system that bases an individual's salary or wage increase on a measure of the person's performance accomplishment during a specific time period is called merit pay.
Continuity	A media scheduling strategy where a continuous pattern of advertising is used over the time span of the advertising campaign is continuity.
Insurance	Insurance refers to a system by which individuals can reduce their exposure to risk of large losses by spreading the risks among a large number of persons.
Grievance	A charge by employees that management is not abiding by the terms of the negotiated labormanagement agreement is the grievance.
Layoff	A layoff is the termination of an employee or (more commonly) a group of employees for business reasons, such as the decision that certain positions are no longer necessary.
Guest worker	Guest worker refers to a foreign worker who is permitted to enter a country temporarily in order to take a job for which there is shortage of domestic labor.
Custodian	Custodian as a financial term, refers to a bank (Custodian bank), agent, or other organization responsible for safeguarding a firm's or individual's financial assets.
Policy	Similar to a script in that a policy can be a less than completely rational decision-making method. Involves the use of a pre-existing set of decision steps for any problem that presents itself.
Wall Street Journal	Dow Jones & Company was founded in 1882 by reporters Charles Dow, Edward Jones and Charles Bergstresser. Jones converted the small Customers' Afternoon Letter into The Wall Street Journal, first published in 1889, and began delivery of the Dow Jones News Service via telegraph. The Journal featured the Jones 'Average', the first of several indexes of stock and bond prices on the New York Stock Exchange.
Journal	Book of original entry, in which transactions are recorded in a general ledger system, is referred to as a journal.
International Business	International business refers to any firm that engages in international trade or investment.
Prentice Hall	Prentice Hall is a leading educational publisher. It is an imprint of the Pearson Education

Company, based in New Jersey, USA.

Hygiene factors	Hygiene factors refers to job factors that can cause dissatisfaction if missing but do not necessarily motivate employees if increased.
Respondent	Respondent refers to a term often used to describe the party charged in an administrative proceeding. The party adverse to the appellant in a case appealed to a higher court.
Stock option	A stock option is a specific type of option that uses the stock itself as an underlying instrument to determine the option's pay-off and therefore its value.
Stock	In financial terminology, stock is the capital raized by a corporation, through the issuance and sale of shares.
Market	A market is, as defined in economics, a social arrangement that allows buyers and sellers to discover information and carry out a voluntary exchange of goods or services.
Evaluation	The consumer's appraisal of the product or brand on important attributes is called evaluation.
Organizational Behavior	The study of human behavior in organizational settings, the interface between human behavior and the organization, and the organization itself is called organizational behavior.
Manufacturing	Production of goods primarily by the application of labor and capital to raw materials and other intermediate inputs, in contrast to agriculture, mining, forestry, fishing, and services a manufacturing.
Entrepreneur	The owner/operator. The person who organizes, manages, and assumes the risks of a firm, taking a new idea or a new product and turning it into a successful business is an entrepreneur.
Apple Computer	Apple Computer has been a major player in the evolution of personal computing since its founding in 1976. The Apple II microcomputer, introduced in 1977, was a hit with home users.
Bill Gates	Bill Gates is the co-founder, chairman, former chief software architect, and former CEO of Microsoft Corporation. He is one of the best-known entrepreneurs of the personal computer revolution and he is widely respected for his foresight and ambition.
Microsoft	Microsoft is a multinational computer technology corporation with 2004 global annual sales of US$39.79 billion and 71,553 employees in 102 countries and regions as of July 2006. It develops, manufactures, licenses, and supports a wide range of software products for computing devices.
Economic development	Increase in the economic standard of living of a country's population, normally accomplished by increasing its stocks of physical and human capital and improving its technology is an economic development.
Correlation	A correlation is the measure of the extent to which two economic or statistical variables move together, normalized so that its values range from -1 to +1. It is defined as the covariance of the two variables divided by the square root of the product of their variances.
Preference	The act of a debtor in paying or securing one or more of his creditors in a manner more favorable to them than to other creditors or to the exclusion of such other creditors is a preference. In the absence of statute, a preference is perfectly good, but to be legal it must be bona fide, and not a mere subterfuge of the debtor to secure a future benefit to himself or to prevent the application of his property to his debts.
Points	Loan origination fees that may be deductible as interest by a buyer of property. A seller of property who pays points reduces the selling price by the amount of the points paid for the buyer.

Go to **Cram101.com** for the Practice Tests for this Chapter.

Plea	A plea is an answer to a declaration or complaint or any material allegation of fact therein that, if untrue, would defeat the action. In criminal procedure, a plea is the matter that the accused, on his arraignment, alleges in answer to the charge against him.
Scientific management	Studying workers to find the most efficient ways of doing things and then teaching people those techniques is scientific management.
Corporation	A legal entity chartered by a state or the Federal government that is distinct and separate from the individuals who own it is a corporation. This separation gives the corporation unique powers which other legal entities lack.
Cooperative	A business owned and controlled by the people who use it, producers, consumers, or workers with similar needs who pool their resources for mutual gain is called cooperative.
Labor	People's physical and mental talents and efforts that are used to help produce goods and services are called labor.
Labor union	A group of workers organized to advance the interests of the group is called a labor union.
Union	A worker association that bargains with employers over wages and working conditions is called a union.
Employee Stock Ownership Plans	Like profit sharing, Employee Stock Ownership Plans are based on the total organization's performance, but are measured in terms of stock price.
Employee stock ownership plan	Employee Stock Ownership Plan is a qualified employee-benefit plan in which employees are entitled and encouraged to invest in shares of the company's stock and often at a favorable price. The employer's contributions are tax deductible for the employer and tax deferred for the employee.
Divestiture	In finance and economics, divestiture is the reduction of some kind of asset, for either financial or social goals. A divestment is the opposite of an investment.
Customer satisfaction	Customer satisfaction is a business term which is used to capture the idea of measuring how satisfied an enterprise's customers are with the organization's efforts in a marketplace.
United Food and Commercial Workers Union	The United Food and Commercial Workers Union is a labor union representing approximately 1.3 million workers in the United States and Canada in many industries, including agriculture, health care, meatpacking, poultry and food processing, manufacturing, textile and chemical trades, and retail food.
Expense	In accounting, an expense represents an event in which an asset is used up or a liability is incurred. In terms of the accounting equation, expenses reduce owners' equity.
Loyalty	Marketers tend to define customer loyalty as making repeat purchases. Some argue that it should be defined attitudinally as a strongly positive feeling about the brand.
United airlines	United Airlines is a major airline of the United States headquartered in unincorporated Elk Grove Township, Illinois, near Chicago's O'Hare International Airport, the airline's largest traffic hub, with 650 daily departures. On February 1, 2006, it emerged from Chapter 11 bankruptcy protection under which it had operated since December 9, 2002, the largest and longest airline bankruptcy case in history.
Contract	A contract is a "promise" or an "agreement" that is enforced or recognized by the law. In the civil law, a contract is considered to be part of the general law of obligations.
Southwest airlines	Southwest Airlines is a low-fare airline in the United States. It is the third-largest airline in the world, by number of passengers carried, and the largest in the United States by number of passengers carried domestically.
Organization	The set of values that helps the organization's employees understand which actions are

Go to Cram101.com for the Practice Tests for this Chapter.

culture	considered acceptable and which unacceptable is referred to as the organization culture.
Shares	Shares refer to an equity security, representing a shareholder's ownership of a corporation. Shares are one of a finite number of equal portions in the capital of a company, entitling the owner to a proportion of distributed, non-reinvested profits known as dividends and to a portion of the value of the company in case of liquidation.
Assessment	Collecting information and providing feedback to employees about their behavior, communication style, or skills is an assessment.

Commerce	Commerce is the exchange of something of value between two entities. It is the central mechanism from which capitalism is derived.
Firm	An organization that employs resources to produce a good or service for profit and owns and operates one or more plants is referred to as a firm.
Customer service	The ability of logistics management to satisfy users in terms of time, dependability, communication, and convenience is called the customer service.
Service	Service refers to a "non tangible product" that is not embodied in a physical good and that typically effects some change in another product, person, or institution. Contrasts with good.
Property	Assets defined in the broadest legal sense. Property includes the unrealized receivables of a cash basis taxpayer, but not services rendered.
Applicant	In many tribunal and administrative law suits, the person who initiates the claim is called the applicant.
Industry	A group of firms that produce identical or similar products is an industry. It is also used specifically to refer to an area of economic production focused on manufacturing which involves large amounts of capital investment before any profit can be realized, also called "heavy industry".
Organization culture	The set of values that helps the organization's employees understand which actions are considered acceptable and which unacceptable is referred to as the organization culture.
Customer satisfaction	Customer satisfaction is a business term which is used to capture the idea of measuring how satisfied an enterprise's customers are with the organization's efforts in a marketplace.
Profit	Profit refers to the return to the resource entrepreneurial ability; total revenue minus total cost.
Stock	In financial terminology, stock is the capital raized by a corporation, through the issuance and sale of shares.
Equity theory	Equity theory, in Business seeks to describe a relationship between employees motivation and their perception of being treated fairly. The theory suggests that employees seek to ascribe values to their inputs and outputs.
Equity	Equity is the name given to the set of legal principles, in countries following the English common law tradition, which supplement strict rules of law where their application would operate harshly, so as to achieve what is sometimes referred to as "natural justice."
Forming	The first stage of team development, where the team is formed and the objectives for the team are set is referred to as forming.
Contribution	In business organization law, the cash or property contributed to a business by its owners is referred to as contribution.
Loyalty	Marketers tend to define customer loyalty as making repeat purchases. Some argue that it should be defined attitudinally as a strongly positive feeling about the brand.
Inputs	The inputs used by a firm or an economy are the labor, raw materials, electricity and other resources it uses to produce its outputs.
Intrinsic reward	Motivating events which occur as a natural part of the learning experience is a intrinsic reward.
Psychological contract	A person's set of expectations regarding what he or she will contribute to the organization and what the organization, in return, will provide to the individual is called psychological contract.

Go to **Cram101.com** for the Practice Tests for this Chapter.

Assessment	Collecting information and providing feedback to employees about their behavior, communication style, or skills is an assessment.
Contract	A contract is a "promise" or an "agreement" that is enforced or recognized by the law. In the civil law, a contract is considered to be part of the general law of obligations.
Labor	People's physical and mental talents and efforts that are used to help produce goods and services are called labor.
Labor market	Any arrangement that brings buyers and sellers of labor services together to agree on conditions of work and pay is called a labor market.
Market	A market is, as defined in economics, a social arrangement that allows buyers and sellers to discover information and carry out a voluntary exchange of goods or services.
Avon	Avon is an American cosmetics, perfume and toy seller with markets in over 135 countries across the world and a sales of $7.74 billion worldwide.
Charles Schwab	Charles Schwab is the world's second-largest discount broker. Besides discount brokerage, the firm offers mutual funds, annuities, bond trading, and now mortgages through its Charles Schwab Bank.
Chief information officer	The chief information officer is a job title for the head of information technology group within an organization. They often report to the chief executive officer or chief financial officer.
Level playing field	The objective of those who advocate protection on the grounds the foreign firms have an unfair advantage. A level playing field would remove such advantages, although it is not usually clear what sorts of advantage would be permitted to remain.
Status quo	Status quo is a Latin term meaning the present, current, existing state of affairs.
Security	Security refers to a claim on the borrower future income that is sold by the borrower to the lender. A security is a type of transferable interest representing financial value.
Evaluation	The consumer's appraisal of the product or brand on important attributes is called evaluation.
Human resources	Human resources refers to the individuals within the firm, and to the portion of the firm's organization that deals with hiring, firing, training, and other personnel issues.
Consultant	A professional that provides expert advice in a particular field or area in which customers occassionaly require this type of knowledge is a consultant.
Assignment	A transfer of property or some right or interest is referred to as assignment.
Overtime	Overtime is the amount of time someone works beyond normal working hours.
Complexity	The technical sophistication of the product and hence the amount of understanding required to use it is referred to as complexity. It is the opposite of simplicity.
Scope	Scope of a project is the sum total of all projects products and their requirements or features.
Expectancy theory	A process theory that proposes that motivation depends on individuals' expectations about their ability to perform tasks and receive desired rewards is called expectancy theory.
Operation	A standardized method or technique that is performed repetitively, often on different materials resulting in different finished goods is called an operation.
Shell	One of the original Seven Sisters, Royal Dutch/Shell is the world's third-largest oil company by revenue, and a major player in the petrochemical industry and the solar energy business. Shell has six core businesses: Exploration and Production, Gas and Power, Downstream,

Go to **Cram101.com** for the Practice Tests for this Chapter.

	Chemicals, Renewables, and Trading/Shipping, and operates in more than 140 countries.
Preference	The act of a debtor in paying or securing one or more of his creditors in a manner more favorable to them than to other creditors or to the exclusion of such other creditors is a preference. In the absence of statute, a preference is perfectly good, but to be legal it must be bona fide, and not a mere subterfuge of the debtor to secure a future benefit to himself or to prevent the application of his property to his debts.
Publicity	Publicity refers to any information about an individual, product, or organization that's distributed to the public through the media and that's not paid for or controlled by the seller.
Valence	Valence refers to the emotional value associated with a stimulus; e.g., a familiar face can have positive valence.
Promotion	Promotion refers to all the techniques sellers use to motivate people to buy products or services. An attempt by marketers to inform people about products and to persuade them to participate in an exchange.
Tangible	Having a physical existence is referred to as the tangible. Personal property other than real estate, such as cars, boats, stocks, or other assets.
Technology	The body of knowledge and techniques that can be used to combine economic resources to produce goods and services is called technology.
Confirmed	When the seller's bank agrees to assume liability on the letter of credit issued by the buyer's bank the transaction is confirmed.The term means that the credit is not only backed up by the issuing foreign bank, but that payment is also guaranteed by the notifying American bank.
Manufacturing	Production of goods primarily by the application of labor and capital to raw materials and other intermediate inputs, in contrast to agriculture, mining, forestry, fishing, and services a manufacturing.
Production	The creation of finished goods and services using the factors of production: land, labor, capital, entrepreneurship, and knowledge.
Variable	A variable is something measured by a number; it is used to analyze what happens to other things when the size of that number changes.
Organizational goals	Objectives that management seeks to achieve in pursuing the firm's purpose are organizational goals.
Classical conditioning	A simple form of learning that links a conditioned response with an unconditioned stimulus is referred to as classical conditioning.
Reinforcement theory	A motivation theory based on the relationship between a given behavior and its consequences is referred to as the reinforcement theory.
Operant conditioning	Operant conditioning is the modification of behavior brought about over time by the consequences of said behavior. Operant conditioning is distinguished from Pavlovian conditioning in that operant conditioning deals with voluntary behavior explained by its consequences, while Pavlovian conditioning deals with involuntary behavior triggered by its antecedents.
Frequency	Frequency refers to the speed of the up and down movements of a fluctuating economic variable; that is, the number of times per unit of time that the variable completes a cycle of up and down movement.
Supervisor	A Supervisor is an employee of an organization with some of the powers and responsibilities of management, occupying a role between true manager and a regular employee. A Supervisor

	position is typically the first step towards being promoted into a management role.
Gain	In finance, gain is a profit or an increase in value of an investment such as a stock or bond. Gain is calculated by fair market value or the proceeds from the sale of the investment minus the sum of the purchase price and all costs associated with it.
Wage	The payment for the service of a unit of labor, per unit time. In trade theory, it is the only payment to labor, usually unskilled labor. In empirical work, wage data may exclude other compenzation, which must be added to get the total cost of employment.
Social learning	Social learning occurs when people observe the behaviors of others, recognize their consequences, and alter their own behavior as a result.
Behavior modification	Behavior modification is a technique of altering an individual's reactions to stimuli through positive reinforcement and the extinction of maladaptive behavior.
Organizational Behavior	The study of human behavior in organizational settings, the interface between human behavior and the organization, and the organization itself is called organizational behavior.
Performance management	The means through which managers ensure that employees' activities and outputs are congruent with the organization's goals is referred to as performance management.
Management	Management characterizes the process of leading and directing all or part of an organization, often a business, through the deployment and manipulation of resources. Early twentieth-century management writer Mary Parker Follett defined management as "the art of getting things done through people."
Intervention	Intervention refers to an activity in which a government buys or sells its currency in the foreign exchange market in order to affect its currency's exchange rate.
American Management Association	American Management Association International is the world's largest membership-based management development and executive training organization. Their products include instructor led seminars, workshops, conferences, customized corporate programs, online learning, books, newsletters, research surveys and reports.
Performance improvement	Performance improvement is the concept of measuring the output of a particular process or procedure then modifying the process or procedure in order to increase the output, increase efficiency, or increase the effectiveness of the process or procedure.
Productivity	Productivity refers to the total output of goods and services in a given period of time divided by work hours.
Drawback	Drawback refers to rebate of import duties when the imported good is re-exported or used as input to the production of an exported good.
Compromise	Compromise occurs when the interaction is moderately important to meeting goals and the goals are neither completely compatible nor completely incompatible.
Argument	The discussion by counsel for the respective parties of their contentions on the law and the facts of the case being tried in order to aid the jury in arriving at a correct and just conclusion is called argument.
Attribution theory	Attribution theory suggests that we attribute causes to behavior based on observations of certain characteristics of that behavior. Employees observe their own behavior, determine whether it is a response to external or internal factors, and shape their future motivated behavior accordingly.
Attribution	Under certain circumstances, the tax law applies attribution rules to assign to one taxpayer the ownership interest of another taxpayer.
Incentive	An incentive is any factor (financial or non-financial) that provides a motive for a

Go to Cram101.com for the Practice Tests for this Chapter.

	particular course of action, or counts as a reason for preferring one choice to the alternatives.
Product line	A group of products that are physically similar or are intended for a similar market are called the product line.
Marketing	Promoting and selling products or services to customers, or prospective customers, is referred to as marketing.
Research and development	The use of resources for the deliberate discovery of new information and ways of doing things, together with the application of that information in inventing new products or processes is referred to as research and development.
Stock option	A stock option is a specific type of option that uses the stock itself as an underlying instrument to determine the option's pay-off and therefore its value.
Option	A contract that gives the purchaser the option to buy or sell the underlying financial instrument at a specified price, called the exercise price or strike price, within a specific period of time.
A share	In finance the term A share has two distinct meanings, both relating to securities. The first is a designation for a 'class' of common or preferred stock. A share of common or preferred stock typically has enhanced voting rights or other benefits compared to the other forms of shares that may have been created. The equity structure, or how many types of shares are offered, is determined by the corporate charter.
Product development	In business and engineering, new product development is the complete process of bringing a new product to market. There are two parallel aspects to this process : one involves product engineering ; the other marketing analysis. Marketers see new product development as the first stage in product life cycle management, engineers as part of Product Lifecycle Management.
Distribution	Distribution in economics, the manner in which total output and income is distributed among individuals or factors.
Acquisition	A company's purchase of the property and obligations of another company is an acquisition.
Public company	A public company is a company owned by the public rather than by a relatively few individuals. There are two different meanings for this term: (1) A company that is owned by stockholders who are members of the general public and trade shares publicly, often through a listing on a stock exchange. Ownership is open to anyone that has the money and inclination to buy shares in the company. It is differentiated from privately held companies where the shares are held by a small group of individuals, who are often members of one or a small group of families or otherwise related individuals, or other companies. The variant of this type of company in the United Kingdom and Ireland is known as a public limited compan, and (2) A government-owned corporation. This meaning of a "public company" comes from the fact that government debt is sometimes referred to as "public debt" although there are no "public bonds", government finance is sometimes called "public finance", among similar uses. This is the less-common meaning.
Entrepreneur	The owner/operator. The person who organizes, manages, and assumes the risks of a firm, taking a new idea or a new product and turning it into a successful business is an entrepreneur.
Forbes	David Churbuck founded online Forbes in 1996. The site drew attention when it uncovered Stephen Glass' journalistic fraud in The New Republic in 1998, a scoop that gave credibility to internet journalism.
Points	Loan origination fees that may be deductible as interest by a buyer of property. A seller of

property who pays points reduces the selling price by the amount of the points paid for the buyer.

Management	Management characterizes the process of leading and directing all or part of an organization, often a business, through the deployment and manipulation of resources. Early twentieth-century management writer Mary Parker Follett defined management as "the art of getting things done through people."
Empowerment	Giving employees the authority and responsibility to respond quickly to customer requests is called empowerment.
Manufacturing	Production of goods primarily by the application of labor and capital to raw materials and other intermediate inputs, in contrast to agriculture, mining, forestry, fishing, and services a manufacturing.
Industry	A group of firms that produce identical or similar products is an industry. It is also used specifically to refer to an area of economic production focused on manufacturing which involves large amounts of capital investment before any profit can be realized, also called "heavy industry".
Long run	In economic models, the long run time frame assumes no fixed factors of production. Firms can enter or leave the marketplace, and the cost (and availability) of land, labor, raw materials, and capital goods can be assumed to vary.
Expense	In accounting, an expense represents an event in which an asset is used up or a liability is incurred. In terms of the accounting equation, expenses reduce owners' equity.
Firm	An organization that employs resources to produce a good or service for profit and owns and operates one or more plants is referred to as a firm.
Assignment	A transfer of property or some right or interest is referred to as assignment.
Supervisor	A Supervisor is an employee of an organization with some of the powers and responsibilities of management, occupying a role between true manager and a regular employee. A Supervisor position is typically the first step towards being promoted into a management role.
Production	The creation of finished goods and services using the factors of production: land, labor, capital, entrepreneurship, and knowledge.
Operation	A standardized method or technique that is performed repetitively, often on different materials resulting in different finished goods is called an operation.
Downsizing	The process of eliminating managerial and non-managerial positions are called downsizing.
Continuity	A media scheduling strategy where a continuous pattern of advertising is used over the time span of the advertising campaign is continuity.
Turnover	Turnover in a financial context refers to the rate at which a provider of goods cycles through its average inventory. Turnover in a human resources context refers to the characteristic of a given company or industry, relative to rate at which an employer gains and loses staff.
Alternative work arrangements	Independent contractors, on-call workers, and contract company workers who are not employed full-time by the company are alternative work arrangements.
Performance management	The means through which managers ensure that employees' activities and outputs are congruent with the organization's goals is referred to as performance management.
Behavior modification	Behavior modification is a technique of altering an individual's reactions to stimuli through positive reinforcement and the extinction of maladaptive behavior.
Organizational Behavior	The study of human behavior in organizational settings, the interface between human behavior and the organization, and the organization itself is called organizational behavior.

Go to **Cram101.com** for the Practice Tests for this Chapter.

Job satisfaction	Job satisfaction describes how content an individual is with his or her job. It is a relatively recent term since in previous centuries the jobs available to a particular person were often predetermined by the occupation of that person's parent.
Labor	People's physical and mental talents and efforts that are used to help produce goods and services are called labor.
Trend	Trend refers to the long-term movement of an economic variable, such as its average rate of increase or decrease over enough years to encompass several business cycles.
Adam Smith	Adam Smith (baptized June 5, 1723 O.S. (June 16 N.S.) – July 17, 1790) was a Scottish political economist and moral philosopher. His Inquiry into the Nature and Causes of the Wealth of Nations was one of the earliest attempts to study the historical development of industry and commerce in Europe. That work helped to create the modern academic discipline of economics
Division of labor	Division of labor is generally speaking the specialization of cooperative labor in specific, circumscribed tasks and roles, intended to increase efficiency of output.
Accounting	A system that collects and processes financial information about an organization and reports that information to decision makers is referred to as accounting.
Economy	The income, expenditures, and resources that affect the cost of running a business and household are called an economy.
Industrial revolution	The Industrial Revolution is the stream of new technology and the resulting growth of output that began in England toward the end of the 18th century.
Scientific management	Studying workers to find the most efficient ways of doing things and then teaching people those techniques is scientific management.
Peak	Peak refers to the point in the business cycle when an economic expansion reaches its highest point before turning down. Contrasts with trough.
Assembly line	An assembly line is a manufacturing process in which interchangeable parts are added to a product in a sequential manner to create a finished product.
Gain	In finance, gain is a profit or an increase in value of an investment such as a stock or bond. Gain is calculated by fair market value or the proceeds from the sale of the investment minus the sum of the purchase price and all costs associated with it.
Productivity	Productivity refers to the total output of goods and services in a given period of time divided by work hours.
Interest	In finance and economics, interest is the price paid by a borrower for the use of a lender's money. In other words, interest is the amount of paid to "rent" money for a period of time.
Automation	Automation allows machines to do work previously accomplished by people.
Wall Street Journal	Dow Jones & Company was founded in 1882 by reporters Charles Dow, Edward Jones and Charles Bergstresser. Jones converted the small Customers' Afternoon Letter into The Wall Street Journal, first published in 1889, and began delivery of the Dow Jones News Service via telegraph. The Journal featured the Jones 'Average', the first of several indexes of stock and bond prices on the New York Stock Exchange.
Journal	Book of original entry, in which transactions are recorded in a general ledger system, is referred to as a journal.
Service	Service refers to a "non tangible product" that is not embodied in a physical good and that typically effects some change in another product, person, or institution. Contrasts with good.

Specialist	A specialist is a trader who makes a market in one or several stocks and holds the limit order book for those stocks.
Corporation	A legal entity chartered by a state or the Federal government that is distinct and separate from the individuals who own it is a corporation. This separation gives the corporation unique powers which other legal entities lack.
Production line	A production line is a set of sequential operations established in a factory whereby materials are put through a refining process to produce an end-product that is suitable for onward consumption; or components are assembled to make a finished article.
Regulation	Regulation refers to restrictions state and federal laws place on business with regard to the conduct of its activities.
Occupational Safety and Health Administration	The United States Occupational Safety and Health Administration is an agency of the United States Department of Labor. It was created by Congress under the Occupational Safety and Health Act, signed by President Richard M. Nixon, on December 29, 1970.
Administration	Administration refers to the management and direction of the affairs of governments and institutions; a collective term for all policymaking officials of a government; the execution and implementation of public policy.
Personnel	A collective term for all of the employees of an organization. Personnel is also commonly used to refer to the personnel management function or the organizational unit responsible for administering personnel programs.
Job enlargement	A job enrichment strategy that involves combining a series of tasks into one challenging and interesting assignment is referred to as job enlargement.
Job rotation	A job enrichment strategy that involves moving employees from one job to another is a job rotation.
Insurance	Insurance refers to a system by which individuals can reduce their exposure to risk of large losses by spreading the risks among a large number of persons.
Ford	Ford is an American company that manufactures and sells automobiles worldwide. Ford introduced methods for large-scale manufacturing of cars, and large-scale management of an industrial workforce, especially elaborately engineered manufacturing sequences typified by the moving assembly lines.
Job enrichment	A motivational strategy that emphasizes motivating the worker through the job itself is called job enrichment.
Horizontal loading	Loading of items of like character in horizontal layers throughout the holds of a ship is horizontal loading.
Instrument	Instrument refers to an economic variable that is controlled by policy makers and can be used to influence other variables, called targets. Examples are monetary and fiscal policies used to achieve external and internal balance.
Supply	Supply is the aggregate amount of any material good that can be called into being at a certain price point; it comprises one half of the equation of supply and demand. In classical economic theory, a curve representing supply is one of the factors that produce price.
Objection	In the trial of a case the formal remonstrance made by counsel to something that has been said or done, in order to obtain the court's ruling thereon is an objection.
Job characteristics theory	Job characteristics theory identifies three critical psychological states: experienced meaningfulness of the work, experienced responsibility for work outcomes, and knowledge of results.

Property	Assets defined in the broadest legal sense. Property includes the unrealized receivables of a cash basis taxpayer, but not services rendered.
Core	A core is the set of feasible allocations in an economy that cannot be improved upon by subset of the set of the economy's consumers (a coalition). In construction, when the force in an element is within a certain center section, the core, the element will only be under compression.
Motorola	The Six Sigma quality system was developed at Motorola even though it became most well known because of its use by General Electric. It was created by engineer Bill Smith, under the direction of Bob Galvin (son of founder Paul Galvin) when he was running the company.
Xerox	Xerox was founded in 1906 as "The Haloid Company" manufacturing photographic paper and equipment. The company came to prominence in 1959 with the introduction of the first plain paper photocopier using the process of xerography (electrophotography) developed by Chester Carlson, the Xerox 914.
Extension	Extension refers to an out-of-court settlement in which creditors agree to allow the firm more time to meet its financial obligations. A new repayment schedule will be developed, subject to the acceptance of creditors.
Human Relations Movement	Human relations movement refers to the period following the Hawthorne Studies, that was based on the assumption that employee satisfaction is a key determinant of performance. It marked the beginning of organizational development.
License	A license in the sphere of Intellectual Property Rights (IPR) is a document, contract or agreement giving permission or the 'right' to a legally-definable entity to do something (such as manufacture a product or to use a service), or to apply something (such as a trademark), with the objective of achieving commercial gain.
International firm	International firm refers to those firms who have responded to stiff competition domestically by expanding their sales abroad. They may start a production facility overseas and send some of their managers, who report to a global division, to that country.
Asset	An item of property, such as land, capital, money, a share in ownership, or a claim on others for future payment, such as a bond or a bank deposit is an asset.
Quality circle	A quality circle is a volunteer group composed of workers who meet together to discuss workplace improvement, and make presentations to management with their ideas.
Hierarchy	A system of grouping people in an organization according to rank from the top down in which all subordinate managers must report to one person is called a hierarchy.
Authority	Authority in agency law, refers to an agent's ability to affect his principal's legal relations with third parties. Also used to refer to an actor's legal power or ability to do something. In addition, sometimes used to refer to a statute, case, or other legal source that justifies a particular result.
Telecommuting	Telecommuting is a work arrangement in which employees enjoy limited flexibility in working location and hours.
Job sharing	Situation in which the duties and hours of one job position are carried out by two people is job sharing.
Compressed schedule	A set of work schedules that use non-traditional methods of completing a 40 hour work week is called the compressed schedule.
Shell	One of the original Seven Sisters, Royal Dutch/Shell is the world's third-largest oil company by revenue, and a major player in the petrochemical industry and the solar energy business. Shell has six core businesses: Exploration and Production, Gas and Power, Downstream,

Go to **Cram101.com** for the Practice Tests for this Chapter.

	Chemicals, Renewables, and Trading/Shipping, and operates in more than 140 countries.
Amoco	Amoco was formed as Standard Oil (Indiana) in 1889 by John D. Rockefeller as part of the Standard Oil trust. In 1910, with the rise in popularity of the automobile, Amoco decided to specialize in providing gas to everyday families and their cars. In 1911, the year it became independent from the Standard Oil trust, the company sold 88% of the gasoline and kerosene sold in the midwest.
Flexible work schedule	A flexible work schedule is a shedule in which an employee has a forty hour work week but can set their own schedule within the limits set by the employer.
Flextime	A scheduling method that gives employees control over their work schedule is flextime; usually involves some 'core' times when employees must be at work, and a set of 'flextime' that can be adjustable for various employees.
Compressed work schedule	A compressed work schedule is a work schedule set by a firm where an employee works forty hours in less than five business days.
Core time	Core time in a flextime plan, the period when all employees are expected to be at their job stations.
Utility	Utility refers to the want-satisfying power of a good or service; the satisfaction or pleasure a consumer obtains from the consumption of a good or service.
Market	A market is, as defined in economics, a social arrangement that allows buyers and sellers to discover information and carry out a voluntary exchange of goods or services.
United airlines	United Airlines is a major airline of the United States headquartered in unincorporated Elk Grove Township, Illinois, near Chicago's O'Hare International Airport, the airline's largest traffic hub, with 650 daily departures. On February 1, 2006, it emerged from Chapter 11 bankruptcy protection under which it had operated since December 9, 2002, the largest and longest airline bankruptcy case in history.
Technology	The body of knowledge and techniques that can be used to combine economic resources to produce goods and services is called technology.
Consultant	A professional that provides expert advice in a particular field or area in which customers occassionaly require this type of knowledge is a consultant.
Standing	Standing refers to the legal requirement that anyone seeking to challenge a particular action in court must demonstrate that such action substantially affects his legitimate interests before he will be entitled to bring suit.
Proactive	To be proactive is to act before a situation becomes a source of confrontation or crisis. It is the opposite of "retroactive," which refers to actions taken after an event.
Accord	An agreement whereby the parties agree to accept something different in satisfaction of the original contract is an accord.
Participative management	Participative management or participatory management is the practice of empowering employees to participate in organizational decision making.
Compressed workweek	A situation in which employees work a full forty-hour week in fewer than the traditional five days is referred to as compressed workweek.
Bethlehem Steel	During its life, Bethlehem Steel was one of the largest shipbuilding companies in the world and was one of the most powerful symbols of American manufacturing leadership. It was the second largest steel producer in the United States, but following its 2001 bankruptcy, the company was dissolved and the remaining assets sold to International Steel Group in 2003.
Inception	The date and time on which coverage under an insurance policy takes effect is inception. Also

Go to **Cram101.com** for the Practice Tests for this Chapter.

	refers to the date at which a stock or mutual fund was first traded.
Custodian	Custodian as a financial term, refers to a bank (Custodian bank), agent, or other organization responsible for safeguarding a firm's or individual's financial assets.
Credit	Credit refers to a recording as positive in the balance of payments, any transaction that gives rise to a payment into the country, such as an export, the sale of an asset, or borrowing from abroad.
Standard market	A site where companies test market a product through normal distribution channels and monitor the results is a standard market.
Comprehensive	A comprehensive refers to a layout accurate in size, color, scheme, and other necessary details to show how a final ad will look. For presentation only, never for reproduction.
Screening	Screening in economics refers to a strategy of combating adverse selection, one of the potential decision-making complications in cases of asymmetric information.
Applicant	In many tribunal and administrative law suits, the person who initiates the claim is called the applicant.
Prentice Hall	Prentice Hall is a leading educational publisher. It is an imprint of the Pearson Education Company, based in New Jersey, USA.
Harvard Business Review	Harvard Business Review is a research-based magazine written for business practitioners, it claims a high ranking business readership and enjoys the reverence of academics, executives, and management consultants. It has been the frequent publishing home for well known scholars and management thinkers.
Motivating potential score	The extent to which the core characteristics of a job creates motivating conditions is the motivating potential score.
Inventory	Tangible property held for sale in the normal course of business or used in producing goods or services for sale is an inventory.
Yield	The interest rate that equates a future value or an annuity to a given present value is a yield.
Task significance	The measure of how much of a job has a substantial impact on the lives of other people, whether these people are in the immediate organization or in the world at large is task significance.
Task identity	The degree to which employees perceive how their job impacts the overall production of a product or service is task identity.
Human resources	Human resources refers to the individuals within the firm, and to the portion of the firm's organization that deals with hiring, firing, training, and other personnel issues.

Promotion	Promotion refers to all the techniques sellers use to motivate people to buy products or services. An attempt by marketers to inform people about products and to persuade them to participate in an exchange.
Honda	With more than 14 million internal combustion engines built each year, Honda is the largest engine-maker in the world. In 2004, the company began to produce diesel motors, which were both very quiet whilst not requiring particulate filters to pass pollution standards. It is arguable, however, that the foundation of their success is the motorcycle division.
Production	The creation of finished goods and services using the factors of production: land, labor, capital, entrepreneurship, and knowledge.
Human resources	Human resources refers to the individuals within the firm, and to the portion of the firm's organization that deals with hiring, firing, training, and other personnel issues.
Applicant	In many tribunal and administrative law suits, the person who initiates the claim is called the applicant.
Screening	Screening in economics refers to a strategy of combating adverse selection, one of the potential decision-making complications in cases of asymmetric information.
Assembly line	An assembly line is a manufacturing process in which interchangeable parts are added to a product in a sequential manner to create a finished product.
Assessor	An assessor is an expert who calculates the value of property. The value calculated by the assessor is then used as the basis for determining the amounts to be paid or assessed for tax or insurance purposes.
Project manager	Project manager refers to a manager responsible for a temporary work project that involves the participation of other people from various functions and levels of the organization.
Open position	An obligation to take or make delivery of an asset or currency in the future without cover, that is, without a matching obligation in the other direction that protects them from effects of change in the price of the asset or currency is an open position.
Administrator	Administrator refers to the personal representative appointed by a probate court to settle the estate of a deceased person who died.
Context	The effect of the background under which a message often takes on more and richer meaning is a context. Context is especially important in cross-cultural interactions because some cultures are said to be high context or low context.
Performance management	The means through which managers ensure that employees' activities and outputs are congruent with the organization's goals is referred to as performance management.
Management	Management characterizes the process of leading and directing all or part of an organization, often a business, through the deployment and manipulation of resources. Early twentieth-century management writer Mary Parker Follett defined management as "the art of getting things done through people."
Social learning	Social learning occurs when people observe the behaviors of others, recognize their consequences, and alter their own behavior as a result.
Utility	Utility refers to the want-satisfying power of a good or service; the satisfaction or pleasure a consumer obtains from the consumption of a good or service.
Specificity	The property that a policy measure applies to one or a group of enterprises or industries, as opposed to all industries, is called specificity.
Incentive	An incentive is any factor (financial or non-financial) that provides a motive for a particular course of action, or counts as a reason for preferring one choice to the

	alternatives.
Neiman Marcus	Neiman Marcus is an upscale, specialty, retail department store, operated by the Neiman Marcus Group in the United States. In 1927, Neiman Marcus premiered the first weekly retail fashion show in the United States.
Productivity	Productivity refers to the total output of goods and services in a given period of time divided by work hours.
Interest	In finance and economics, interest is the price paid by a borrower for the use of a lender's money. In other words, interest is the amount of paid to "rent" money for a period of time.
Complexity	The technical sophistication of the product and hence the amount of understanding required to use it is referred to as complexity. It is the opposite of simplicity.
Consideration	Consideration in contract law, a basic requirement for an enforceable agreement under traditional contract principles, defined in this text as legal value, bargained for and given in exchange for an act or promise. In corporation law, cash or property contributed to a corporation in exchange for shares, or a promise to contribute such cash or property.
Subsidiary	A company that is controlled by another company or corporation is a subsidiary.
Evaluation	The consumer's appraisal of the product or brand on important attributes is called evaluation.
Innovation	Innovation refers to the first commercially successful introduction of a new product, the use of a new method of production, or the creation of a new form of business organization.
Core	A core is the set of feasible allocations in an economy that cannot be improved upon by subset of the set of the economy's consumers (a coalition). In construction, when the force in an element is within a certain center section, the core, the element will only be under compression.
Consultant	A professional that provides expert advice in a particular field or area in which customers occassionaly require this type of knowledge is a consultant.
Short run	Short run refers to a period of time that permits an increase or decrease in current production volume with existing capacity, but one that is too short to permit enlargement of that capacity itself (eg, the building of new plants, training of additional workers, etc.).
Expense	In accounting, an expense represents an event in which an asset is used up or a liability is incurred. In terms of the accounting equation, expenses reduce owners' equity.
Alcoa	Alcoa (NYSE: AA) is the world's leading producer of alumina, primary and fabricated aluminum, with operations in 43 countries. (It is followed in this by a former subsidiary, Alcan, the second-leading producer.)
Performance appraisal	An evaluation in which the performance level of employees is measured against established standards to make decisions about promotions, compenzation, additional training, or firing is referred to as performance appraisal.
Liability	A liability is a present obligation of the enterprise arizing from past events, the settlement of which is expected to result in an outflow from the enterprise of resources embodying economic benefits.
Balance	In banking and accountancy, the outstanding balance is the amount of money owned, (or due), that remains in a deposit account (or a loan account) at a given date, after all past remittances, payments and withdrawal have been accounted for. It can be positive (then, in the balance sheet of a firm, it is an asset) or negative (a liability).
Assessment	Collecting information and providing feedback to employees about their behavior,

communication style, or skills is an assessment.

Supervisor	A Supervisor is an employee of an organization with some of the powers and responsibilities of management, occupying a role between true manager and a regular employee. A Supervisor position is typically the first step towards being promoted into a management role.
Alternative work arrangements	Independent contractors, on-call workers, and contract company workers who are not employed full-time by the company are alternative work arrangements.
Performance measurement	The process by which someone evaluates an employee's work behaviors by measurement and comparison with previously established standards, documents the results, and communicates the results to the employee is called performance measurement.
Management system	A management system is the framework of processes and procedures used to ensure that an organization can fulfill all tasks required to achieve its objectives.
Quality management	Quality management is a method for ensuring that all the activities necessary to design, develop and implement a product or service are effective and efficient with respect to the system and its performance.
Frequency	Frequency refers to the speed of the up and down movements of a fluctuating economic variable; that is, the number of times per unit of time that the variable completes a cycle of up and down movement.
Policy	Similar to a script in that a policy can be a less than completely rational decision-making method. Involves the use of a pre-existing set of decision steps for any problem that presents itself.
Total quality management	The broad set of management and control processes designed to focus an entire organization and all of its employees on providing products or services that do the best possible job of satisfying the customer is called total quality management.
Distribution	Distribution in economics, the manner in which total output and income is distributed among individuals or factors.
Performance feedback	The process of providing employees with information regarding their performance effectiveness is referred to as performance feedback.
Operation	A standardized method or technique that is performed repetitively, often on different materials resulting in different finished goods is called an operation.
Gain	In finance, gain is a profit or an increase in value of an investment such as a stock or bond. Gain is calculated by fair market value or the proceeds from the sale of the investment minus the sum of the purchase price and all costs associated with it.
Layoff	A layoff is the termination of an employee or (more commonly) a group of employees for business reasons, such as the decision that certain positions are no longer necessary.
Training and development	All attempts to improve productivity by increasing an employee's ability to perform is training and development.
Chase Manhattan	The Chase Manhattan Bank was formed by the merger of the Chase National Bank and the Bank of the Manhattan Company in 1955.
Nestle	Nestle is the world's biggest food and beverage company. In the 1860s, a pharmacist, developed a food for babies who were unable to be breastfed. His first success was a premature infant who could not tolerate his own mother's milk nor any of the usual substitutes. The value of the new product was quickly recognized when his new formula saved the child's life.

Go to **Cram101.com** for the Practice Tests for this Chapter.

Technology	The body of knowledge and techniques that can be used to combine economic resources to produce goods and services is called technology.
Business Week	Business Week is a business magazine published by McGraw-Hill. It was first published in 1929 under the direction of Malcolm Muir, who was serving as president of the McGraw-Hill Publishing company at the time. It is considered to be the standard both in industry and among students.
Financial capital	Common stock, preferred stock, bonds, and retained earnings are financial capital. Financial capital appears on the corporate balance sheet under long-term liabilities and equity.
British Airways	British Airways is the largest airline of the United Kingdom. It is also one of the largest airlines in the world, with the greatest number of flights from Europe to North America. Its main bases are London Heathrow (LHR) and London Gatwick (LGW).
Human capital	Human capital refers to the stock of knowledge and skill, embodied in an individual as a result of education, training, and experience that makes them more productive. The stock of knowledge and skill embodied in the population of an economy.
Capital	Capital generally refers to financial wealth, especially that used to start or maintain a business. In classical economics, capital is one of four factors of production, the others being land and labor and entrepreneurship.
Asset	An item of property, such as land, capital, money, a share in ownership, or a claim on others for future payment, such as a bond or a bank deposit is an asset.
Information technology	Information technology refers to technology that helps companies change business by allowing them to use new methods.
Firm	An organization that employs resources to produce a good or service for profit and owns and operates one or more plants is referred to as a firm.
Corporate goal	A strategic performance target that the entire organization must reach to pursue its vision is a corporate goal.
Complaint	The pleading in a civil case in which the plaintiff states his claim and requests relief is called complaint. In the common law, it is a formal legal document that sets out the basic facts and legal reasons that the filing party (the plaintiffs) believes are sufficient to support a claim against another person, persons, entity or entities (the defendants) that entitles the plaintiff(s) to a remedy (either money damages or injunctive relief).
Security	Security refers to a claim on the borrower future income that is sold by the borrower to the lender. A security is a type of transferable interest representing financial value.
Continuous improvement	The constant effort to eliminate waste, reduce response time, simplify the design of both products and processes, and improve quality and customer service is referred to as continuous improvement.
Leadership	Management merely consists of leadership applied to business situations; or in other words: management forms a sub-set of the broader process of leadership.
Openness	Openness refers to the extent to which an economy is open, often measured by the ratio of its trade to GDP.
Trust	An arrangement in which shareholders of independent firms agree to give up their stock in exchange for trust certificates that entitle them to a share of the trust's common profits.
Extension	Extension refers to an out-of-court settlement in which creditors agree to allow the firm more time to meet its financial obligations. A new repayment schedule will be developed, subject to the acceptance of creditors.

Manufacturing	Production of goods primarily by the application of labor and capital to raw materials and other intermediate inputs, in contrast to agriculture, mining, forestry, fishing, and services a manufacturing.
Performance plan	Performance plan refers to an understanding between an employee and a manager concerning what and how a job is to be done such that both parties know what is expected and how success is defined and measured.
Job analysis	Job analysis refers to a study of what is done by employees who hold various job titles. It refers to various methodologies for analyzing the requirements of a job.
Comprehensive	A comprehensive refers to a layout accurate in size, color, scheme, and other necessary details to show how a final ad will look. For presentation only, never for reproduction.
Equal employment opportunity	The government's attempt to ensure that all individuals have an equal opportunity for employment, regardless of race, color, religion, sex, age, disability, or national origin is equal employment opportunity.
Behaviorally Anchored Rating Scale	A performance appraisal approach that describes observable job behaviors, each of which is evaluated to determine good versus bad performance is referred to as behaviorally anchored rating scale.
Graphic rating scale	A scale that lists a variety of dimensions thought to be related to high performance outcomes in a given job and that one is expected to exhibit is referred to as the graphic rating scale.
Learning organization	A firm, which values continuous learning and is consistently looking to adapt and change with its environment is referred to as learning organization.
Shell	One of the original Seven Sisters, Royal Dutch/Shell is the world's third-largest oil company by revenue, and a major player in the petrochemical industry and the solar energy business. Shell has six core businesses: Exploration and Production, Gas and Power, Downstream, Chemicals, Renewables, and Trading/Shipping, and operates in more than 140 countries.
Americans with Disabilities Act	The Americans with Disabilities Act of 1990 is a wide-ranging civil rights law that prohibits discrimination based on disability.
International trade	The export of goods and services from a country and the import of goods and services into a country is referred to as the international trade.
Time management	Time Management refers to tools or techniques for planning and scheduling time, usually with the aim to increase the effectiveness and/or efficiency of personal and corporate time use.
Trade theory	The body of economic thought that seeks to explain why and how countries engage in international trade and the welfare implication of that trade, encompassing especially the Ricardian Model, the Heckscher-Ohlin Model, and the New Trade Theory.
Managing diversity	Building systems and a climate that unite different people in a common pursuit without undermining their individual strengths is managing diversity.
BellSouth	BellSouth is currently the only "Baby Bell" that does not operate pay telephones. By 2003, the payphone operation was discontinued because it had become too unprofitable, most likely due to the increased availability of cell phones. Cincinnati Bell has taken their place for payphones in northern BellSouth territory; independents have set in further south.
Mentor	An experienced employee who supervises, coaches, and guides lower-level employees by introducing them to the right people and generally being their organizational sponsor is a mentor.
Board of	The group of individuals elected by the stockholders of a corporation to oversee its

directors	operations is a board of directors.
Business case	The business case addresses, at a high level, the business need that a project seeks to resolve. It includes the reasons for the project, the expected business benefits, the options considered (with reasons for rejecting or carrying forward each option), the expected costs of the project, a gap analysis and the expected risks.
Contribution	In business organization law, the cash or property contributed to a business by its owners is referred to as contribution.
Exchange	The trade of things of value between buyer and seller so that each is better off after the trade is called the exchange.
Compliance	A type of influence process where a receiver accepts the position advocated by a source to obtain favorable outcomes or to avoid punishment is the compliance.
Wage	The payment for the service of a unit of labor, per unit time. In trade theory, it is the only payment to labor, usually unskilled labor. In empirical work, wage data may exclude other compenzation, which must be added to get the total cost of employment.
Bottom line	The bottom line is net income on the last line of a income statement.
Loyalty	Marketers tend to define customer loyalty as making repeat purchases. Some argue that it should be defined attitudinally as a strongly positive feeling about the brand.
Labor	People's physical and mental talents and efforts that are used to help produce goods and services are called labor.
Labor union	A group of workers organized to advance the interests of the group is called a labor union.
Inflation	An increase in the overall price level of an economy, usually as measured by the CPI or by the implicit price deflator is called inflation.
Market	A market is, as defined in economics, a social arrangement that allows buyers and sellers to discover information and carry out a voluntary exchange of goods or services.
Union	A worker association that bargains with employers over wages and working conditions is called a union.
Extrinsic reward	Extrinsic reward refers to something given to you by someone else as recognition for good work; extrinsic rewards include pay increases, praise, and promotions.
Incentive system	An incentive system refers to plans in which employees can earn additional compenzation in return for certain types of performance.
Employee stock option	An employee stock option is a stock option for the company's own stock that is often offered to upper-level employees as part of the executive compenzation package, especially by American corporations. An employee stock option is identical to a call option on the company's stock, with some extra restrictions.
Earnings per share	Earnings per share refers to annual profit of the corporation divided by the number of shares outstanding.
Return on equity	Net profit after taxes per dollar of equity capital is referred to as return on equity.
Stock option	A stock option is a specific type of option that uses the stock itself as an underlying instrument to determine the option's pay-off and therefore its value.
Merit pay	A compenzation system that bases an individual's salary or wage increase on a measure of the person's performance accomplishment during a specific time period is called merit pay.
Base pay	Base pay is the fixed compenzation paid to an employee for performance of specific job responsibilities. It is typically paid as a salary, hourly or piece rate.

Equity	Equity is the name given to the set of legal principles, in countries following the English common law tradition, which supplement strict rules of law where their application would operate harshly, so as to achieve what is sometimes referred to as "natural justice."
Profit	Profit refers to the return to the resource entrepreneurial ability; total revenue minus total cost.
Option	A contract that gives the purchaser the option to buy or sell the underlying financial instrument at a specified price, called the exercise price or strike price, within a specific period of time.
Stock	In financial terminology, stock is the capital raized by a corporation, through the issuance and sale of shares.
Grant	Grant refers to an intergovernmental transfer of funds . Since the New Deal, state and local governments have become increasingly dependent upon federal grants for an almost infinite variety of programs.
Fund	Independent accounting entity with a self-balancing set of accounts segregated for the purposes of carrying on specific activities is referred to as a fund.
Senior executive	Senior executive means a chief executive officer, chief operating officer, chief financial officer and anyone in charge of a principal business unit or function.
Corporation	A legal entity chartered by a state or the Federal government that is distinct and separate from the individuals who own it is a corporation. This separation gives the corporation unique powers which other legal entities lack.
Objection	In the trial of a case the formal remonstrance made by counsel to something that has been said or done, in order to obtain the court's ruling thereon is an objection.
Revenue	Revenue is a U.S. business term for the amount of money that a company receives from its activities, mostly from sales of products and/or services to customers.
Analyst	Analyst refers to a person or tool with a primary function of information analysis, generally with a more limited, practical and short term set of goals than a researcher.
Shareholder	A shareholder is an individual or company (including a corporation) that legally owns one or more shares of stock in a joined stock company.
Shares	Shares refer to an equity security, representing a shareholder's ownership of a corporation. Shares are one of a finite number of equal portions in the capital of a company, entitling the owner to a proportion of distributed, non-reinvested profits known as dividends and to a portion of the value of the company in case of liquidation.
Quality improvement	Quality is inversely proportional to variability thus quality Improvement is the reduction of variability in products and processes.
Institutional investors	Institutional investors refers to large organizations such as pension funds, mutual funds, insurance companies, and banks that invest their own funds or the funds of others.
Compensation package	The total array of money, incentives, benefits, perquisites, and awards provided by the organization to an employee is the compensation package.
Insurance	Insurance refers to a system by which individuals can reduce their exposure to risk of large losses by spreading the risks among a large number of persons.
Social Security	Social security primarily refers to a field of social welfare concerned with social protection, or protection against socially recognized conditions, including poverty, old age, disability, unemployment, families with children and others.
Health insurance	Health insurance is a type of insurance whereby the insurer pays the medical costs of the

Go to **Cram101.com** for the Practice Tests for this Chapter.

	insured if the insured becomes sick due to covered causes, or due to accidents. The insurer may be a private organization or a government agency.
Deductible	The dollar sum of costs that an insured individual must pay before the insurer begins to pay is called deductible.
General Motors	General Motors is the world's largest automaker. Founded in 1908, today it employs about 327,000 people around the world. With global headquarters in Detroit, it manufactures its cars and trucks in 33 countries.
Toyota	Toyota is a Japanese multinational corporation that manufactures automobiles, trucks and buses. Toyota is the world's second largest automaker by sales. Toyota also provides financial services through its subsidiary, Toyota Financial Services, and participates in other lines of business.
Supply	Supply is the aggregate amount of any material good that can be called into being at a certain price point; it comprises one half of the equation of supply and demand. In classical economic theory, a curve representing supply is one of the factors that produce price.
Nissan	Nissan is Japan's second largest car company after Toyota. Nissan is among the top three Asian rivals of the "big three" in the US.
Privilege	Generally, a legal right to engage in conduct that would otherwise result in legal liability is a privilege. Privileges are commonly classified as absolute or conditional. Occasionally, privilege is also used to denote a legal right to refrain from particular behavior.
Service	Service refers to a "non tangible product" that is not embodied in a physical good and that typically effects some change in another product, person, or institution. Contrasts with good.
Internal Revenue Service	In 1862, during the Civil War, President Lincoln and Congress created the office of Commissioner of Internal Revenue and enacted an income tax to pay war expenses. The position of Commissioner still exists today. The Commissioner is the head of the Internal Revenue Service.
General Electric	In 1876, Thomas Alva Edison opened a new laboratory in Menlo Park, New Jersey. Out of the laboratory was to come perhaps the most famous invention of all—a successful development of the incandescent electric lamp. By 1890, Edison had organized his various businesses into the Edison General Electric Company.
Administrative cost	An administrative cost is all executive, organizational, and clerical costs associated with the general management of an organization rather than with manufacturing, marketing, or selling
Attachment	Attachment in general, the process of taking a person's property under an appropriate judicial order by an appropriate officer of the court. Used for a variety of purposes, including the acquisition of jurisdiction over the property seized and the securing of property that may be used to satisfy a debt.
Trend	Trend refers to the long-term movement of an economic variable, such as its average rate of increase or decrease over enough years to encompass several business cycles.
Administration	Administration refers to the management and direction of the affairs of governments and institutions; a collective term for all policymaking officials of a government; the execution and implementation of public policy.
Committee	A long-lasting, sometimes permanent team in the organization structure created to deal with tasks that recur regularly is the committee.
Task force	A temporary team or committee formed to solve a specific short-term problem involving several

Go to Cram101.com for the Practice Tests for this Chapter.

departments is the task force.

National Labor Relations Board	The National Labor Relations Board is an independent agency of the United States Government charged with conducting elections for labor union representation and with investigating and remedying unfair labor practices.
National Labor Relations Act	The National Labor Relations Act is a 1935 United States federal law that protects the rights of most workers in the private sector to organize labor unions, to engage in collective bargaining, and to take part in strikes and other forms of concerted activity in support of their demands.
Labor relations	The field of labor relations looks at the relationship between management and workers, particularly groups of workers represented by a labor union.
Coercion	Economic coercion is when an agent puts economic pressure onto the victim. The most common example of this is cutting off the supply to an essential resource, such as water.
Cost of living	The amount of money it takes to buy the goods and services that a typical family consumes is the cost of living.
Balance sheet	A statement of the assets, liabilities, and net worth of a firm or individual at some given time often at the end of its "fiscal year," is referred to as a balance sheet.
Assignment	A transfer of property or some right or interest is referred to as assignment.
Expatriate	Employee sent by his or her company to live and manage operations in a different country is called an expatriate.
Domestic	From or in one's own country. A domestic producer is one that produces inside the home country. A domestic price is the price inside the home country. Opposite of 'foreign' or 'world.'.
Consumption	In Keynesian economics consumption refers to personal consumption expenditure, i.e., the purchase of currently produced goods and services out of income, out of savings (net worth), or from borrowed funds. It refers to that part of disposable income that does not go to saving.
Management by objectives	Management by objectives is a process of agreeing upon objectives within an organization so that management and employees buy in to the objectives and understand what they are.
Personnel	A collective term for all of the employees of an organization. Personnel is also commonly used to refer to the personnel management function or the organizational unit responsible for administering personnel programs.
Foundation	A Foundation is a type of philanthropic organization set up by either individuals or institutions as a legal entity (either as a corporation or trust) with the purpose of distributing grants to support causes in line with the goals of the foundation.
Economy	The income, expenditures, and resources that affect the cost of running a business and household are called an economy.
Organizational Behavior	The study of human behavior in organizational settings, the interface between human behavior and the organization, and the organization itself is called organizational behavior.
Overtime	Overtime is the amount of time someone works beyond normal working hours.
Attrition	The practice of not hiring new employees to replace older employees who either quit or retire is referred to as attrition.
New economy	New economy, this term was used in the late 1990's to suggest that globalization and/or innovations in information technology had changed the way that the world economy works.

Go to Cram101.com for the Practice Tests for this Chapter.

Gap	In December of 1995, Gap became the first major North American retailer to accept independent monitoring of the working conditions in a contract factory producing its garments. Gap is the largest specialty retailer in the United States.
Cost advantage	Possession of a lower cost of production or operation than a competing firm or country is cost advantage.
Industry	A group of firms that produce identical or similar products is an industry. It is also used specifically to refer to an area of economic production focused on manufacturing which involves large amounts of capital investment before any profit can be realized, also called "heavy industry".
BMW	BMW is an independent German company and manufacturer of automobiles and motorcycles. BMW is the world's largest premium carmaker and is the parent company of the BMW MINI and Rolls-Royce car brands, and, formerly, Rover.
Precedent	A previously decided court decision that is recognized as authority for the disposition of future decisions is a precedent.

Trend	Trend refers to the long-term movement of an economic variable, such as its average rate of increase or decrease over enough years to encompass several business cycles.
Profit	Profit refers to the return to the resource entrepreneurial ability; total revenue minus total cost.
Free trade	Free trade refers to a situation in which there are no artificial barriers to trade, such as tariffs and quotas. Usually used, often only implicitly, with frictionless trade, so that it implies that there are no barriers to trade of any kind.
Recession	A significant decline in economic activity. In the U.S., recession is approximately defined as two successive quarters of falling GDP, as judged by NBER.
Industry	A group of firms that produce identical or similar products is an industry. It is also used specifically to refer to an area of economic production focused on manufacturing which involves large amounts of capital investment before any profit can be realized, also called "heavy industry".
Operation	A standardized method or technique that is performed repetitively, often on different materials resulting in different finished goods is called an operation.
Consolidation	The combination of two or more firms, generally of equal size and market power, to form an entirely new entity is a consolidation.
Automation	Automation allows machines to do work previously accomplished by people.
Technology	The body of knowledge and techniques that can be used to combine economic resources to produce goods and services is called technology.
Consultant	A professional that provides expert advice in a particular field or area in which customers occassionaly require this type of knowledge is a consultant.
Depression	Depression refers to a prolonged period characterized by high unemployment, low output and investment, depressed business confidence, falling prices, and widespread business failures. A milder form of business downturn is a recession.
Firm	An organization that employs resources to produce a good or service for profit and owns and operates one or more plants is referred to as a firm.
Incentive	An incentive is any factor (financial or non-financial) that provides a motive for a particular course of action, or counts as a reason for preferring one choice to the alternatives.
Objection	In the trial of a case the formal remonstrance made by counsel to something that has been said or done, in order to obtain the court's ruling thereon is an objection.
Union	A worker association that bargains with employers over wages and working conditions is called a union.
Physical demands	Stressors associated with the job's physical setting, such as the adequacy of temperature and lighting and the physical requirements the job makes on the employee are called physical demands.
Complexity	The technical sophistication of the product and hence the amount of understanding required to use it is referred to as complexity. It is the opposite of simplicity.
Contribution	In business organization law, the cash or property contributed to a business by its owners is referred to as contribution.
Eustress	Eustress is defined as stress that is healthful or gives one a feeling of fulfillment.
Security	Security refers to a claim on the borrower future income that is sold by the borrower to the

Go to **Cram101.com** for the Practice Tests for this Chapter.

lender. A security is a type of transferable interest representing financial value.

Red tape	Red tape is a derisive term for excessive regulations or rigid conformity to formal rules that are considered redundant or bureaucratic and hinders or prevents action or decision-making.
Expense	In accounting, an expense represents an event in which an asset is used up or a liability is incurred. In terms of the accounting equation, expenses reduce owners' equity.
Productivity	Productivity refers to the total output of goods and services in a given period of time divided by work hours.
Job satisfaction	Job satisfaction describes how content an individual is with his or her job. It is a relatively recent term since in previous centuries the jobs available to a particular person were often predetermined by the occupation of that person's parent.
Loyalty	Marketers tend to define customer loyalty as making repeat purchases. Some argue that it should be defined attitudinally as a strongly positive feeling about the brand.
Personnel	A collective term for all of the employees of an organization. Personnel is also commonly used to refer to the personnel management function or the organizational unit responsible for administering personnel programs.
Internal locus of control	People tend to ascribe their chances of future successes or failures either to internal or external causes. Persons with an internal locus of control see themselves as responsible for the outcomes of their own actions.
Management	Management characterizes the process of leading and directing all or part of an organization, often a business, through the deployment and manipulation of resources. Early twentieth-century management writer Mary Parker Follett defined management as "the art of getting things done through people."
Interpersonal demands	Interpersonal demands refer to stressors associated with group pressures, leadership, and personality conflicts.
Leadership	Management merely consists of leadership applied to business situations; or in other words: management forms a sub-set of the broader process of leadership.
Turnover	Turnover in a financial context refers to the rate at which a provider of goods cycles through its average inventory. Turnover in a human resources context refers to the characteristic of a given company or industry, relative to rate at which an employer gains and loses staff.
Controller	Controller refers to the financial executive primarily responsible for management accounting and financial accounting. Also called chief accounting officer.
Agent	A person who makes economic decisions for another economic actor. A hired manager operates as an agent for a firm's owner.
Senior executive	Senior executive means a chief executive officer, chief operating officer, chief financial officer and anyone in charge of a principal business unit or function.
Distribution	Distribution in economics, the manner in which total output and income is distributed among individuals or factors.
Labor	People's physical and mental talents and efforts that are used to help produce goods and services are called labor.
Role ambiguity	Uncertainty of specifications for a role is role ambiguity. This occurs when duties for a role are not specified. The resolution to role ambiguity may lie in precise role descriptions (job descriptions) or a simplification of the tasks.

Role conflict	Role conflict is a special form of social conflict that takes place when one is forced to take on two different and incompatible roles at the same time.
Creep	Creep is a problem in project management where the initial objectives of the project are jeopardized by a gradual increase in overall objectives as the project progresses.
Disney	Disney is one of the largest media and entertainment corporations in the world. Founded on October 16, 1923 by brothers Walt and Roy Disney as a small animation studio, today it is one of the largest Hollywood studios and also owns nine theme parks and several television networks, including the American Broadcasting Company (ABC).
Context	The effect of the background under which a message often takes on more and richer meaning is a context. Context is especially important in cross-cultural interactions because some cultures are said to be high context or low context.
Assignment	A transfer of property or some right or interest is referred to as assignment.
Promotion	Promotion refers to all the techniques sellers use to motivate people to buy products or services. An attempt by marketers to inform people about products and to persuade them to participate in an exchange.
Journal	Book of original entry, in which transactions are recorded in a general ledger system, is referred to as a journal.
Points	Loan origination fees that may be deductible as interest by a buyer of property. A seller of property who pays points reduces the selling price by the amount of the points paid for the buyer.
Investment banker	Investment banker refers to a financial organization that specializes in selling primary offerings of securities. Investment bankers can also perform other financial functions, such as advising clients, negotiating mergers and takeovers, and selling secondary offerings.
Investment	Investment refers to spending for the production and accumulation of capital and additions to inventories. In a financial sense, buying an asset with the expectation of making a return.
Economic cost	Economic cost refers to payments made or incomes forgone to obtain and retain the services of a resource.
Time management	Time Management refers to tools or techniques for planning and scheduling time, usually with the aim to increase the effectiveness and/or efficiency of personal and corporate time use.
Organizational strategy	The process of positioning the Organization in the competitive environment and implementing actions to compete successfully is an organizational strategy.
Stress management	An active approach to deal with stress that is influencing behavior is stress management.
Enabling	Enabling refers to giving workers the education and tools they need to assume their new decision-making powers.
Flexible work schedule	A flexible work schedule is a shedule in which an employee has a forty hour work week but can set their own schedule within the limits set by the employer.
Policy	Similar to a script in that a policy can be a less than completely rational decision-making method. Involves the use of a pre-existing set of decision steps for any problem that presents itself.
Delegation	Delegation is the handing of a task over to another person, usually a subordinate. It is the assignment of authority and responsibility to another person to carry out specific activities.
Collateral	Property that is pledged to the lender to guarantee payment in the event that the borrower is

unable to make debt payments is called collateral.

Financial perspective	Financial perspective is one of the four standard perspectives used with the Balanced Scorecard. Financial perspective measures inform an organization whether strategy execution, which is detailed through measures in the other three perspectives, is leading to improved bottom line results.
Long run	In economic models, the long run time frame assumes no fixed factors of production. Firms can enter or leave the marketplace, and the cost (and availability) of land, labor, raw materials, and capital goods can be assumed to vary.
Supervisor	A Supervisor is an employee of an organization with some of the powers and responsibilities of management, occupying a role between true manager and a regular employee. A Supervisor position is typically the first step towards being promoted into a management role.
Overtime	Overtime is the amount of time someone works beyond normal working hours.
Labor force	In economics the labor force is the group of people who have a potential for being employed.
Realization	Realization is the sale of assets when an entity is being liquidated.
Workforce diversity	The similarities and differences in such characteristics as age, gender, ethnic heritage, physical abilities and disabilities, race, and sexual orientation among the employees of organizations is called workforce diversity.
Tradeoff	The sacrifice of some or all of one economic goal, good, or service to achieve some other goal, good, or service is a tradeoff.
Controlling	A management function that involves determining whether or not an organization is progressing toward its goals and objectives, and taking corrective action if it is not is called controlling.
Enron	Enron Corportaion's global reputation was undermined by persistent rumours of bribery and political pressure to secure contracts in Central America, South America, Africa, and the Philippines. Especially controversial was its $3 billion contract with the Maharashtra State Electricity Board in India, where it is alleged that Enron officials used political connections within the Clinton and Bush administrations to exert pressure on the board.
Fraud	Tax fraud falls into two categories: civil and criminal. Under civil fraud, the IRS may impose as a penalty of an amount equal to as much as 75 percent of the underpayment.
New economy	New economy, this term was used in the late 1990's to suggest that globalization and/or innovations in information technology had changed the way that the world economy works.
Economy	The income, expenditures, and resources that affect the cost of running a business and household are called an economy.
Teamwork	That which occurs when group members work together in ways that utilize their skills well to accomplish a purpose is called teamwork.
Graduation	Termination of a country's eligibility for GSP tariff preferences on the grounds that it has progressed sufficiently, in terms of per capita income or another measure, that it is no longer in need to special and differential treatment is graduation.
Derivative	A derivative is a generic term for specific types of investments from which payoffs over time are derived from the performance of assets (such as commodities, shares or bonds), interest rates, exchange rates, or indices (such as a stock market index, consumer price index (CPI) or an index of weather conditions).
Insurance	Insurance refers to a system by which individuals can reduce their exposure to risk of large losses by spreading the risks among a large number of persons.

Go to **Cram101.com** for the Practice Tests for this Chapter.

Buyer	A buyer refers to a role in the buying center with formal authority and responsibility to select the supplier and negotiate the terms of the contract.
Mentor	An experienced employee who supervises, coaches, and guides lower-level employees by introducing them to the right people and generally being their organizational sponsor is a mentor.
Stock	In financial terminology, stock is the capital raized by a corporation, through the issuance and sale of shares.
Deregulation	The lessening or complete removal of government regulations on an industry, especially concerning the price that firms are allowed to charge and leaving price to be determined by market forces a deregulation.
Service	Service refers to a "non tangible product" that is not embodied in a physical good and that typically effects some change in another product, person, or institution. Contrasts with good.
Competitiveness	Competitiveness usually refers to characteristics that permit a firm to compete effectively with other firms due to low cost or superior technology, perhaps internationally.
Channel	Channel, in communications (sometimes called communications channel), refers to the medium used to convey information from a sender (or transmitter) to a receiver.
Accounting	A system that collects and processes financial information about an organization and reports that information to decision makers is referred to as accounting.
Gain	In finance, gain is a profit or an increase in value of an investment such as a stock or bond. Gain is calculated by fair market value or the proceeds from the sale of the investment minus the sum of the purchase price and all costs associated with it.
Administrator	Administrator refers to the personal representative appointed by a probate court to settle the estate of a deceased person who died.
Bankruptcy	Bankruptcy is a legally declared inability or impairment of ability of an individual or organization to pay their creditors.
Fund	Independent accounting entity with a self-balancing set of accounts segregated for the purposes of carrying on specific activities is referred to as a fund.
Termination	The ending of a corporation that occurs only after the winding-up of the corporation's affairs, the liquidation of its assets, and the distribution of the proceeds to the claimants are referred to as a termination.
Claim in bankruptcy	A Claim in Bankruptcy, in United States bankruptcy law, is a document filed with the Court so as to register a claim against the assets of the bankruptcy estate. The claim sets out the amount owing as of the date of the bankruptcy and, if releveant, any priority status . Although a document called a Claim in Bankruptcy is used in proceedings in both Canada and the United States, in the United States, the document is properly termed a Proof of Claim. The form is different although they share many similar aspects.
Performance management	The means through which managers ensure that employees' activities and outputs are congruent with the organization's goals is referred to as performance management.
Management system	A management system is the framework of processes and procedures used to ensure that an organization can fulfill all tasks required to achieve its objectives.
Organizational communication	Thee process by which information is exchanged in the organizational setting is organizational communication.

Technology	The body of knowledge and techniques that can be used to combine economic resources to produce goods and services is called technology.
Proprietary	Proprietary indicates that a party, or proprietor, exercises private ownership, control or use over an item of property, usually to the exclusion of other parties. Where a party, holds or claims proprietary interests in relation to certain types of property (eg. a creative literary work, or software), that property may also be the subject of intellectual property law (eg. copyright or patents).
Firm	An organization that employs resources to produce a good or service for profit and owns and operates one or more plants is referred to as a firm.
Reuters	Reuters is best known as a news service that provides reports from around the world to newspapers and broadcasters. Its main focus is on supplying the financial markets with information and trading products.
Subsidiary	A company that is controlled by another company or corporation is a subsidiary.
Labor	People's physical and mental talents and efforts that are used to help produce goods and services are called labor.
Cost structure	The relative proportion of an organization's fixed, variable, and mixed costs is referred to as cost structure.
Leadership	Management merely consists of leadership applied to business situations; or in other words: management forms a sub-set of the broader process of leadership.
Buyer	A buyer refers to a role in the buying center with formal authority and responsibility to select the supplier and negotiate the terms of the contract.
Competitor	Other organizations in the same industry or type of business that provide a good or service to the same set of customers is referred to as a competitor.
Service	Service refers to a "non tangible product" that is not embodied in a physical good and that typically effects some change in another product, person, or institution. Contrasts with good.
Analyst	Analyst refers to a person or tool with a primary function of information analysis, generally with a more limited, practical and short term set of goals than a researcher.
Stakeholder	A stakeholder is an individual or group with a vested interest in or expectation for organizational performance. Usually stakeholders can either have an effect on or are affected by an organization.
Performance appraisal	An evaluation in which the performance level of employees is measured against established standards to make decisions about promotions, compenzation, additional training, or firing is referred to as performance appraisal.
Organizational Behavior	The study of human behavior in organizational settings, the interface between human behavior and the organization, and the organization itself is called organizational behavior.
Exchange	The trade of things of value between buyer and seller so that each is better off after the trade is called the exchange.
Organizational communication	Thee process by which information is exchanged in the organizational setting is organizational communication.
Organizational goals	Objectives that management seeks to achieve in pursuing the firm's purpose are organizational goals.
Purchasing	Purchasing refers to the function in a firm that searches for quality material resources, finds the best suppliers, and negotiates the best price for goods and services.

International Business	International business refers to any firm that engages in international trade or investment.
Big Business	Big business is usually used as a pejorative reference to the significant economic and political power which large and powerful corporations (especially multinational corporations), are capable of wielding.
Marketing	Promoting and selling products or services to customers, or prospective customers, is referred to as marketing.
Mistake	In contract law a mistake is incorrect understanding by one or more parties to a contract and may be used as grounds to invalidate the agreement. Common law has identified three different types of mistake in contract: unilateral mistake, mutual mistake, and common mistake.
Customs	Customs is an authority or agency in a country responsible for collecting customs duties and for controlling the flow of people, animals and goods (including personal effects and hazardous items) in and out of the country.
Body language	Body language is a broad term for forms of communication using body movements or gestures instead of, or in addition to, sounds, verbal language, or other forms of communication.
Users	Users refer to people in the organization who actually use the product or service purchased by the buying center.
Caterpillar	Caterpillar is a United States based corporation headquartered in Peoria, Illinois. Caterpillar is "the world's largest manufacturer of construction and mining equipment, diesel and natural gas engines, and industrial gas turbines."
Context	The effect of the background under which a message often takes on more and richer meaning is a context. Context is especially important in cross-cultural interactions because some cultures are said to be high context or low context.
Financial market	In economics, a financial market is a mechanism which allows people to trade money for securities or commodities such as gold or other precious metals. In general, any commodity market might be considered to be a financial market, if the usual purpose of traders is not the immediate consumption of the commodity, but rather as a means of delaying or accelerating consumption over time.
Market	A market is, as defined in economics, a social arrangement that allows buyers and sellers to discover information and carry out a voluntary exchange of goods or services.
Consideration	Consideration in contract law, a basic requirement for an enforceable agreement under traditional contract principles, defined in this text as legal value, bargained for and given in exchange for an act or promise. In corporation law, cash or property contributed to a corporation in exchange for shares, or a promise to contribute such cash or property.
Operation	A standardized method or technique that is performed repetitively, often on different materials resulting in different finished goods is called an operation.
Policy	Similar to a script in that a policy can be a less than completely rational decision-making method. Involves the use of a pre-existing set of decision steps for any problem that presents itself.
Task force	A temporary team or committee formed to solve a specific short-term problem involving several departments is the task force.
Industry	A group of firms that produce identical or similar products is an industry. It is also used specifically to refer to an area of economic production focused on manufacturing which involves large amounts of capital investment before any profit can be realized, also called "heavy industry".

Management	Management characterizes the process of leading and directing all or part of an organization, often a business, through the deployment and manipulation of resources. Early twentieth-century management writer Mary Parker Follett defined management as "the art of getting things done through people."
Receiver	A person that is appointed as a custodian of other people's property by a court of law or a creditor of the owner, pending a lawsuit or reorganization is called a receiver.
Nonverbal communication	The many additional ways that communication is accomplished beyond the oral or written word is referred to as nonverbal communication.
Communication network	A communication network refer to networks that form spontaneously and naturally as the interactions among workers continue over time.
Channel	Channel, in communications (sometimes called communications channel), refers to the medium used to convey information from a sender (or transmitter) to a receiver.
Mass media	Mass media refers to non-personal channels of communication that allow a message to be sent to many individuals at one time.
Authority	Authority in agency law, refers to an agent's ability to affect his principal's legal relations with third parties. Also used to refer to an actor's legal power or ability to do something. In addition, sometimes used to refer to a statute, case, or other legal source that justifies a particular result.
Expense	In accounting, an expense represents an event in which an asset is used up or a liability is incurred. In terms of the accounting equation, expenses reduce owners' equity.
Corporation	A legal entity chartered by a state or the Federal government that is distinct and separate from the individuals who own it is a corporation. This separation gives the corporation unique powers which other legal entities lack.
Grant	Grant refers to an intergovernmental transfer of funds . Since the New Deal, state and local governments have become increasingly dependent upon federal grants for an almost infinite variety of programs.
Points	Loan origination fees that may be deductible as interest by a buyer of property. A seller of property who pays points reduces the selling price by the amount of the points paid for the buyer.
Interest	In finance and economics, interest is the price paid by a borrower for the use of a lender's money. In other words, interest is the amount of paid to "rent" money for a period of time.
Brief	Brief refers to a statement of a party's case or legal arguments, usually prepared by an attorney. Also used to make legal arguments before appellate courts.
Feedback loop	Feedback loop consists of a response and feedback. It is a system where outputs are fed back into the system as inputs, increasing or decreasing effects.
Channel noise	A disturbance in communication that is primarily a function of the medium is called the channel noise.
Principal	In agency law, one under whose direction an agent acts and for whose benefit that agent acts is a principal.
Hearing	A hearing is a proceeding before a court or other decision-making body or officer. A hearing is generally distinguished from a trial in that it is usually shorter and often less formal.
Effective communication	When the intended meaning equals the perceived meaning it is called effective communication.
Innovation	Innovation refers to the first commercially successful introduction of a new product, the use

143

of a new method of production, or the creation of a new form of business organization.

Intranet	Intranet refers to a companywide network, closed to public access, that uses Internet-type technology. A set of communications links within one company that travel over the Internet but are closed to public access.
Information technology	Information technology refers to technology that helps companies change business by allowing them to use new methods.
Telecommuting	Telecommuting is a work arrangement in which employees enjoy limited flexibility in working location and hours.
Electronic mail	Electronic mail refers to electronic written communication between individuals using computers connected to the Internet.
Personnel	A collective term for all of the employees of an organization. Personnel is also commonly used to refer to the personnel management function or the organizational unit responsible for administering personnel programs.
Manufacturing	Production of goods primarily by the application of labor and capital to raw materials and other intermediate inputs, in contrast to agriculture, mining, forestry, fishing, and services a manufacturing.
Distribution	Distribution in economics, the manner in which total output and income is distributed among individuals or factors.
Motorola	The Six Sigma quality system was developed at Motorola even though it became most well known because of its use by General Electric. It was created by engineer Bill Smith, under the direction of Bob Galvin (son of founder Paul Galvin) when he was running the company.
Productivity	Productivity refers to the total output of goods and services in a given period of time divided by work hours.
Information system	An information system is a system whether automated or manual, that comprises people, machines, and/or methods organized to collect, process, transmit, and disseminate data that represent user information.
Loyalty	Marketers tend to define customer loyalty as making repeat purchases. Some argue that it should be defined attitudinally as a strongly positive feeling about the brand.
Promotion	Promotion refers to all the techniques sellers use to motivate people to buy products or services. An attempt by marketers to inform people about products and to persuade them to participate in an exchange.
Supervisor	A Supervisor is an employee of an organization with some of the powers and responsibilities of management, occupying a role between true manager and a regular employee. A Supervisor position is typically the first step towards being promoted into a management role.
Management system	A management system is the framework of processes and procedures used to ensure that an organization can fulfill all tasks required to achieve its objectives.
Liability	A liability is a present obligation of the enterprise arizing from past events, the settlement of which is expected to result in an outflow from the enterprise of resources embodying economic benefits.
Security	Security refers to a claim on the borrower future income that is sold by the borrower to the lender. A security is a type of transferable interest representing financial value.
Press release	A written public news announcement normally distributed to major news services is referred to as press release.
Best practice	Best practice is a management idea which asserts that there is a technique, method, process,

activity, incentive or reward that is more effective at delivering a particular outcome than any other technique, method, process, etc.

Eli Lilly — Eli Lilly is a global pharmaceutical company and one of the world's largest corporations. Eli Lilly was the first distributor of methadone, an analgesic used frequently in the treatment of heroin, opium and other opioid and narcotic drug addictions.

Value system — A value system refers to how an individual or a group of individuals organize their ethical or ideological values. A well-defined value system is a moral code.

Chain network — In this type of network, each member communicates with the person above and below, except for the individuals on each end who communicate with only one person are chain network.

Chain of command — An unbroken line of authority that links all individuals in the organization and specifies who reports to whom is a chain of command. The concept of chain of command also implies that higher rank alone does not entitle a person to give commands.

Hierarchy — A system of grouping people in an organization according to rank from the top down in which all subordinate managers must report to one person is called a hierarchy.

Circle network — Circle network refers to a type of network where each member communicates with the people on both sides but with no one else.

Frequency — Frequency refers to the speed of the up and down movements of a fluctuating economic variable; that is, the number of times per unit of time that the variable completes a cycle of up and down movement.

Organization chart — Organization chart refers to a visual device, which shows the relationship and divides the organization's work; it shows who is accountable for the completion of specific work and who reports to whom.

Downward communication — Downward communication refers to communication flows from a company or boss down to the affected employees.

Upward communication — A communication channel that allows for relatively free movement of messages from those lower in the organization to those at higher levels is an upward communication.

Task performance — The quantity and quality of work produced is referred to as the task performance. Actions taken to ensure that the work group reaches its goals.

Vertical communication — Communication between one level of authority and another within an organization is vertical communication.

Protocol — Protocol refers to a statement that, before product development begins, identifies a well-defined target market; specific customers' needs, wants, and preferences; and what the product will be and do.

Horizontal communication — The lateral or diagonal exchange of messages among peers or coworkers is referred to as horizontal communication.

Liaison — An individual who serves as a bridge between groups, tying groups together and facilitating the communication flow needed to integrate group activities is a liaison.

Tying — Tying is the practice of making the sale of one good (the tying good) to the de facto or de jure customer conditional on the purchase of a second distinctive good.

Trade show — A type of exhibition or forum where manufacturers can display their products to current as well as prospective buyers is referred to as trade show.

Turnover — Turnover in a financial context refers to the rate at which a provider of goods cycles through its average inventory. Turnover in a human resources context refers to the characteristic of a given company or industry, relative to rate at which an employer gains

and loses staff.

Integration	Economic integration refers to reducing barriers among countries to transactions and to movements of goods, capital, and labor, including harmonization of laws, regulations, and standards. Integrated markets theoretically function as a unified market.
Evaluation	The consumer's appraisal of the product or brand on important attributes is called evaluation.
Jargon	Jargon is terminology, much like slang, that relates to a specific activity, profession, or group. It develops as a kind of shorthand, to express ideas that are frequently discussed between members of a group, and can also have the effect of distinguishing those belonging to a group from those who are not.
Enron	Enron Corportaion's global reputation was undermined by persistent rumours of bribery and political pressure to secure contracts in Central America, South America, Africa, and the Philippines. Especially controversial was its $3 billion contract with the Maharashtra State Electricity Board in India, where it is alleged that Enron officials used political connections within the Clinton and Bush administrations to exert pressure on the board.
Accounting	A system that collects and processes financial information about an organization and reports that information to decision makers is referred to as accounting.
Selective attention	A perceptual process in which consumers choose to attend to some stimuli and not others is referred to as selective attention.
Value judgment	Value judgment refers to an opinion of what is desirable or undesirable; belief regarding what ought or ought not to be.
Credibility	The extent to which a source is perceived as having knowledge, skill, or experience relevant to a communication topic and can be trusted to give an unbiased opinion or present objective information on the issue is called credibility.
Verification	Verification refers to the final stage of the creative process where the validity or truthfulness of the insight is determined. The feedback portion of communication in which the receiver sends a message to the source indicating receipt of the message and the degree to which he or she understood the message.
Supply	Supply is the aggregate amount of any material good that can be called into being at a certain price point; it comprises one half of the equation of supply and demand. In classical economic theory, a curve representing supply is one of the factors that produce price.
Bankruptcy	Bankruptcy is a legally declared inability or impairment of ability of an individual or organization to pay their creditors.
Kmart	Kmart is an international chain of discount department stores in the United States, Australia, and New Zealand. Kmart merged with Sears in early 2005, creating the Sears Holdings Corporation.
Stock	In financial terminology, stock is the capital raized by a corporation, through the issuance and sale of shares.
Investment	Investment refers to spending for the production and accumulation of capital and additions to inventories. In a financial sense, buying an asset with the expectation of making a return.
Distortion	Distortion refers to any departure from the ideal of perfect competition that interferes with economic agents maximizing social welfare when they maximize their own.
Trust	An arrangement in which shareholders of independent firms agree to give up their stock in exchange for trust certificates that entitle them to a share of the trust's common profits.

Formal communication channel	Formal communication channel refers to a communication channel that flows within the chain of command or task responsibility defined by the organization.
Communication channel	The pathways through which messages are communicated are called a communication channel.
Drawback	Drawback refers to rebate of import duties when the imported good is re-exported or used as input to the production of an exported good.
Balance	In banking and accountancy, the outstanding balance is the amount of money owned, (or due), that remains in a deposit account (or a loan account) at a given date, after all past remittances, payments and withdrawal have been accounted for. It can be positive (then, in the balance sheet of a firm, it is an asset) or negative (a liability).
Production	The creation of finished goods and services using the factors of production: land, labor, capital, entrepreneurship, and knowledge.
General Electric	In 1876, Thomas Alva Edison opened a new laboratory in Menlo Park, New Jersey. Out of the laboratory was to come perhaps the most famous invention of all—a successful development of the incandescent electric lamp. By 1890, Edison had organized his various businesses into the Edison General Electric Company.
Complaint	The pleading in a civil case in which the plaintiff states his claim and requests relief is called complaint. In the common law, it is a formal legal document that sets out the basic facts and legal reasons that the filing party (the plaintiffs) believes are sufficient to support a claim against another person, persons, entity or entities (the defendants) that entitles the plaintiff(s) to a remedy (either money damages or injunctive relief).
Gatekeeper	Gatekeeper refers to an individual who has a strategic position in the network that allows him or her to control information moving in either direction through a channel.
Profit	Profit refers to the return to the resource entrepreneurial ability; total revenue minus total cost.
Annual report	An annual report is prepared by corporate management that presents financial information including financial statements, footnotes, and the management discussion and analysis.
Slowdown	A slowdown is an industrial action in which employees perform their duties but seek to reduce productivity or efficiency in their performance of these duties. A slowdown may be used as either a prelude or an alternative to a strike, as it is seen as less disruptive as well as less risky and costly for workers and their union.
Downturn	A decline in a stock market or economic cycle is a downturn.
Compaq	Compaq was founded in February 1982 by Rod Canion, Jim Harris and Bill Murto, three senior managers from semiconductor manufacturer Texas Instruments. Each invested $1,000 to form the company. Their first venture capital came from Ben Rosen and Sevin-Rosen partners. It is often told that the architecture of the original PC was first sketched out on a placemat by the founders while dining in the Houston restaurant, House of Pies.
Nike	Because Nike creates goods for a wide range of sports, they have competition from every sports and sports fashion brand there is. Nike has no direct competitors because there is no single brand which can compete directly with their range of sports and non-sports oriented gear, except for Reebok.
Initial public offering	Firms in the process of becoming publicly traded companies will issue shares of stock using an initial public offering, which is merely the process of selling stock for the first time to interested investors.

Wireless communication	Wireless communication refers to a method of communication that uses low-powered radio waves to transmit data between devices. The term refers to communication without cables or cords, chiefly using radio frequency and infrared waves. Common uses include the various communications defined by the IrDA, the wireless networking of computers and cellular mobile phones.
Layoff	A layoff is the termination of an employee or (more commonly) a group of employees for business reasons, such as the decision that certain positions are no longer necessary.
Heir	In common law jurisdictions an heir is a person who is entitled to receive a share of the decedent's property via the rules of inheritance in the jurisdiction where the decedent died or owned property at the time of his death.
Participatory management	Participatory management is the practice of empowering employees to participate in organizational decision making. This practice grew out of the human relations movement in the 1920s, and is based on some of the principles discovered by scholars doing research in management and organization studies.
Foundation	A Foundation is a type of philanthropic organization set up by either individuals or institutions as a legal entity (either as a corporation or trust) with the purpose of distributing grants to support causes in line with the goals of the foundation.
International firm	International firm refers to those firms who have responded to stiff competition domestically by expanding their sales abroad. They may start a production facility overseas and send some of their managers, who report to a global division, to that country.
Trial	An examination before a competent tribunal, according to the law of the land, of the facts or law put in issue in a cause, for the purpose of determining such issue is a trial. When the court hears and determines any issue of fact or law for the purpose of determining the rights of the parties, it may be considered a trial.
Main product	Product from a joint production process that has a high sales value compared with the sales values of all other products of the joint production process is referred to as main product.
Closing	The finalization of a real estate sales transaction that passes title to the property from the seller to the buyer is referred to as a closing. Closing is a sales term which refers to the process of making a sale. It refers to reaching the final step, which may be an exchange of money or acquiring a signature.
Gap	In December of 1995, Gap became the first major North American retailer to accept independent monitoring of the working conditions in a contract factory producing its garments. Gap is the largest specialty retailer in the United States.
Warehouse	Warehouse refers to a location, often decentralized, that a firm uses to store, consolidate, age, or mix stock; house product-recall programs; or ease tax burdens.

Productivity	Productivity refers to the total output of goods and services in a given period of time divided by work hours.
Customer service	The ability of logistics management to satisfy users in terms of time, dependability, communication, and convenience is called the customer service.
Service	Service refers to a "non tangible product" that is not embodied in a physical good and that typically effects some change in another product, person, or institution. Contrasts with good.
Group dynamics	The term group dynamics implies that individual behaviors may differ depending on individuals' current or prospective connections to a sociological group. Group dynamics is the field of study within the social sciences that focuses on the nature of groups. Urges to belong or to identify may make for distinctly different attitudes (recognized or unrecognized), and the influence of a group may rapidly become strong, influencing or overwhelming individual proclivities and actions.
Group performance factors	Group performance factors refers to composition, size, norms, and cohesiveness. They affect the success of the group in fulfilling its goals.
Lockheed Martin	Lockheed Martin is the world's largest defense contractor (by defense revenue). As of 2005, 95% of revenues came from the U.S. Department of Defense, other U.S. federal government agencies, and foreign military customers.
Subcontractor	A subcontractor is an individual or in many cases a business that signs a contract to perform part or all of the obligations of another's contract. A subcontractor is hired by a general or prime contractor to perform a specific task as part of the overall project.
Users	Users refer to people in the organization who actually use the product or service purchased by the buying center.
Exchange	The trade of things of value between buyer and seller so that each is better off after the trade is called the exchange.
General Motors	General Motors is the world's largest automaker. Founded in 1908, today it employs about 327,000 people around the world. With global headquarters in Detroit, it manufactures its cars and trucks in 33 countries.
Product design	Product Design is defined as the idea generation, concept development, testing and manufacturing or implementation of a physical object or service. It is possibly the evolution of former discipline name - Industrial Design.
Collaboration	Collaboration occurs when the interaction between groups is very important to goal attainment and the goals are compatible. Wherein people work together —applying both to the work of individuals as well as larger collectives and societies.
Consultant	A professional that provides expert advice in a particular field or area in which customers occassionaly require this type of knowledge is a consultant.
Aid	Assistance provided by countries and by international institutions such as the World Bank to developing countries in the form of monetary grants, loans at low interest rates, in kind, or a combination of these is called aid. Aid can also refer to assistance of any type rendered to benefit some group or individual.
Applicant	In many tribunal and administrative law suits, the person who initiates the claim is called the applicant.
General Electric	In 1876, Thomas Alva Edison opened a new laboratory in Menlo Park, New Jersey. Out of the laboratory was to come perhaps the most famous invention of all—a successful development of

the incandescent electric lamp. By 1890, Edison had organized his various businesses into the Edison General Electric Company.

Management	Management characterizes the process of leading and directing all or part of an organization, often a business, through the deployment and manipulation of resources. Early twentieth-century management writer Mary Parker Follett defined management as "the art of getting things done through people."
Shares	Shares refer to an equity security, representing a shareholder's ownership of a corporation. Shares are one of a finite number of equal portions in the capital of a company, entitling the owner to a proportion of distributed, non-reinvested profits known as dividends and to a portion of the value of the company in case of liquidation.
Jack Welch	In 1986, GE acquired NBC. During the 90s, Jack Welch helped to modernize GE by emphasizing a shift from manufacturing to services. He also made hundreds of acquisitions and made a push to dominate markets abroad. Welch adopted the Six Sigma quality program in late 1995.
Smart card	A stored-value card that contains a computer chip that allows it to be loaded with digital cash from the owner's bank account whenever needed is called a smart card.
Technology	The body of knowledge and techniques that can be used to combine economic resources to produce goods and services is called technology.
Forming	The first stage of team development, where the team is formed and the objectives for the team are set is referred to as forming.
Social identity	Social identity is a theory formed by Henri Tajfel and John Turner to understand the psychological basis of intergroup discrimination. It is composed of three elements: categorization, identification, and comparison
Composition	An out-of-court settlement in which creditors agree to accept a fractional settlement on their original claim is referred to as composition.
Organizational Behavior	The study of human behavior in organizational settings, the interface between human behavior and the organization, and the organization itself is called organizational behavior.
Motivation and productivity	The stage of group development in which members cooperate, help each other, and work toward accomplishing tasks is motivation and productivity.
Control and organization	Control and organization refers to the stage of group development where the group is mature; members work together and are flexible, adaptive, and self-correcting.
Strike	The withholding of labor services by an organized group of workers is referred to as a strike.
Union	A worker association that bargains with employers over wages and working conditions is called a union.
Organizational goals	Objectives that management seeks to achieve in pursuing the firm's purpose are organizational goals.
Innovation	Innovation refers to the first commercially successful introduction of a new product, the use of a new method of production, or the creation of a new form of business organization.
Policy	Similar to a script in that a policy can be a less than completely rational decision-making method. Involves the use of a pre-existing set of decision steps for any problem that presents itself.
Manufacturing	Production of goods primarily by the application of labor and capital to raw materials and other intermediate inputs, in contrast to agriculture, mining, forestry, fishing, and services a manufacturing.

Go to **Cram101.com** for the Practice Tests for this Chapter.

Distribution	Distribution in economics, the manner in which total output and income is distributed among individuals or factors.
Competitor	Other organizations in the same industry or type of business that provide a good or service to the same set of customers is referred to as a competitor.
Supply	Supply is the aggregate amount of any material good that can be called into being at a certain price point; it comprises one half of the equation of supply and demand. In classical economic theory, a curve representing supply is one of the factors that produce price.
Market	A market is, as defined in economics, a social arrangement that allows buyers and sellers to discover information and carry out a voluntary exchange of goods or services.
Firm	An organization that employs resources to produce a good or service for profit and owns and operates one or more plants is referred to as a firm.
Annual report	An annual report is prepared by corporate management that presents financial information including financial statements, footnotes, and the management discussion and analysis.
Affinity group	Collections of employees from the same level in the organization who meet on a regular basis to share information, capture emerging opportunities, and solve problems are called an affinity group.
Task group	Task group refers to a relatively temporary, formal group established to do a specific task.
Command group	Command group refers to a relatively permanent, formal group with functional reporting relationships; usually included in the organization chart.
Organization chart	Organization chart refers to a visual device, which shows the relationship and divides the organization's work; it shows who is accountable for the completion of specific work and who reports to whom.
Personnel	A collective term for all of the employees of an organization. Personnel is also commonly used to refer to the personnel management function or the organizational unit responsible for administering personnel programs.
Federal Express	The company officially began operations on April 17, 1973, utilizing a network of 14 Dassault Falcon 20s which connected 25 U.S. cities. FedEx, the first cargo airline to use jet aircraft for its services, expanded greatly after the deregulation of the cargo airlines sector. Federal Express use of the hub-spoke distribution paradigm in air freight enabled it to become a world leader in its field.
Organization structure	The system of task, reporting, and authority relationships within which the organization does its work is referred to as the organization structure.
Formal organization	Formal organization refers to the structure that details lines of responsibility, authority, and position; that is, the structure shown on organization charts.
Hierarchy	A system of grouping people in an organization according to rank from the top down in which all subordinate managers must report to one person is called a hierarchy.
Interest	In finance and economics, interest is the price paid by a borrower for the use of a lender's money. In other words, interest is the amount of paid to "rent" money for a period of time.
Facilitator	A facilitator is someone who skilfully helps a group of people understand their common objectives and plan to achieve them without personally taking any side of the argument.
Information system	An information system is a system whether automated or manual, that comprises people, machines, and/or methods organized to collect, process, transmit, and disseminate data that represent user information.
Brief	Brief refers to a statement of a party's case or legal arguments, usually prepared by an

Go to **Cram101.com** for the Practice Tests for this Chapter.

	attorney. Also used to make legal arguments before appellate courts.
Argument	The discussion by counsel for the respective parties of their contentions on the law and the facts of the case being tried in order to aid the jury in arriving at a correct and just conclusion is called argument.
Trust	An arrangement in which shareholders of independent firms agree to give up their stock in exchange for trust certificates that entitle them to a share of the trust's common profits.
Budget	Budget refers to an account, usually for a year, of the planned expenditures and the expected receipts of an entity. For a government, the receipts are tax revenues.
Vendor	A person who sells property to a vendee is a vendor. The words vendor and vendee are more commonly applied to the seller and purchaser of real estate, and the words seller and buyer are more commonly applied to the seller and purchaser of personal property.
Contribution	In business organization law, the cash or property contributed to a business by its owners is referred to as contribution.
Synergy	Corporate synergy occurs when corporations interact congruently. A corporate synergy refers to a financial benefit that a corporation expects to realize when it merges with or acquires another corporation.
Homogeneous	In the context of procurement/purchasing, homogeneous is used to describe goods that do not vary in their essential characteristic irrespective of the source of supply.
Variable	A variable is something measured by a number; it is used to analyze what happens to other things when the size of that number changes.
Authority	Authority in agency law, refers to an agent's ability to affect his principal's legal relations with third parties. Also used to refer to an actor's legal power or ability to do something. In addition, sometimes used to refer to a statute, case, or other legal source that justifies a particular result.
Joint venture	Joint venture refers to an undertaking by two parties for a specific purpose and duration, taking any of several legal forms.
Industry	A group of firms that produce identical or similar products is an industry. It is also used specifically to refer to an area of economic production focused on manufacturing which involves large amounts of capital investment before any profit can be realized, also called "heavy industry".
Complexity	The technical sophistication of the product and hence the amount of understanding required to use it is referred to as complexity. It is the opposite of simplicity.
Social loafing	Social loafing is a tendency for a team member to put out less effort than they would if they were working alone. Freeloading such as this can occur when members' performance melds in and they can hide in the crowd.
Leadership	Management merely consists of leadership applied to business situations; or in other words: management forms a sub-set of the broader process of leadership.
Maturity	Maturity refers to the final payment date of a loan or other financial instrument, after which point no further interest or principal need be paid.
Maturity stage	The third stage of the product life cycle is called the maturity stage. This is when sales growth slows due to heavy competition, alternative product options or changing buyer or user preferences.
Central Intelligence	The primary function of the Central Intelligence Agency is obtaining and analyzing information about foreign governments, corporations, and individuals, and reporting such

Go to **Cram101.com** for the Practice Tests for this Chapter.

Agency	information to the various branches of the Government. A second function is overtly and covertly disseminating information, both true and false, that influences others to make decisions favorable to the United States Government.
Security	Security refers to a claim on the borrower future income that is sold by the borrower to the lender. A security is a type of transferable interest representing financial value.
Executive branch	The executive branch is the part of government charged with implementing or enforcing the laws. Consists of the President and Vice President.
Cabinet	The heads of the executive departments of a jurisdiction who report to and advise its chief executive; examples would include the president's cabinet, the governor's cabinet, and the mayor's cabinet.
Research and development	The use of resources for the deliberate discovery of new information and ways of doing things, together with the application of that information in inventing new products or processes is referred to as research and development.
Primary factor	Primary factor refers to an input that exists as a stock, providing services that contribute to production. The stock is not used up in production, although it may deteriorate with use, providing a smaller flow of services later.
Groupthink	Groupthink is a situation in which pressures for cohesion and togetherness are so strong as to produce narrowly considered and bad decisions; this can be especially true via conformity pressures in groups.
Interdependence	The extent to which departments depend on each other for resources or materials to accomplish their tasks is referred to as interdependence.
Teamwork	That which occurs when group members work together in ways that utilize their skills well to accomplish a purpose is called teamwork.
Cooperative	A business owned and controlled by the people who use it, producers, consumers, or workers with similar needs who pool their resources for mutual gain is called cooperative.
Delegation	Delegation is the handing of a task over to another person, usually a subordinate. It is the assignment of authority and responsibility to another person to carry out specific activities.
Oracle	In 2004, sales at Oracle grew at a rate of 14.5% to $6.2 billion, giving it 41.3% and the top share of the relational-database market. Their main competitors in the database arena are IBM DB2 and Microsoft SQL Server, and to a lesser extent Sybase, Teradata, Informix, and MySQL. In the applications arena, their main competitor is SAP.
Profit	Profit refers to the return to the resource entrepreneurial ability; total revenue minus total cost.
Compatibility	Compatibility refers to used to describe a product characteristic, it means a good fit with other products used by the consumer or with the consumer's lifestyle. Used in a technical context, it means the ability of systems to work together.
Accommodation	Accommodation is a term used to describe a delivery of nonconforming goods meant as a partial performance of a contract for the sale of goods, where a full performance is not possible.
Warehouse	Warehouse refers to a location, often decentralized, that a firm uses to store, consolidate, age, or mix stock; house product-recall programs; or ease tax burdens.
Welfare	Welfare refers to the economic well being of an individual, group, or economy. For individuals, it is conceptualized by a utility function. For groups, including countries and the world, it is a tricky philosophical concept, since individuals fare differently.

Go to **Cram101.com** for the Practice Tests for this Chapter.

163

Compromise	Compromise occurs when the interaction is moderately important to meeting goals and the goals are neither completely compatible nor completely incompatible.
Negotiation	Negotiation is the process whereby interested parties resolve disputes, agree upon courses of action, bargain for individual or collective advantage, and/or attempt to craft outcomes which serve their mutual interests.
Labor	People's physical and mental talents and efforts that are used to help produce goods and services are called labor.
Contract	A contract is a "promise" or an "agreement" that is enforced or recognized by the law. In the civil law, a contract is considered to be part of the general law of obligations.
Expense	In accounting, an expense represents an event in which an asset is used up or a liability is incurred. In terms of the accounting equation, expenses reduce owners' equity.
Conflict resolution	Conflict resolution is the process of resolving a dispute or a conflict. Successful conflict resolution occurs by providing each side's needs, and adequately addressing their interests so that they are each satisfied with the outcome. Conflict resolution aims to end conflicts before they start or lead to physical fighting.
Status quo	Status quo is a Latin term meaning the present, current, existing state of affairs.
Conflict management	Conflict management refers to the long-term management of intractable conflicts. It is the label for the variety of ways by which people handle grievances -- standing up for what they consider to be right and against what they consider to be wrong.
Conflict stimulation	Conflict stimulation refers to the creation and constructive use of conflict by a manager.
Superordinate goal	Superordinate goal refers to an organizational goal that is more important to the well-being of the organization and its members than the more specific goals of interacting parties.
Linking role	A position for a person or group that serves to coordinate the activities of two or more organizational groups is referred to as the linking role.
Affiliation	A relationship with other websites in which a company can cross-promote and is credited for sales that accrue through their site is an affiliation.
Bond	Bond refers to a debt instrument, issued by a borrower and promising a specified stream of payments to the purchaser, usually regular interest payments plus a final repayment of principal.
Frequency	Frequency refers to the speed of the up and down movements of a fluctuating economic variable; that is, the number of times per unit of time that the variable completes a cycle of up and down movement.
Corporation	A legal entity chartered by a state or the Federal government that is distinct and separate from the individuals who own it is a corporation. This separation gives the corporation unique powers which other legal entities lack.
Bayer	Bayer is a German chemical and pharmaceutical company founded in 1863. By 1899, their trademark Aspirin was registered worldwide for the Bayer brand of acetylsalicylic acid, but through the widespread use to describe all brands of the compound, and Bayer's inability to protect its trademark the word "aspirin" lost its trademark status in the United States and some other countries.
Human resources	Human resources refers to the individuals within the firm, and to the portion of the firm's organization that deals with hiring, firing, training, and other personnel issues.
Proactive	To be proactive is to act before a situation becomes a source of confrontation or crisis. It

Go to **Cram101.com** for the Practice Tests for this Chapter.

Go to **Cram101.com** for the Practice Tests for this Chapter.
And, **NEVER** highlight a book again!

is the opposite of "retroactive," which refers to actions taken after an event.

Supervisor	A Supervisor is an employee of an organization with some of the powers and responsibilities of management, occupying a role between true manager and a regular employee. A Supervisor position is typically the first step towards being promoted into a management role.
Option	A contract that gives the purchaser the option to buy or sell the underlying financial instrument at a specified price, called the exercise price or strike price, within a specific period of time.
Span of control	Span of control refers to the optimum number of subordinates a manager supervises or should supervise.
Performance measurement	The process by which someone evaluates an employee's work behaviors by measurement and comparison with previously established standards, documents the results, and communicates the results to the employee is called performance measurement.
Production	The creation of finished goods and services using the factors of production: land, labor, capital, entrepreneurship, and knowledge.
Quota	A government-imposed restriction on quantity, or sometimes on total value, used to restrict the import of something to a specific quantity is called a quota.
Divisional organization	A form of organization that breaks the company into two or more business units (commonly called divisions) is called divisional organization.
Restructuring	Restructuring is the corporate management term for the act of partially dismantling and reorganizing a company for the purpose of making it more efficient and therefore more profitable.
Stock	In financial terminology, stock is the capital raized by a corporation, through the issuance and sale of shares.
Points	Loan origination fees that may be deductible as interest by a buyer of property. A seller of property who pays points reduces the selling price by the amount of the points paid for the buyer.
Assessment	Collecting information and providing feedback to employees about their behavior, communication style, or skills is an assessment.
Inventory	Tangible property held for sale in the normal course of business or used in producing goods or services for sale is an inventory.
Interpersonal skills	Interpersonal skills are used to communicate with, understand, and motivate individuals and groups.
Regulation	Regulation refers to restrictions state and federal laws place on business with regard to the conduct of its activities.
Business Week	Business Week is a business magazine published by McGraw-Hill. It was first published in 1929 under the direction of Malcolm Muir, who was serving as president of the McGraw-Hill Publishing company at the time. It is considered to be the standard both in industry and among students.
Wall Street Journal	Dow Jones & Company was founded in 1882 by reporters Charles Dow, Edward Jones and Charles Bergstresser. Jones converted the small Customers' Afternoon Letter into The Wall Street Journal, first published in 1889, and began delivery of the Dow Jones News Service via telegraph. The Journal featured the Jones 'Average', the first of several indexes of stock and bond prices on the New York Stock Exchange.
Journal	Book of original entry, in which transactions are recorded in a general ledger system, is

referred to as a journal.

Forbes David Churbuck founded online Forbes in 1996. The site drew attention when it uncovered Stephen Glass' journalistic fraud in The New Republic in 1998, a scoop that gave credibility to internet journalism.

Go to **Cram101.com** for the Practice Tests for this Chapter.
And, **NEVER** highlight a book again!

Production	The creation of finished goods and services using the factors of production: land, labor, capital, entrepreneurship, and knowledge.
Integration	Economic integration refers to reducing barriers among countries to transactions and to movements of goods, capital, and labor, including harmonization of laws, regulations, and standards. Integrated markets theoretically function as a unified market.
Industry	A group of firms that produce identical or similar products is an industry. It is also used specifically to refer to an area of economic production focused on manufacturing which involves large amounts of capital investment before any profit can be realized, also called "heavy industry".
Teamwork	That which occurs when group members work together in ways that utilize their skills well to accomplish a purpose is called teamwork.
Autonomous work groups	Groups used to integrate an organization's technical and social systems for the benefit of large systems are referred to as autonomous work groups.
Management	Management characterizes the process of leading and directing all or part of an organization, often a business, through the deployment and manipulation of resources. Early twentieth-century management writer Mary Parker Follett defined management as "the art of getting things done through people."
Participative management	Participative management or participatory management is the practice of empowering employees to participate in organizational decision making.
Brief	Brief refers to a statement of a party's case or legal arguments, usually prepared by an attorney. Also used to make legal arguments before appellate courts.
Task force	A temporary team or committee formed to solve a specific short-term problem involving several departments is the task force.
Committee	A long-lasting, sometimes permanent team in the organization structure created to deal with tasks that recur regularly is the committee.
Supervisor	A Supervisor is an employee of an organization with some of the powers and responsibilities of management, occupying a role between true manager and a regular employee. A Supervisor position is typically the first step towards being promoted into a management role.
Holding	The holding is a court's determination of a matter of law based on the issue presented in the particular case. In other words: under this law, with these facts, this result.
Authority	Authority in agency law, refers to an agent's ability to affect his principal's legal relations with third parties. Also used to refer to an actor's legal power or ability to do something. In addition, sometimes used to refer to a statute, case, or other legal source that justifies a particular result.
Turnover	Turnover in a financial context refers to the rate at which a provider of goods cycles through its average inventory. Turnover in a human resources context refers to the characteristic of a given company or industry, relative to rate at which an employer gains and loses staff.
Personnel	A collective term for all of the employees of an organization. Personnel is also commonly used to refer to the personnel management function or the organizational unit responsible for administering personnel programs.
Workflow	Workflow refers to automated systems that electronically route documents to the next person in the process.
Synergy	Corporate synergy occurs when corporations interact congruently. A corporate synergy refers to a financial benefit that a corporation expects to realize when it merges with or acquires

	another corporation.
Service	Service refers to a "non tangible product" that is not embodied in a physical good and that typically effects some change in another product, person, or institution. Contrasts with good.
Journal	Book of original entry, in which transactions are recorded in a general ledger system, is referred to as a journal.
Trust	An arrangement in which shareholders of independent firms agree to give up their stock in exchange for trust certificates that entitle them to a share of the trust's common profits.
Partnership	In the common law, a partnership is a type of business entity in which partners share with each other the profits or losses of the business undertaking in which they have all invested.
Facilitator	A facilitator is someone who skilfully helps a group of people understand their common objectives and plan to achieve them without personally taking any side of the argument.
Controller	Controller refers to the financial executive primarily responsible for management accounting and financial accounting. Also called chief accounting officer.
Gain	In finance, gain is a profit or an increase in value of an investment such as a stock or bond. Gain is calculated by fair market value or the proceeds from the sale of the investment minus the sum of the purchase price and all costs associated with it.
Core	A core is the set of feasible allocations in an economy that cannot be improved upon by subset of the set of the economy's consumers (a coalition). In construction, when the force in an element is within a certain center section, the core, the element will only be under compression.
Pfizer	Pfizer is the world's largest pharmaceutical company based in New York City. It produces the number-one selling drug Lipitor (atorvastatin, used to lower blood cholesterol).
Eastman Chemical Company	Eastman Chemical Company is a large supplier of industrial chemicals. It was formerly the chemical division of the Eastman Kodak Company and known as Tennessee Eastman, but was spun off by Kodak in an effort by that company to reduce its operations to its "core" photographic businesses
Productivity	Productivity refers to the total output of goods and services in a given period of time divided by work hours.
Profit	Profit refers to the return to the resource entrepreneurial ability; total revenue minus total cost.
Specific performance	A contract remedy whereby the defendant is ordered to perform according to the terms of his contract is referred to as specific performance.
Performance target	A task established for an employee that provides the comparative basis for performance appraisal is a performance target.
Corporation	A legal entity chartered by a state or the Federal government that is distinct and separate from the individuals who own it is a corporation. This separation gives the corporation unique powers which other legal entities lack.
Insurance	Insurance refers to a system by which individuals can reduce their exposure to risk of large losses by spreading the risks among a large number of persons.
Cisco Systems	While Cisco Systems was not the first company to develop and sell a router (a device that forwards computer traffic from one network to another), it did create the first commercially successful multi-protocol router to allow previously incompatible computers to communicate using different network protocols.

Manufacturing	Production of goods primarily by the application of labor and capital to raw materials and other intermediate inputs, in contrast to agriculture, mining, forestry, fishing, and services a manufacturing.
Mutual fund	A mutual fund is a form of collective investment that pools money from many investors and invests the money in stocks, bonds, short-term money market instruments, and/or other securities. In a mutual fund, the fund manager trades the fund's underlying securities, realizing capital gains or loss, and collects the dividend or interest income.
Instrument	Instrument refers to an economic variable that is controlled by policy makers and can be used to influence other variables, called targets. Examples are monetary and fiscal policies used to achieve external and internal balance.
Innovation	Innovation refers to the first commercially successful introduction of a new product, the use of a new method of production, or the creation of a new form of business organization.
Operation	A standardized method or technique that is performed repetitively, often on different materials resulting in different finished goods is called an operation.
Market	A market is, as defined in economics, a social arrangement that allows buyers and sellers to discover information and carry out a voluntary exchange of goods or services.
Fund	Independent accounting entity with a self-balancing set of accounts segregated for the purposes of carrying on specific activities is referred to as a fund.
Firm	An organization that employs resources to produce a good or service for profit and owns and operates one or more plants is referred to as a firm.
Collaboration	Collaboration occurs when the interaction between groups is very important to goal attainment and the goals are compatible. Wherein people work together —applying both to the work of individuals as well as larger collectives and societies.
Technology	The body of knowledge and techniques that can be used to combine economic resources to produce goods and services is called technology.
Organization culture	The set of values that helps the organization's employees understand which actions are considered acceptable and which unacceptable is referred to as the organization culture.
Contribution	In business organization law, the cash or property contributed to a business by its owners is referred to as contribution.
Global competition	Global competition exists when competitive conditions across national markets are linked strongly enough to form a true international market and when leading competitors compete head to head in many different countries.
Motorola	The Six Sigma quality system was developed at Motorola even though it became most well known because of its use by General Electric. It was created by engineer Bill Smith, under the direction of Bob Galvin (son of founder Paul Galvin) when he was running the company.
Policy	Similar to a script in that a policy can be a less than completely rational decision-making method. Involves the use of a pre-existing set of decision steps for any problem that presents itself.
Management philosophy	Management philosophy refers to a philosophy that links key goal-related issues with key collaboration issues to come up with general ways by which the firm will manage its affairs.
Job satisfaction	Job satisfaction describes how content an individual is with his or her job. It is a relatively recent term since in previous centuries the jobs available to a particular person were often predetermined by the occupation of that person's parent.
Abandonment	Abandonment in law, is the relinquishment of an interest, claim, privilege or possession.

Go to **Cram101.com** for the Practice Tests for this Chapter.

	This broad meaning has a number of applications in different branches of law.
Management team	A management team is directly responsible for managing the day-to-day operations (and profitability) of a company.
Quality circle	A quality circle is a volunteer group composed of workers who meet together to discuss workplace improvement, and make presentations to management with their ideas.
Interest	In finance and economics, interest is the price paid by a borrower for the use of a lender's money. In other words, interest is the amount of paid to "rent" money for a period of time.
Digital Equipment Corporation	Digital Equipment Corporation was a pioneering company in the American computer industry. Its PDP and VAX products were arguably the most popular mini-computers for the scientific and engineering communities during the 70s and 80s.
Matrix structure	An organizational structure which typically crosses a functional approach with a product or service-based design, often resulting in employees having two bosses is the matrix structure.
Product development	In business and engineering, new product development is the complete process of bringing a new product to market. There are two parallel aspects to this process : one involves product engineering ; the other marketing analysis. Marketers see new product development as the first stage in product life cycle management, engineers as part of Product Lifecycle Management.
General Electric	In 1876, Thomas Alva Edison opened a new laboratory in Menlo Park, New Jersey. Out of the laboratory was to come perhaps the most famous invention of all—a successful development of the incandescent electric lamp. By 1890, Edison had organized his various businesses into the Edison General Electric Company.
Product development teams	Combinations of work teams and problem-solving teams that create new designs for products or services that will satisfy customer needs are product development teams.
Electronic mail	Electronic mail refers to electronic written communication between individuals using computers connected to the Internet.
Utility	Utility refers to the want-satisfying power of a good or service; the satisfaction or pleasure a consumer obtains from the consumption of a good or service.
Warrant	A warrant is a security that entitles the holder to buy or sell a certain additional quantity of an underlying security at an agreed-upon price, at the holder's discretion.
Organizational structure	Organizational structure is the way in which the interrelated groups of an organization are constructed. From a managerial point of view the main concerns are ensuring effective communication and coordination.
Preparation	Preparation refers to usually the first stage in the creative process. It includes education and formal training.
Hierarchy	A system of grouping people in an organization according to rank from the top down in which all subordinate managers must report to one person is called a hierarchy.
Union	A worker association that bargains with employers over wages and working conditions is called a union.
Consultant	A professional that provides expert advice in a particular field or area in which customers occassionaly require this type of knowledge is a consultant.
Leadership	Management merely consists of leadership applied to business situations; or in other words: management forms a sub-set of the broader process of leadership.
Mission	Mission statement refers to an outline of the fundamental purposes of an organization.

Go to **Cram101.com** for the Practice Tests for this Chapter.

statement	
Continuous improvement	The constant effort to eliminate waste, reduce response time, simplify the design of both products and processes, and improve quality and customer service is referred to as continuous improvement.
Customer satisfaction	Customer satisfaction is a business term which is used to capture the idea of measuring how satisfied an enterprise's customers are with the organization's efforts in a marketplace.
Staffing	Staffing refers to a management function that includes hiring, motivating, and retaining the best people available to accomplish the company's objectives.
Composition	An out-of-court settlement in which creditors agree to accept a fractional settlement on their original claim is referred to as composition.
Management system	A management system is the framework of processes and procedures used to ensure that an organization can fulfill all tasks required to achieve its objectives.
Hierarchical organization	A hierarchical organization is an organization structured in a way such that every entity in the organization, except one, is subordinate to a single other entity. This is the dominant mode of organization among large organizations; most corporations, governments, and organized religions are hierarchical organizations.
Draft	A signed, written order by which one party instructs another party to pay a specified sum to a third party, at sight or at a specific date is a draft.
Security	Security refers to a claim on the borrower future income that is sold by the borrower to the lender. A security is a type of transferable interest representing financial value.
Interpersonal skills	Interpersonal skills are used to communicate with, understand, and motivate individuals and groups.
Anticipation	In finance, anticipation is where debts are paid off early, generally in order to pay less interest.
Intermediaries	Intermediaries specialize in information either to bring together two parties to a transaction or to buy in order to sell again.
Peak	Peak refers to the point in the business cycle when an economic expansion reaches its highest point before turning down. Contrasts with trough.
Regulation	Regulation refers to restrictions state and federal laws place on business with regard to the conduct of its activities.
Loyalty	Marketers tend to define customer loyalty as making repeat purchases. Some argue that it should be defined attitudinally as a strongly positive feeling about the brand.
Performance feedback	The process of providing employees with information regarding their performance effectiveness is referred to as performance feedback.
Performance appraisal	An evaluation in which the performance level of employees is measured against established standards to make decisions about promotions, compenzation, additional training, or firing is referred to as performance appraisal.
External customers	Dealers, who buy products to sell to others, and ultimate customers, who buy products for their own personal use are referred to as external customers.
Lease	A contract for the possession and use of land or other property, including goods, on one side, and a recompense of rent or other income on the other is the lease.
General manager	A manager who is responsible for several departments that perform different functions is called general manager.

Go to **Cram101.com** for the Practice Tests for this Chapter.

Incentive	An incentive is any factor (financial or non-financial) that provides a motive for a particular course of action, or counts as a reason for preferring one choice to the alternatives.
Ethical dilemma	An ethical dilemma is a situation that often involves an apparent conflict between moral imperatives, in which to obey one would result in transgressing another.
Press release	A written public news announcement normally distributed to major news services is referred to as press release.
Strategic goal	A strategic goal is a broad statement of where an organization wants to be in the future; pertains to the organization as a whole rather than to specific divisions or departments.
Virtual team	A group of physically dispersed people who work as a team via alternative communication modes is called virtual team.
Cooperative	A business owned and controlled by the people who use it, producers, consumers, or workers with similar needs who pool their resources for mutual gain is called cooperative.
Specialist	A specialist is a trader who makes a market in one or several stocks and holds the limit order book for those stocks.
Enabling	Enabling refers to giving workers the education and tools they need to assume their new decision-making powers.
Foundation	A Foundation is a type of philanthropic organization set up by either individuals or institutions as a legal entity (either as a corporation or trust) with the purpose of distributing grants to support causes in line with the goals of the foundation.
Annual report	An annual report is prepared by corporate management that presents financial information including financial statements, footnotes, and the management discussion and analysis.
Organizational Behavior	The study of human behavior in organizational settings, the interface between human behavior and the organization, and the organization itself is called organizational behavior.
Complexity	The technical sophistication of the product and hence the amount of understanding required to use it is referred to as complexity. It is the opposite of simplicity.
Effective groups	Groups that achieve high levels of task performance, member satisfaction, and team viability are effective groups.

Go to **Cram101.com** for the Practice Tests for this Chapter.
And, **NEVER** highlight a book again!

Leadership	Management merely consists of leadership applied to business situations; or in other words: management forms a sub-set of the broader process of leadership.
Pizza Hut	Pizza Hut is the world's largest pizza restaurant chain with nearly 34,000 restaurants, delivery-carry out units, and kiosks in 100 countries
Harvard Business Review	Harvard Business Review is a research-based magazine written for business practitioners, it claims a high ranking business readership and enjoys the reverence of academics, executives, and management consultants. It has been the frequent publishing home for well known scholars and management thinkers.
Balance	In banking and accountancy, the outstanding balance is the amount of money owned, (or due), that remains in a deposit account (or a loan account) at a given date, after all past remittances, payments and withdrawal have been accounted for. It can be positive (then, in the balance sheet of a firm, it is an asset) or negative (a liability).
Mistake	In contract law a mistake is incorrect understanding by one or more parties to a contract and may be used as grounds to invalidate the agreement. Common law has identified three different types of mistake in contract: unilateral mistake, mutual mistake, and common mistake.
Property	Assets defined in the broadest legal sense. Property includes the unrealized receivables of a cash basis taxpayer, but not services rendered.
Organizational goals	Objectives that management seeks to achieve in pursuing the firm's purpose are organizational goals.
Authority	Authority in agency law, refers to an agent's ability to affect his principal's legal relations with third parties. Also used to refer to an actor's legal power or ability to do something. In addition, sometimes used to refer to a statute, case, or other legal source that justifies a particular result.
Management	Management characterizes the process of leading and directing all or part of an organization, often a business, through the deployment and manipulation of resources. Early twentieth-century management writer Mary Parker Follett defined management as "the art of getting things done through people."
Staffing	Staffing refers to a management function that includes hiring, motivating, and retaining the best people available to accomplish the company's objectives.
Controlling	A management function that involves determining whether or not an organization is progressing toward its goals and objectives, and taking corrective action if it is not is called controlling.
Policy	Similar to a script in that a policy can be a less than completely rational decision-making method. Involves the use of a pre-existing set of decision steps for any problem that presents itself.
Stakeholder	A stakeholder is an individual or group with a vested interest in or expectation for organizational performance. Usually stakeholders can either have an effect on or are affected by an organization.
Stockholder	A stockholder is an individual or company (including a corporation) that legally owns one or more shares of stock in a joined stock company. The shareholders are the owners of a corporation. Companies listed at the stock market strive to enhance shareholder value.
Budget	Budget refers to an account, usually for a year, of the planned expenditures and the expected receipts of an entity. For a government, the receipts are tax revenues.
Coalition	An informal alliance among managers who support a specific goal is called coalition.
Deed	A deed is a legal instrument used to grant a right. The deed is best known as the method of

transferring title to real estate from one person to another.

Business plan	A detailed written statement that describes the nature of the business, the target market, the advantages the business will have in relation to competition, and the resources and qualifications of the owner is referred to as a business plan.
Trait approach	This approach attempted to identify stable and enduring character traits that differentiated effective leaders from nonleaders is called trait approach.
Industry	A group of firms that produce identical or similar products is an industry. It is also used specifically to refer to an area of economic production focused on manufacturing which involves large amounts of capital investment before any profit can be realized, also called "heavy industry".
Competitor	Other organizations in the same industry or type of business that provide a good or service to the same set of customers is referred to as a competitor.
Corporate culture	The whole collection of beliefs, values, and behaviors of a firm that send messages to those within and outside the company about how business is done is the corporate culture.
Acquisition	A company's purchase of the property and obligations of another company is an acquisition.
Firm	An organization that employs resources to produce a good or service for profit and owns and operates one or more plants is referred to as a firm.
Fortune magazine	Fortune magazine is America's longest-running business magazine. Currently owned by media conglomerate Time Warner, it was founded in 1930 by Henry Luce. It is known for its regular features ranking companies by revenue.
Interest	In finance and economics, interest is the price paid by a borrower for the use of a lender's money. In other words, interest is the amount of paid to "rent" money for a period of time.
Assessment	Collecting information and providing feedback to employees about their behavior, communication style, or skills is an assessment.
Profit	Profit refers to the return to the resource entrepreneurial ability; total revenue minus total cost.
Behavioral approach	Behavioral approach refers to approach to leadership that tries to identify behaviors that differentiated effective leaders from nonleaders. It uses rules of thumb, suboptimizing, and satisfying in making decisions.
Leadership grid	A leadership grid evaluates leadership behavior along two dimensions, concern for production and concern for people, and suggests that effective leadership styles include high levels of both behaviors.
Supervisor	A Supervisor is an employee of an organization with some of the powers and responsibilities of management, occupying a role between true manager and a regular employee. A Supervisor position is typically the first step towards being promoted into a management role.
Productivity	Productivity refers to the total output of goods and services in a given period of time divided by work hours.
Samsung	On November 30, 2005 Samsung pleaded guilty to a charge it participated in a worldwide DRAM price fixing conspiracy during 1999-2002 that damaged competition and raized PC prices.
Sony	Sony is a multinational corporation and one of the world's largest media conglomerates founded in Tokyo, Japan. One of its divisions Sony Electronics is one of the leading manufacturers of electronics, video, communications, and information technology products for the consumer and professional markets.
Market leader	The market leader is dominant in its industry. It has substantial market share and often

	extensive distribution arrangements with retailers. It typically is the industry leader in developing innovative new business models and new products (although not always).
Market	A market is, as defined in economics, a social arrangement that allows buyers and sellers to discover information and carry out a voluntary exchange of goods or services.
Manufacturing	Production of goods primarily by the application of labor and capital to raw materials and other intermediate inputs, in contrast to agriculture, mining, forestry, fishing, and services a manufacturing.
Innovation	Innovation refers to the first commercially successful introduction of a new product, the use of a new method of production, or the creation of a new form of business organization.
Patent	The legal right to the proceeds from and control over the use of an invented product or process, granted for a fixed period of time, usually 20 years. Patent is one form of intellectual property that is subject of the TRIPS agreement.
Corporate governance	Corporate governance is the set of processes, customs, policies, laws and institutions affecting the way a corporation is directed, administered or controlled.
Board of directors	The group of individuals elected by the stockholders of a corporation to oversee its operations is a board of directors.
Pay for Performance	A one-time cash payment to an investment center manager as a reward for meeting a predetermined criterion on a specified performance measure is referred to as pay for performance.
Consideration	Consideration in contract law, a basic requirement for an enforceable agreement under traditional contract principles, defined in this text as legal value, bargained for and given in exchange for an act or promise. In corporation law, cash or property contributed to a corporation in exchange for shares, or a promise to contribute such cash or property.
Trust	An arrangement in which shareholders of independent firms agree to give up their stock in exchange for trust certificates that entitle them to a share of the trust's common profits.
Channel	Channel, in communications (sometimes called communications channel), refers to the medium used to convey information from a sender (or transmitter) to a receiver.
International Harvester	International Harvester was an American corporation based in Chicago that produced a multitude of agricultural machinery and vehicles. In 1924, International Harvester introduced the Farmall tractor, a smaller general-purpose tractor, to fend off competition from the Ford Motor Company's Fordson tractors. The Farmall was the first tractor in the United States to incorporate a tricycle-like design (or row-crop front axle), which could be used on tall crops such as cotton and corn.
Corporation	A legal entity chartered by a state or the Federal government that is distinct and separate from the individuals who own it is a corporation. This separation gives the corporation unique powers which other legal entities lack.
Production	The creation of finished goods and services using the factors of production: land, labor, capital, entrepreneurship, and knowledge.
Complexity	The technical sophistication of the product and hence the amount of understanding required to use it is referred to as complexity. It is the opposite of simplicity.
Contingency theory	Any theory that presupposes that there is no theory or method for operating a business that can be applied in all instances is referred to as a contingency theory.
LPC Theory of Leadership	Suggests that a leader's effectiveness depends on the situation is an LPC Theory of Leadership.

Go to **Cram101.com** for the Practice Tests for this Chapter.

Respondent	Respondent refers to a term often used to describe the party charged in an administrative proceeding. The party adverse to the appellant in a case appealed to a higher court.
Evaluation	The consumer's appraisal of the product or brand on important attributes is called evaluation.
Lpc scale	A questionnaire designed to measure relationship-oriented versus task-oriented leadership style according to the leader's choice of adjectives for describing the 'least preferred coworker is called the lpc scale.
Position power	Position power refers to power manager's hold due to their role in the organization. May include a manager's network of contacts, legitimate authority and control over information, rewards, punishments, and the work environment.
Promotion	Promotion refers to all the techniques sellers use to motivate people to buy products or services. An attempt by marketers to inform people about products and to persuade them to participate in an exchange.
Assignment	A transfer of property or some right or interest is referred to as assignment.
Boeing	Boeing is the world's largest aircraft manufacturer by revenue. Headquartered in Chicago, Illinois, Boeing is the second-largest defense contractor in the world. In 2005, the company was the world's largest civil aircraft manufacturer in terms of value.
Kraft Foods	Kraft Foods is the largest food and beverage company headquartered in North America and the second largest in the world. In 1993 the Kraft Foods plant in Boston was hit with a $250,000 fine for violating the Clean Air Act of 1970.
Contribution	In business organization law, the cash or property contributed to a business by its owners is referred to as contribution.
Context	The effect of the background under which a message often takes on more and richer meaning is a context. Context is especially important in cross-cultural interactions because some cultures are said to be high context or low context.
Contingency approach	Contingency approach refers to the dominant perspective in organizational behavior, it argues that there's no single best way to manage behavior. What 'works' in any given context depends on the complex interplay between a variety of person and situational factors.
Nabisco	In 2000 Philip Morris Companies acquired Nabisco; that acquisition was approved by the Federal Trade Commission subject to the divestiture of products in five areas: three Jell-O and Royal brands types of products (dry-mix gelatin dessert, dry-mix pudding, no-bake desserts), intense mints (such as Altoids), and baking powder. Kraft later purchased the company.
Brand	A name, symbol, or design that identifies the goods or services of one seller or group of sellers and distinguishes them from the goods and services of competitors is a brand.
Vendor	A person who sells property to a vendee is a vendor. The words vendor and vendee are more commonly applied to the seller and purchaser of real estate, and the words seller and buyer are more commonly applied to the seller and purchaser of personal property.
Brand manager	A manager who has direct responsibility for one brand or one product line is called a brand manager.
International division	Division responsible for a firm's international activities is an international division.
Operation	A standardized method or technique that is performed repetitively, often on different materials resulting in different finished goods is called an operation.

Go to **Cram101.com** for the Practice Tests for this Chapter.

Revenue	Revenue is a U.S. business term for the amount of money that a company receives from its activities, mostly from sales of products and/or services to customers.
Supportive leadership	That which focuses on subordinate needs, well-being, and promotion of a friendly work climate is supportive leadership.
Participative leadership	Leadership style that consists of managers and employees working together to make decisions is referred to as participative leadership.
Directive leadership	Spells out the what and how of subordinates task and expects subordinates to follow orders is called directive leadership.
Decision tree	In decision theory, a decision tree is a graph of decisions and their possible consequences, (including resource costs and risks) used to create a plan to reach a goal.
Expert system	Computer systems incorporating the decision rules of people recognized as experts in a certain area are refered to as an expert system.
Exchange	The trade of things of value between buyer and seller so that each is better off after the trade is called the exchange.
Variable	A variable is something measured by a number; it is used to analyze what happens to other things when the size of that number changes.
Privilege	Generally, a legal right to engage in conduct that would otherwise result in legal liability is a privilege. Privileges are commonly classified as absolute or conditional. Occasionally, privilege is also used to denote a legal right to refrain from particular behavior.
Compatibility	Compatibility refers to used to describe a product characteristic, it means a good fit with other products used by the consumer or with the consumer's lifestyle. Used in a technical context, it means the ability of systems to work together.
Confirmed	When the seller's bank agrees to assume liability on the letter of credit issued by the buyer's bank the transaction is confirmed. The term means that the credit is not only backed up by the issuing foreign bank, but that payment is also guaranteed by the notifying American bank.
Situational leadership model	Situational leadership model refers to a model of leadership proposed by Hersey and Blanchard that clarifies the interrelation between employee preparedness and effectiveness in leadership.
Situational leadership	Situational leadership refers to a leadership model, which argues that effective leadership involves matching the right combination of task-oriented and relationship-oriented behavior to the maturity level of subordinates.
Human resources	Human resources refers to the individuals within the firm, and to the portion of the firm's organization that deals with hiring, firing, training, and other personnel issues.
Trademark	A distinctive word, name, symbol, device, or combination thereof, which enables consumers to identify favored products or services and which may find protection under state or federal law is a trademark.
Organizational Behavior	The study of human behavior in organizational settings, the interface between human behavior and the organization, and the organization itself is called organizational behavior.
Points	Loan origination fees that may be deductible as interest by a buyer of property. A seller of property who pays points reduces the selling price by the amount of the points paid for the buyer.
Technology	The body of knowledge and techniques that can be used to combine economic resources to produce goods and services is called technology.

Go to **Cram101.com** for the Practice Tests for this Chapter.
And, **NEVER** highlight a book again!

Failure rate	Failure rate is the frequency with an engineered system or component fails, expressed for example in failures per hour. Failure rate is usually time dependent. In the special case when the likelihood of failure remains constant as time passes, failure rate is simply the inverse of the mean time to failure, expressed for example in hours per failure.
Product cycle	Product cycle refers to the life cycle of a new product, which first can be produced only in the country where it was developed, then as it becomes standardized and more familiar, can be produced in other countries and exported back to where it started.
Bottom line	The bottom line is net income on the last line of a income statement.
Core	A core is the set of feasible allocations in an economy that cannot be improved upon by subset of the set of the economy's consumers (a coalition). In construction, when the force in an element is within a certain center section, the core, the element will only be under compression.
Management team	A management team is directly responsible for managing the day-to-day operations (and profitability) of a company.
Customer service	The ability of logistics management to satisfy users in terms of time, dependability, communication, and convenience is called the customer service.
Service	Service refers to a "non tangible product" that is not embodied in a physical good and that typically effects some change in another product, person, or institution. Contrasts with good.
Sales expense	Any cost associated with the marketing or sale of a product or service is a sales expense.
Expense	In accounting, an expense represents an event in which an asset is used up or a liability is incurred. In terms of the accounting equation, expenses reduce owners' equity.

Southwest airlines	Southwest Airlines is a low-fare airline in the United States. It is the third-largest airline in the world, by number of passengers carried, and the largest in the United States by number of passengers carried domestically.
Entrepreneur	The owner/operator. The person who organizes, manages, and assumes the risks of a firm, taking a new idea or a new product and turning it into a successful business is an entrepreneur.
Firm	An organization that employs resources to produce a good or service for profit and owns and operates one or more plants is referred to as a firm.
Competitor	Other organizations in the same industry or type of business that provide a good or service to the same set of customers is referred to as a competitor.
Leadership	Management merely consists of leadership applied to business situations; or in other words: management forms a sub-set of the broader process of leadership.
Service	Service refers to a "non tangible product" that is not embodied in a physical good and that typically effects some change in another product, person, or institution. Contrasts with good.
Hierarchy	A system of grouping people in an organization according to rank from the top down in which all subordinate managers must report to one person is called a hierarchy.
Transformati-nal leadership	The set of abilities that allows the leader to recognize the need for change, to create a vision to guide that change, and to execute that change effectively is referred to as transformational leadership.
Merger	Merger refers to the combination of two firms into a single firm.
Management	Management characterizes the process of leading and directing all or part of an organization, often a business, through the deployment and manipulation of resources. Early twentieth-century management writer Mary Parker Follett defined management as "the art of getting things done through people."
Transactional leadership	Transactional leadership uses conventional reward and punishment to gain compliance from their followers.
Compaq	Compaq was founded in February 1982 by Rod Canion, Jim Harris and Bill Murto, three senior managers from semiconductor manufacturer Texas Instruments. Each invested $1,000 to form the company. Their first venture capital came from Ben Rosen and Sevin-Rosen partners. It is often told that the architecture of the original PC was first sketched out on a placemat by the founders while dining in the Houston restaurant, House of Pies.
Charisma	A form of interpersonal attraction that inspires support and acceptance from others is charisma. It refers especially to a quality in certain people who easily draw the attention and admiration (or even hatred if the charisma is negative) of others due to a "magnetic" quality of personality and/or appearance.
Charismatic leader	A leader who has the ability to motivate subordinates to transcend their expected performance is a charismatic leader.
Continental Airlines	Continental Airlines is an airline of the United States. Based in Houston, Texas, it is the 6th largest airline in the U.S. and the 8th largest in the world. Continental's tagline, since 1998, has been Work Hard, Fly Right.
Standing	Standing refers to the legal requirement that anyone seeking to challenge a particular action in court must demonstrate that such action substantially affects his legitimate interests before he will be entitled to bring suit.
Family business	A family business is a company owned, controlled, and operated by members of one or several

Go to **Cram101.com** for the Practice Tests for this Chapter.

families. Many companies that are now publicly held were founded as family businesses. Many family businesses have non-family members as employees, but, particularly in smaller companies, the top positions are often allocated to family members.

Consumption	In Keynesian economics consumption refers to personal consumption expenditure, i.e., the purchase of currently produced goods and services out of income, out of savings (net worth), or from borrowed funds. It refers to that part of disposable income that does not go to saving.
Industry	A group of firms that produce identical or similar products is an industry. It is also used specifically to refer to an area of economic production focused on manufacturing which involves large amounts of capital investment before any profit can be realized, also called "heavy industry".
Synergy	Corporate synergy occurs when corporations interact congruently. A corporate synergy refers to a financial benefit that a corporation expects to realize when it merges with or acquires another corporation.
Gain	In finance, gain is a profit or an increase in value of an investment such as a stock or bond. Gain is calculated by fair market value or the proceeds from the sale of the investment minus the sum of the purchase price and all costs associated with it.
Supply	Supply is the aggregate amount of any material good that can be called into being at a certain price point; it comprises one half of the equation of supply and demand. In classical economic theory, a curve representing supply is one of the factors that produce price.
Turnover	Turnover in a financial context refers to the rate at which a provider of goods cycles through its average inventory. Turnover in a human resources context refers to the characteristic of a given company or industry, relative to rate at which an employer gains and loses staff.
Labor	People's physical and mental talents and efforts that are used to help produce goods and services are called labor.
News release	A publicity tool consisting of an announcement regarding changes in the company or the product line is called a news release.
Leadership substitutes	Individual, task, and organizational characteristics that tend to outweigh the leader's ability to affect subordinates' satisfaction and performance is referred to as leadership substitutes.
Supervisor	A Supervisor is an employee of an organization with some of the powers and responsibilities of management, occupying a role between true manager and a regular employee. A Supervisor position is typically the first step towards being promoted into a management role.
Facilitator	A facilitator is someone who skilfully helps a group of people understand their common objectives and plan to achieve them without personally taking any side of the argument.
Principal	In agency law, one under whose direction an agent acts and for whose benefit that agent acts is a principal.
Referent power	Referent power is individual power based on a high level of identification with, admiration of, or respect for the powerholder.
Legitimate power	Legitimate power refers to power that is granted by virtue of one's position in the organization.
Authority	Authority in agency law, refers to an agent's ability to affect his principal's legal relations with third parties. Also used to refer to an actor's legal power or ability to do something. In addition, sometimes used to refer to a statute, case, or other legal source

Go to **Cram101.com** for the Practice Tests for this Chapter.
And, **NEVER** highlight a book again!

that justifies a particular result.

Organic organization	A term created by Tom Burns and G.M. Stalker in the late 1950s, an organic organization is an organization which is flexible and values outside knowledge.
Research and development	The use of resources for the deliberate discovery of new information and ways of doing things, together with the application of that information in inventing new products or processes is referred to as research and development.
Assignment	A transfer of property or some right or interest is referred to as assignment.
Promotion	Promotion refers to all the techniques sellers use to motivate people to buy products or services. An attempt by marketers to inform people about products and to persuade them to participate in an exchange.
Coercive power	Coercive power refers to the extent to which a person has the ability to punish or physically or psychologically harm someone else.
Coercion	Economic coercion is when an agent puts economic pressure onto the victim. The most common example of this is cutting off the supply to an essential resource, such as water.
Volkswagen	Volkswagen or VW is an automobile manufacturer based in Wolfsburg, Germany in the state of Lower Saxony. It forms the core of this Group, one of the world's four largest car producers. Its German tagline is "Aus Liebe zum Automobil", which is translated as "For the love of the car" - or, For Love of the People's Cars,".
Niche	In industry, a niche is a situation or an activity perfectly suited to a person. A niche can imply a working position or an area suited to a person who occupies it. Basically, a job where a person is able to succeed and thrive.
Expert power	The extent to which a person controls information that is valuable to someone else is referred to as expert power.
Trust	An arrangement in which shareholders of independent firms agree to give up their stock in exchange for trust certificates that entitle them to a share of the trust's common profits.
Position power	Position power refers to power manager's hold due to their role in the organization. May include a manager's network of contacts, legitimate authority and control over information, rewards, punishments, and the work environment.
Control activities	Control activities are the activities intended to prevent, detect, and correct errors and irregularities relating to business risks. Policies and procedures used by management to meet its objectives.
Loyalty	Marketers tend to define customer loyalty as making repeat purchases. Some argue that it should be defined attitudinally as a strongly positive feeling about the brand.
Overtime	Overtime is the amount of time someone works beyond normal working hours.
Compliance	A type of influence process where a receiver accepts the position advocated by a source to obtain favorable outcomes or to avoid punishment is the compliance.
Employee development	Employee development is the strategic investment, by an organization, in the training of its members.
Channel	Channel, in communications (sometimes called communications channel), refers to the medium used to convey information from a sender (or transmitter) to a receiver.
Infraction	Infraction is an essentially minor violation of law where the penalty upon conviction only consists of monetary forfeiture. A violation of law which could include imprisonment is a crime. It is distinguished from a misdemeanor or a felony in that the penalty for an infraction cannot include any imprisonment.

Complete information	Complete information refers to the assumption that economic agents know everything that they need to know in order to make optimal decisions. Types of incomplete information are uncertainty and asymmetric information.
Credibility	The extent to which a source is perceived as having knowledge, skill, or experience relevant to a communication topic and can be trusted to give an unbiased opinion or present objective information on the issue is called credibility.
Organizational politics	Organizational politics occurs when power sources and influence tactics are used to serve personal goals or motives.
Evaluation	The consumer's appraisal of the product or brand on important attributes is called evaluation.
Termination	The ending of a corporation that occurs only after the winding-up of the corporation's affairs, the liquidation of its assets, and the distribution of the proceeds to the claimants are referred to as a termination.
Boeing	Boeing is the world's largest aircraft manufacturer by revenue. Headquartered in Chicago, Illinois, Boeing is the second-largest defense contractor in the world. In 2005, the company was the world's largest civil aircraft manufacturer in terms of value.
Stock	In financial terminology, stock is the capital raized by a corporation, through the issuance and sale of shares.
Generally accepted accounting principles	Generally accepted accounting principles refers to the standard framework of guidelines for financial accounting. It includes the standards, conventions, and rules accountants follow in recording and summarizing transactions, and in the preparation of financial statements.
Accounting	A system that collects and processes financial information about an organization and reports that information to decision makers is referred to as accounting.
Expense	In accounting, an expense represents an event in which an asset is used up or a liability is incurred. In terms of the accounting equation, expenses reduce owners' equity.
Disclosure	Disclosure means the giving out of information, either voluntarily or to be in compliance with legal regulations or workplace rules.
Short run	Short run refers to a period of time that permits an increase or decrease in current production volume with existing capacity, but one that is too short to permit enlargement of that capacity itself (eg, the building of new plants, training of additional workers, etc.).
Production	The creation of finished goods and services using the factors of production: land, labor, capital, entrepreneurship, and knowledge.
Business Week	Business Week is a business magazine published by McGraw-Hill. It was first published in 1929 under the direction of Malcolm Muir, who was serving as president of the McGraw-Hill Publishing company at the time. It is considered to be the standard both in industry and among students.
Dow Jones Industrial Average	Today, the Dow Jones Industrial Average consists of 30 of the largest and most widely held public companies in the United States. The "industrial" portion of the name is largely historical—many of the 30 modern components have little to do with heavy industry. To compensate for the effects of stock splits and other adjustments, it is currently a weighted average, not the actual average of the prices of its component stocks.
Consideration	Consideration in contract law, a basic requirement for an enforceable agreement under traditional contract principles, defined in this text as legal value, bargained for and given in exchange for an act or promise. In corporation law, cash or property contributed to a

Go to **Cram101.com** for the Practice Tests for this Chapter.
And, **NEVER** highlight a book again!

	corporation in exchange for shares, or a promise to contribute such cash or property.
Organizational goals	Objectives that management seeks to achieve in pursuing the firm's purpose are organizational goals.
Technology	The body of knowledge and techniques that can be used to combine economic resources to produce goods and services is called technology.
Market share	That fraction of an industry's output accounted for by an individual firm or group of firms is called market share.
Market	A market is, as defined in economics, a social arrangement that allows buyers and sellers to discover information and carry out a voluntary exchange of goods or services.
Incentive	An incentive is any factor (financial or non-financial) that provides a motive for a particular course of action, or counts as a reason for preferring one choice to the alternatives.
Restructuring	Restructuring is the corporate management term for the act of partially dismantling and reorganizing a company for the purpose of making it more efficient and therefore more profitable.
Argument	The discussion by counsel for the respective parties of their contentions on the law and the facts of the case being tried in order to aid the jury in arriving at a correct and just conclusion is called argument.
Nonprogrammed decision	Nonprogrammed decision refers to a decision that recurs infrequently and for which there is no previously established decision rule.
Consultant	A professional that provides expert advice in a particular field or area in which customers occassionaly require this type of knowledge is a consultant.
Controlling	A management function that involves determining whether or not an organization is progressing toward its goals and objectives, and taking corrective action if it is not is called controlling.
Tactic	A short-term immediate decision that, in its totality, leads to the achievement of strategic goals is called a tactic.
Senior executive	Senior executive means a chief executive officer, chief operating officer, chief financial officer and anyone in charge of a principal business unit or function.
Coalition	An informal alliance among managers who support a specific goal is called coalition.
Preference	The act of a debtor in paying or securing one or more of his creditors in a manner more favorable to them than to other creditors or to the exclusion of such other creditors is a preference. In the absence of statute, a preference is perfectly good, but to be legal it must be bona fide, and not a mere subterfuge of the debtor to secure a future benefit to himself or to prevent the application of his property to his debts.
Interest	In finance and economics, interest is the price paid by a borrower for the use of a lender's money. In other words, interest is the amount of paid to "rent" money for a period of time.
Reciprocity	An industrial buying practice in which two organizations agree to purchase each other's products and services is called reciprocity.
Impression management	A direct and intentional effort by someone to enhance his or her own image in the eyes of others is called impression management.
Enron	Enron Corportaion's global reputation was undermined by persistent rumours of bribery and political pressure to secure contracts in Central America, South America, Africa, and the Philippines. Especially controversial was its $3 billion contract with the Maharashtra State

Go to **Cram101.com** for the Practice Tests for this Chapter.
And, **NEVER** highlight a book again!

Electricity Board in India, where it is alleged that Enron officials used political connections within the Clinton and Bush administrations to exert pressure on the board.

Economy	The income, expenditures, and resources that affect the cost of running a business and household are called an economy.
Profit	Profit refers to the return to the resource entrepreneurial ability; total revenue minus total cost.
Starbucks	Although it has endured much criticism for its purported monopoly on the global coffee-bean market, Starbucks purchases only 3% of the coffee beans grown worldwide. In 2000 the company introduced a line of fair trade products and now offers three options for socially conscious coffee drinkers. According to Starbucks, they purchased 4.8 million pounds of Certified Fair Trade coffee in fiscal year 2004 and 11.5 million pounds in 2005.
Voting shares	Voting shares are shares that give the stockholder the right to vote on matters of corporate policy making as well as who will compose the members of the board of directors.
Shares	Shares refer to an equity security, representing a shareholder's ownership of a corporation. Shares are one of a finite number of equal portions in the capital of a company, entitling the owner to a proportion of distributed, non-reinvested profits known as dividends and to a portion of the value of the company in case of liquidation.
Polaroid	The Polaroid Corporation was founded in 1937 by Edwin H. Land. It is most famous for its instant film cameras, which reached the market in 1948, and continue to be the company's flagship product line.
Xerox	Xerox was founded in 1906 as "The Haloid Company" manufacturing photographic paper and equipment. The company came to prominence in 1959 with the introduction of the first plain paper photocopier using the process of xerography (electrophotography) developed by Chester Carlson, the Xerox 914.
Wall Street Journal	Dow Jones & Company was founded in 1882 by reporters Charles Dow, Edward Jones and Charles Bergstresser. Jones converted the small Customers' Afternoon Letter into The Wall Street Journal, first published in 1889, and began delivery of the Dow Jones News Service via telegraph. The Journal featured the Jones 'Average', the first of several indexes of stock and bond prices on the New York Stock Exchange.
Journal	Book of original entry, in which transactions are recorded in a general ledger system, is referred to as a journal.
Prejudice	Prejudice is, as the name implies, the process of "pre-judging" something. It implies coming to a judgment on a subject before learning where the preponderance of evidence actually lies, or forming a judgment without direct experience.
Instrument	Instrument refers to an economic variable that is controlled by policy makers and can be used to influence other variables, called targets. Examples are monetary and fiscal policies used to achieve external and internal balance.
Proxy	Proxy refers to a person who is authorized to vote the shares of another person. Also, the written authorization empowering a person to vote the shares of another person.
Layoff	A layoff is the termination of an employee or (more commonly) a group of employees for business reasons, such as the decision that certain positions are no longer necessary.
Stockholder	A stockholder is an individual or company (including a corporation) that legally owns one or more shares of stock in a joined stock company. The shareholders are the owners of a corporation. Companies listed at the stock market strive to enhance shareholder value.
Deutsche Bank	Deutsche Bank was founded in Germany on January 22, 1870 as a specialist bank for foreign

Go to **Cram101.com** for the Practice Tests for this Chapter.

trade. Major projects in its first decades included the Northern Pacific Railroad in the United States (1883) and the Baghdad Railway (1888). It also financed bond offerings of the steel concern Krupp (1885) and introduced the chemical company Bayer on the Berlin stock market.

Organizational Behavior	The study of human behavior in organizational settings, the interface between human behavior and the organization, and the organization itself is called organizational behavior.
Context	The effect of the background under which a message often takes on more and richer meaning is a context. Context is especially important in cross-cultural interactions because some cultures are said to be high context or low context.
Mistake	In contract law a mistake is incorrect understanding by one or more parties to a contract and may be used as grounds to invalidate the agreement. Common law has identified three different types of mistake in contract: unilateral mistake, mutual mistake, and common mistake.
Information technology	Information technology refers to technology that helps companies change business by allowing them to use new methods.
Exchange	The trade of things of value between buyer and seller so that each is better off after the trade is called the exchange.
Appeal	Appeal refers to the act of asking an appellate court to overturn a decision after the trial court's final judgment has been entered.
Product line	A group of products that are physically similar or are intended for a similar market are called the product line.

Customs	Customs is an authority or agency in a country responsible for collecting customs duties and for controlling the flow of people, animals and goods (including personal effects and hazardous items) in and out of the country.
Negotiation	Negotiation is the process whereby interested parties resolve disputes, agree upon courses of action, bargain for individual or collective advantage, and/or attempt to craft outcomes which serve their mutual interests.
Marketing	Promoting and selling products or services to customers, or prospective customers, is referred to as marketing.
Parent company	Parent company refers to the entity that has a controlling influence over another company. It may have its own operations, or it may have been set up solely for the purpose of owning the Subject Company.
Viacom	Viacom is an American-based media conglomerate with various worldwide interests in cable and satellite television networks (MTV Networks and BET), video gaming (part of Sega of America), and movie production and distribution (the Paramount Pictures movie studio and DreamWorks).
Market	A market is, as defined in economics, a social arrangement that allows buyers and sellers to discover information and carry out a voluntary exchange of goods or services.
Prime minister	The Prime Minister of the United Kingdom of Great Britain and Northern Ireland is the head of government and so exercises many of the executive functions nominally vested in the Sovereign, who is head of state. According to custom, the Prime Minister and the Cabinet (which he or she heads) are accountable for their actions to Parliament, of which they are members by (modern) convention.
Household	An economic unit that provides the economy with resources and uses the income received to purchase goods and services that satisfy economic wants is called household.
Standard of living	Standard of living refers to the level of consumption that people enjoy, on the average, and is measured by average income per person.
Advertisement	Advertisement is the promotion of goods, services, companies and ideas, usually by an identified sponsor. Marketers see advertising as part of an overall promotional strategy.
Buying power	The dollar amount available to purchase securities on margin is buying power. The amount is calculated by adding the cash held in the brokerage accounts and the amount that could be spent if securities were fully margined to their limit. If an investor uses their buying power, they are purchasing securities on credit.
Policy	Similar to a script in that a policy can be a less than completely rational decision-making method. Involves the use of a pre-existing set of decision steps for any problem that presents itself.
Industry	A group of firms that produce identical or similar products is an industry. It is also used specifically to refer to an area of economic production focused on manufacturing which involves large amounts of capital investment before any profit can be realized, also called "heavy industry".
Synergy	Corporate synergy occurs when corporations interact congruently. A corporate synergy refers to a financial benefit that a corporation expects to realize when it merges with or acquires another corporation.
Holding	The holding is a court's determination of a matter of law based on the issue presented in the particular case. In other words: under this law, with these facts, this result.
Chief operating officer	A chief operating officer is a corporate officer responsible for managing the day-to-day activities of the corporation. The chief operating officer is one of the highest ranking

Go to **Cram101.com** for the Practice Tests for this Chapter.

	members of an organization, monitoring the daily operations of the company and reporting to the chief executive officer directly.
Firm	An organization that employs resources to produce a good or service for profit and owns and operates one or more plants is referred to as a firm.
Preference	The act of a debtor in paying or securing one or more of his creditors in a manner more favorable to them than to other creditors or to the exclusion of such other creditors is a preference. In the absence of statute, a preference is perfectly good, but to be legal it must be bona fide, and not a mere subterfuge of the debtor to secure a future benefit to himself or to prevent the application of his property to his debts.
Evaluation	The consumer's appraisal of the product or brand on important attributes is called evaluation.
Frequency	Frequency refers to the speed of the up and down movements of a fluctuating economic variable; that is, the number of times per unit of time that the variable completes a cycle of up and down movement.
Context	The effect of the background under which a message often takes on more and richer meaning is a context. Context is especially important in cross-cultural interactions because some cultures are said to be high context or low context.
Decision rule	Decision rule refers to a statement that tells a decision maker which alternative to choose based on the characteristics of the decision situation.
Channel	Channel, in communications (sometimes called communications channel), refers to the medium used to convey information from a sender (or transmitter) to a receiver.
Nonprogrammed decision	Nonprogrammed decision refers to a decision that recurs infrequently and for which there is no previously established decision rule.
Aid	Assistance provided by countries and by international institutions such as the World Bank to developing countries in the form of monetary grants, loans at low interest rates, in kind, or a combination of these is called aid. Aid can also refer to assistance of any type rendered to benefit some group or individual.
Management	Management characterizes the process of leading and directing all or part of an organization, often a business, through the deployment and manipulation of resources. Early twentieth-century management writer Mary Parker Follett defined management as "the art of getting things done through people."
Promotion	Promotion refers to all the techniques sellers use to motivate people to buy products or services. An attempt by marketers to inform people about products and to persuade them to participate in an exchange.
Profit	Profit refers to the return to the resource entrepreneurial ability; total revenue minus total cost.
Expected value	A representative value from a probability distribution arrived at by multiplying each outcome by the associated probability and summing up the values is called the expected value.
Economy	The income, expenditures, and resources that affect the cost of running a business and household are called an economy.
Behavioral approach	Behavioral approach refers to approach to leadership that tries to identify behaviors that differentiated effective leaders from nonleaders. It uses rules of thumb, suboptimizing, and satisfying in making decisions.
Dow Chemical	Dow Chemical is the world's largest producer of plastics, including polystyrene, polyurethanes, polyethylene, polypropylene, and synthetic rubbers. It is also a major

Go to **Cram101.com** for the Practice Tests for this Chapter.

producer of the chemicals calcium chloride, ethylene oxide, and various acrylates, surfactants, and cellulose resins. It produces many agricultural chemicals.

Six sigma	A means to 'delight the customer' by achieving quality through a highly disciplined process to focus on developing and delivering near-perfect products and services is called six sigma. Originally, it was defined as a metric for measuring defects and improving quality; and a methodology to reduce defect levels below 3.4 Defects Per (one) Million Opportunities (DPMO).
Performance gap	This represents the difference in actual performance shown as compared to the desired standard of performance. In employee performance management efforts, this performance gap is often described in terms of needed knowledge and skills which become training and development goals for the employee.
Manufacturing	Production of goods primarily by the application of labor and capital to raw materials and other intermediate inputs, in contrast to agriculture, mining, forestry, fishing, and services a manufacturing.
Compliance	A type of influence process where a receiver accepts the position advocated by a source to obtain favorable outcomes or to avoid punishment is the compliance.
Gap	In December of 1995, Gap became the first major North American retailer to accept independent monitoring of the working conditions in a contract factory producing its garments. Gap is the largest specialty retailer in the United States.
Subcontractor	A subcontractor is an individual or in many cases a business that signs a contract to perform part or all of the obligations of another's contract. A subcontractor is hired by a general or prime contractor to perform a specific task as part of the overall project.
Framing	Framing refers to the tendency for a decision maker to be swayed by whether a decision is pitched as a positive or negative.
Jack Welch	In 1986, GE acquired NBC. During the 90s, Jack Welch helped to modernize GE by emphasizing a shift from manufacturing to services. He also made hundreds of acquisitions and made a push to dominate markets abroad. Welch adopted the Six Sigma quality program in late 1995.
Customer satisfaction	Customer satisfaction is a business term which is used to capture the idea of measuring how satisfied an enterprise's customers are with the organization's efforts in a marketplace.
Composition	An out-of-court settlement in which creditors agree to accept a fractional settlement on their original claim is referred to as composition.
Expense	In accounting, an expense represents an event in which an asset is used up or a liability is incurred. In terms of the accounting equation, expenses reduce owners' equity.
Market share	That fraction of an industry's output accounted for by an individual firm or group of firms is called market share.
Advertising	Advertising refers to paid, nonpersonal communication through various media by organizations and individuals who are in some way identified in the advertising message.
Competitor	Other organizations in the same industry or type of business that provide a good or service to the same set of customers is referred to as a competitor.
Mistake	In contract law a mistake is incorrect understanding by one or more parties to a contract and may be used as grounds to invalidate the agreement. Common law has identified three different types of mistake in contract: unilateral mistake, mutual mistake, and common mistake.
Supervisor	A Supervisor is an employee of an organization with some of the powers and responsibilities of management, occupying a role between true manager and a regular employee. A Supervisor position is typically the first step towards being promoted into a management role.

Perfect information	Perfect information is a term used in economics and game theory to describe a state of complete knowledge about the actions of other players that is instantaneously updated as new information arises.
Consideration	Consideration in contract law, a basic requirement for an enforceable agreement under traditional contract principles, defined in this text as legal value, bargained for and given in exchange for an act or promise. In corporation law, cash or property contributed to a corporation in exchange for shares, or a promise to contribute such cash or property.
Task force	A temporary team or committee formed to solve a specific short-term problem involving several departments is the task force.
Group dynamics	The term group dynamics implies that individual behaviors may differ depending on individuals' current or prospective connections to a sociological group. Group dynamics is the field of study within the social sciences that focuses on the nature of groups. Urges to belong or to identify may make for distinctly different attitudes (recognized or unrecognized), and the influence of a group may rapidly become strong, influencing or overwhelming individual proclivities and actions.
Leadership	Management merely consists of leadership applied to business situations; or in other words: management forms a sub-set of the broader process of leadership.
Market research	Market research is the process of systematic gathering, recording and analyzing of data about customers, competitors and the market. Market research can help create a business plan, launch a new product or service, fine tune existing products and services, expand into new markets etc. It can be used to determine which portion of the population will purchase the product/service, based on variables like age, gender, location and income level. It can be found out what market characteristics your target market has.
Entrepreneur	The owner/operator. The person who organizes, manages, and assumes the risks of a firm, taking a new idea or a new product and turning it into a successful business is an entrepreneur.
Bounded rationality	The understanding that rational decisions are very much bounded or constrained by practical constraints is referred to as bounded rationality.
Inputs	The inputs used by a firm or an economy are the labor, raw materials, electricity and other resources it uses to produce its outputs.
Suboptimizing	Knowingly accepting less than the best possible outcome to avoid unintended negative effects on other aspects of the organization is referred to as suboptimizing.
Satisficing	Satisficing refers to a method for making decisions under bounded rationality; to choose the first option that meets a set of minimal criteria that have been established.
Product line	A group of products that are physically similar or are intended for a similar market are called the product line.
Production	The creation of finished goods and services using the factors of production: land, labor, capital, entrepreneurship, and knowledge.
Long run	In economic models, the long run time frame assumes no fixed factors of production. Firms can enter or leave the marketplace, and the cost (and availability) of land, labor, raw materials, and capital goods can be assumed to vary.
Practical approach	The approach to decision-making that combines the steps of the rational approach with the conditions in the behavioral approach to create a more realistic process for making decisions in organizations is referred to as practical approach.
Conflict model	A very personal approach to decision making because it deals with the personal conflicts that

Go to **Cram101.com** for the Practice Tests for this Chapter.

people experience in particularly difficult decision situations is called conflict model.

Rationalization	Rationalization in economics is an attempt to change a pre-existing ad-hoc workflow into one that is based on a set of published rules.
Compromise	Compromise occurs when the interaction is moderately important to meeting goals and the goals are neither completely compatible nor completely incompatible.
Option	A contract that gives the purchaser the option to buy or sell the underlying financial instrument at a specified price, called the exercise price or strike price, within a specific period of time.
Unconflicted change	Involves making changes in present activities if doing so presents no serious risks are called the unconflicted change.
Vigilant information processing	Involves thoroughly investigating all possible alternatives, weighing their costs and benefits before making a decision, and developing contingency plans is vigilant information processing.
Defensive avoidance	The tendency for decision makers to fail to solve problems because they go out of their way to avoid working on the problem is defensive avoidance.
Contingency planning	The process of preparing alternative courses of action that may be used if the primary plans do not achieve the objectives of the organization is called contingency planning.
Ethical dilemma	An ethical dilemma is a situation that often involves an apparent conflict between moral imperatives, in which to obey one would result in transgressing another.
Gain	In finance, gain is a profit or an increase in value of an investment such as a stock or bond. Gain is calculated by fair market value or the proceeds from the sale of the investment minus the sum of the purchase price and all costs associated with it.
Stock option	A stock option is a specific type of option that uses the stock itself as an underlying instrument to determine the option's pay-off and therefore its value.
Stockholder	A stockholder is an individual or company (including a corporation) that legally owns one or more shares of stock in a joined stock company. The shareholders are the owners of a corporation. Companies listed at the stock market strive to enhance shareholder value.
Stock	In financial terminology, stock is the capital raized by a corporation, through the issuance and sale of shares.
Interest	In finance and economics, interest is the price paid by a borrower for the use of a lender's money. In other words, interest is the amount of paid to "rent" money for a period of time.
Escalation	Regarding the structure of tariffs. In the context of a trade war, escalation refers to the increase in tariffs that occurs as countries retaliate again and again.
Escalation of commitment	Escalation of commitment is the phenomenon where people increase their investment in a decision despite new evidence suggesting that the decision was probably wrong.
Corporation	A legal entity chartered by a state or the Federal government that is distinct and separate from the individuals who own it is a corporation. This separation gives the corporation unique powers which other legal entities lack.
Multinational corporations	Firms that own production facilities in two or more countries and produce and sell their products globally are referred to as multinational corporations.
Multinational corporation	An organization that manufactures and markets products in many different countries and has multinational stock ownership and multinational management is referred to as multinational corporation.

Food and Drug Administration	The Food and Drug Administration is an agency of the United States Department of Health and Human Services and is responsible for regulating food (human and animal), dietary supplements, drugs (human and animal), cosmetics, medical devices (human and animal) and radiation emitting devices (including non-medical devices), biologics, and blood products in the United States.
Administration	Administration refers to the management and direction of the affairs of governments and institutions; a collective term for all policymaking officials of a government; the execution and implementation of public policy.
Trial	An examination before a competent tribunal, according to the law of the land, of the facts or law put in issue in a cause, for the purpose of determining such issue is a trial. When the court hears and determines any issue of fact or law for the purpose of determining the rights of the parties, it may be considered a trial.
Investment	Investment refers to spending for the production and accumulation of capital and additions to inventories. In a financial sense, buying an asset with the expectation of making a return.
Welfare	Welfare refers to the economic well being of an individual, group, or economy. For individuals, it is conceptualized by a utility function. For groups, including countries and the world, it is a tricky philosophical concept, since individuals fare differently.
Groupthink	Groupthink is a situation in which pressures for cohesion and togetherness are so strong as to produce narrowly considered and bad decisions; this can be especially true via conformity pressures in groups.
Argument	The discussion by counsel for the respective parties of their contentions on the law and the facts of the case being tried in order to aid the jury in arriving at a correct and just conclusion is called argument.
Trend	Trend refers to the long-term movement of an economic variable, such as its average rate of increase or decrease over enough years to encompass several business cycles.
Counterargument	A type of thought or cognitive response a receiver has that is counter or opposed to the position advocated in a message is referred to as counterargument.
Transcript	A copy of writing is referred to as a transcript. It is the official record of proceedings in a trial or hearing.
Drawback	Drawback refers to rebate of import duties when the imported good is re-exported or used as input to the production of an exported good.
Prejudice	Prejudice is, as the name implies, the process of "pre-judging" something. It implies coming to a judgment on a subject before learning where the preponderance of evidence actually lies, or forming a judgment without direct experience.
Scientific management	Studying workers to find the most efficient ways of doing things and then teaching people those techniques is scientific management.
General manager	A manager who is responsible for several departments that perform different functions is called general manager.
Organizational structure	Organizational structure is the way in which the interrelated groups of an organization are constructed. From a managerial point of view the main concerns are ensuring effective communication and coordination.
Organization structure	The system of task, reporting, and authority relationships within which the organization does its work is referred to as the organization structure.
Idea generation	Developing a pool of concepts as candidates for new products is called idea generation.

Go to **Cram101.com** for the Practice Tests for this Chapter.

Nominal group technique	Nominal group technique refers to a more elaborate attempt to separate the generation from the evaluation of ideas in group settings. With the nominal group method, ideas are generated in private and circulated among the group later.
Delphi Technique	Delphi technique refers to an elaborate attempt to reduce group criticism and increase the generation of good decision options. Ideas are generated in private, anonymously collated and presented to the group.
Nominal group	A nominal category or a nominal group is a group of objects or ideas that can be collectively grouped on the basis of shared, arbitrary characteristic.
Brainstorming	Brainstorming refers to a technique designed to overcome our natural tendency to evaluate and criticize ideas and thereby reduce the creative output of those ideas. People are encouraged to produce ideas/options without criticizing, often at a very fast pace to minimize our natural tendency to criticize.
Brief	Brief refers to a statement of a party's case or legal arguments, usually prepared by an attorney. Also used to make legal arguments before appellate courts.
Contribution	In business organization law, the cash or property contributed to a business by its owners is referred to as contribution.
Principal	In agency law, one under whose direction an agent acts and for whose benefit that agent acts is a principal.
Complexity	The technical sophistication of the product and hence the amount of understanding required to use it is referred to as complexity. It is the opposite of simplicity.
Acquisition	A company's purchase of the property and obligations of another company is an acquisition.
Game theory	The modeling of strategic interactions among agents, used in economic models where the numbers of interacting agents is small enough that each has a perceptible influence on the others is called game theory.
Demographic characteristic	The vital statistics of a population group or a derived sample, such as: age, sex, education, ethnic heritage, education, income, housing is referred to as a demographic characteristic.
Demographic	A demographic is a term used in marketing and broadcasting, to describe a demographic grouping or a market segment.
Variable	A variable is something measured by a number; it is used to analyze what happens to other things when the size of that number changes.
Authoritarianism	The belief that power and status differences are appropriate within hierarchical social systems such as organizations is referred to as authoritarianism.
Machiavellianism	Machiavellianism refers to a personality trait. People who possess this trait behave to gain power and to control the behavior of others.
Brand	A name, symbol, or design that identifies the goods or services of one seller or group of sellers and distinguishes them from the goods and services of competitors is a brand.
Export	In economics, an export is any good or commodity, shipped or otherwise transported out of a country, province, town to another part of the world in a legitimate fashion, typically for use in trade or sale.
Asset	An item of property, such as land, capital, money, a share in ownership, or a claim on others for future payment, such as a bond or a bank deposit is an asset.
Union	A worker association that bargains with employers over wages and working conditions is called a union.

Go to **Cram101.com** for the Practice Tests for this Chapter.

Go to **Cram101.com** for the Practice Tests for this Chapter.
And, **NEVER** highlight a book again!

Labor	People's physical and mental talents and efforts that are used to help produce goods and services are called labor.
Analytic approach	Type of assessment of HRM effectiveness that involves determining the impact of, or the financial costs and benefits of, a program or practice is referred to as analytic approach.
Consultant	A professional that provides expert advice in a particular field or area in which customers occassionaly require this type of knowledge is a consultant.
Pram model	This model guides the negotiator through the four steps of planning for agreement, building relationships, reaching agreements, and maintaining relationships is referred to as pram model.
Trust	An arrangement in which shareholders of independent firms agree to give up their stock in exchange for trust certificates that entitle them to a share of the trust's common profits.
Points	Loan origination fees that may be deductible as interest by a buyer of property. A seller of property who pays points reduces the selling price by the amount of the points paid for the buyer.
Lease	A contract for the possession and use of land or other property, including goods, on one side, and a recompense of rent or other income on the other is the lease.
Partnership	In the common law, a partnership is a type of business entity in which partners share with each other the profits or losses of the business undertaking in which they have all invested.
Operation	A standardized method or technique that is performed repetitively, often on different materials resulting in different finished goods is called an operation.
Continuity	A media scheduling strategy where a continuous pattern of advertising is used over the time span of the advertising campaign is continuity.
Insurance	Insurance refers to a system by which individuals can reduce their exposure to risk of large losses by spreading the risks among a large number of persons.
Security	Security refers to a claim on the borrower future income that is sold by the borrower to the lender. A security is a type of transferable interest representing financial value.
Warehouse	Warehouse refers to a location, often decentralized, that a firm uses to store, consolidate, age, or mix stock; house product-recall programs; or ease tax burdens.
Cooperative	A business owned and controlled by the people who use it, producers, consumers, or workers with similar needs who pool their resources for mutual gain is called cooperative.
Technology	The body of knowledge and techniques that can be used to combine economic resources to produce goods and services is called technology.
Recovery	Characterized by rizing output, falling unemployment, rizing profits, and increasing economic activity following a decline is a recovery.
Complaint	The pleading in a civil case in which the plaintiff states his claim and requests relief is called complaint. In the common law, it is a formal legal document that sets out the basic facts and legal reasons that the filing party (the plaintiffs) believes are sufficient to support a claim against another person, persons, entity or entities (the defendants) that entitles the plaintiff(s) to a remedy (either money damages or injunctive relief).
Chief information officer	The chief information officer is a job title for the head of information technology group within an organization. They often report to the chief executive officer or chief financial officer.
Realization	Realization is the sale of assets when an entity is being liquidated.

Merger	Merger refers to the combination of two firms into a single firm.
Organizational Behavior	The study of human behavior in organizational settings, the interface between human behavior and the organization, and the organization itself is called organizational behavior.
Excess capacity	Excess capacity refers to plant resources that are underused when imperfectly competitive firms produce less output than that associated with purely competitive firms, who by definiation, are achieving minimum average total cost.
Information technology	Information technology refers to technology that helps companies change business by allowing them to use new methods.
Enron	Enron Corportaion's global reputation was undermined by persistent rumours of bribery and political pressure to secure contracts in Central America, South America, Africa, and the Philippines. Especially controversial was its $3 billion contract with the Maharashtra State Electricity Board in India, where it is alleged that Enron officials used political connections within the Clinton and Bush administrations to exert pressure on the board.
Physical asset	A physical asset is an item of economic value that has a tangible or material existence. A physical asset usually refers to cash, equipment, inventory and properties owned by a business.
Accounting	A system that collects and processes financial information about an organization and reports that information to decision makers is referred to as accounting.
Analyst	Analyst refers to a person or tool with a primary function of information analysis, generally with a more limited, practical and short term set of goals than a researcher.
Financial statement	Financial statement refers to a summary of all the transactions that have occurred over a particular period.
Financial institution	A financial institution acts as an agent that provides financial services for its clients. Financial institutions generally fall under financial regulation from a government authority.
Cash flow statement	A cash flow statement is a financial report that shows incoming and outgoing money during a particular period (often monthly or quarterly). The statement shows how changes in balance sheet and income accounts affected cash and cash equivalents and breaks the analysis down according to operating, investing, and financing activities.
Balance sheet	A statement of the assets, liabilities, and net worth of a firm or individual at some given time often at the end of its "fiscal year," is referred to as a balance sheet.
Cash flow	In finance, cash flow refers to the amounts of cash being received and spent by a business during a defined period of time, sometimes tied to a specific project. Most of the time they are being used to determine gaps in the liquid position of a company.
Balance	In banking and accountancy, the outstanding balance is the amount of money owned, (or due), that remains in a deposit account (or a loan account) at a given date, after all past remittances, payments and withdrawal have been accounted for. It can be positive (then, in the balance sheet of a firm, it is an asset) or negative (a liability).
Testimony	In some contexts, the word bears the same import as the word evidence, but in most connections it has a much narrower meaning. Testimony are the words heard from the witness in court, and evidence is what the jury considers it worth.
Hearing	A hearing is a proceeding before a court or other decision-making body or officer. A hearing is generally distinguished from a trial in that it is usually shorter and often less formal.
Bankruptcy	Bankruptcy is a legally declared inability or impairment of ability of an individual or organization to pay their creditors.

Go to **Cram101.com** for the Practice Tests for this Chapter.

Go to **Cram101.com** for the Practice Tests for this Chapter.
And, **NEVER** highlight a book again!

Estate	An estate is the totality of the legal rights, interests, entitlements and obligations attaching to property. In the context of wills and probate, it refers to the totality of the property which the deceased owned or in which some interest was held.
Fund	Independent accounting entity with a self-balancing set of accounts segregated for the purposes of carrying on specific activities is referred to as a fund.
Board of directors	The group of individuals elected by the stockholders of a corporation to oversee its operations is a board of directors.
Committee	A long-lasting, sometimes permanent team in the organization structure created to deal with tasks that recur regularly is the committee.
Privilege	Generally, a legal right to engage in conduct that would otherwise result in legal liability is a privilege. Privileges are commonly classified as absolute or conditional. Occasionally, privilege is also used to denote a legal right to refrain from particular behavior.

Organization structure	The system of task, reporting, and authority relationships within which the organization does its work is referred to as the organization structure.
Driving force	The key external pressure that will shape the future for an organization is a driving force. The driving force in an industry are the main underlying causes of changing industry and competitive conditions.
Business unit	The lowest level of the company which contains the set of functions that carry a product through its life span from concept through manufacture, distribution, sales and service is a business unit.
New economy	New economy, this term was used in the late 1990's to suggest that globalization and/or innovations in information technology had changed the way that the world economy works.
Integration	Economic integration refers to reducing barriers among countries to transactions and to movements of goods, capital, and labor, including harmonization of laws, regulations, and standards. Integrated markets theoretically function as a unified market.
Convergence	The blending of various facets of marketing functions and communication technology to create more efficient and expanded synergies is a convergence.
Steve Case	Steve Case is a businessman best known as the co-founder and former chief executive officer and chairman of America Online (AOL). He reached his highest profile when he played an instrumental role in AOL's merger with Time Warner in 2000.
Synergy	Corporate synergy occurs when corporations interact congruently. A corporate synergy refers to a financial benefit that a corporation expects to realize when it merges with or acquires another corporation.
Economy	The income, expenditures, and resources that affect the cost of running a business and household are called an economy.
Firm	An organization that employs resources to produce a good or service for profit and owns and operates one or more plants is referred to as a firm.
Technology	The body of knowledge and techniques that can be used to combine economic resources to produce goods and services is called technology.
Hedge	Hedge refers to a process of offsetting risk. In the foreign exchange market, hedgers use the forward market to cover a transaction or open position and thereby reduce exchange risk. The term applies most commonly to trade.
Industry	A group of firms that produce identical or similar products is an industry. It is also used specifically to refer to an area of economic production focused on manufacturing which involves large amounts of capital investment before any profit can be realized, also called "heavy industry".
Time Warner	Time Warner is the world's largest media company with major Internet, publishing, film, telecommunications and television divisions.
Revenue	Revenue is a U.S. business term for the amount of money that a company receives from its activities, mostly from sales of products and/or services to customers.
Brand	A name, symbol, or design that identifies the goods or services of one seller or group of sellers and distinguishes them from the goods and services of competitors is a brand.
New Line Cinema	Unlike other independent studios such as Orion Pictures, Carolco Pictures, or Cannon Films, New Line Cinema has grown and prospered to become one of Hollywood's major film studios, culminating in the hit The Lord of the Rings film trilogy film trilogy that brought added prestige to the studio.

Go to **Cram101.com** for the Practice Tests for this Chapter.

Advertising	Advertising refers to paid, nonpersonal communication through various media by organizations and individuals who are in some way identified in the advertising message.
Promotion	Promotion refers to all the techniques sellers use to motivate people to buy products or services. An attempt by marketers to inform people about products and to persuade them to participate in an exchange.
Merger	Merger refers to the combination of two firms into a single firm.
Reorganization	Reorganization occurs, among other instances, when one corporation acquires another in a merger or acquisition, a single corporation divides into two or more entities, or a corporation makes a substantial change in its capital structure.
Strategic planning	The process of determining the major goals of the organization and the policies and strategies for obtaining and using resources to achieve those goals is called strategic planning.
Authority	Authority in agency law, refers to an agent's ability to affect his principal's legal relations with third parties. Also used to refer to an actor's legal power or ability to do something. In addition, sometimes used to refer to a statute, case, or other legal source that justifies a particular result.
Shareholder value	For a publicly traded company, shareholder value is the part of its capitalization that is equity as opposed to long-term debt. In the case of only one type of stock, this would roughly be the number of outstanding shares times current shareprice.
Shareholder	A shareholder is an individual or company (including a corporation) that legally owns one or more shares of stock in a joined stock company.
Slump	A decline in performance, in a firm is a slump in sales or profits, or in a country is a slump in output or employment.
Stock	In financial terminology, stock is the capital raized by a corporation, through the issuance and sale of shares.
Management	Management characterizes the process of leading and directing all or part of an organization, often a business, through the deployment and manipulation of resources. Early twentieth-century management writer Mary Parker Follett defined management as "the art of getting things done through people."
Organizational goals	Objectives that management seeks to achieve in pursuing the firm's purpose are organizational goals.
Action plan	Action plan refers to a written document that includes the steps the trainee and manager will take to ensure that training transfers to the job.
Microsoft	Microsoft is a multinational computer technology corporation with 2004 global annual sales of US$39.79 billion and 71,553 employees in 102 countries and regions as of July 2006. It develops, manufactures, licenses, and supports a wide range of software products for computing devices.
Organization chart	Organization chart refers to a visual device, which shows the relationship and divides the organization's work; it shows who is accountable for the completion of specific work and who reports to whom.
Gain	In finance, gain is a profit or an increase in value of an investment such as a stock or bond. Gain is calculated by fair market value or the proceeds from the sale of the investment minus the sum of the purchase price and all costs associated with it.
Labor	People's physical and mental talents and efforts that are used to help produce goods and services are called labor.

Division of labor	Division of labor is generally speaking the specialization of cooperative labor in specific, circumscribed tasks and roles, intended to increase efficiency of output.
Foundation	A Foundation is a type of philanthropic organization set up by either individuals or institutions as a legal entity (either as a corporation or trust) with the purpose of distributing grants to support causes in line with the goals of the foundation.
Product line	A group of products that are physically similar or are intended for a similar market are called the product line.
Expense	In accounting, an expense represents an event in which an asset is used up or a liability is incurred. In terms of the accounting equation, expenses reduce owners' equity.
Chrysler	The Chrysler Corporation was an American automobile manufacturer that existed independently from 1925–1998. The company was formed by Walter Percy Chrysler on June 6, 1925, with the remaining assets of Maxwell Motor Company.
Margin	A deposit by a buyer in stocks with a seller or a stockbroker, as security to cover fluctuations in the market in reference to stocks that the buyer has purchased but for which he has not paid is a margin. Commodities are also traded on margin.
Mitsubishi	In a statement, the Mitsubishi says that forced labor is inconsistent with the company's values, and that the various lawsuits targeting Mitsubishi are misdirected. Instead, a spokesman says the Mitsubishi of World War II is not the same Mitsubishi of today. The conglomerate also rejected a Chinese slave labor lawsuit demand by saying it bore no responsibility since it was national policy to employ Chinese laborers."
Shares	Shares refer to an equity security, representing a shareholder's ownership of a corporation. Shares are one of a finite number of equal portions in the capital of a company, entitling the owner to a proportion of distributed, non-reinvested profits known as dividends and to a portion of the value of the company in case of liquidation.
Chief executive officer	A chief executive officer is the highest-ranking corporate officer or executive officer of a corporation, or agency. In closely held corporations, it is general business culture that the office chief executive officer is also the chairman of the board.
Board of directors	The group of individuals elected by the stockholders of a corporation to oversee its operations is a board of directors.
Staff unit	A group that assists the line units by performing specialized services for the organization is called a staff unit.
Manufacturing	Production of goods primarily by the application of labor and capital to raw materials and other intermediate inputs, in contrast to agriculture, mining, forestry, fishing, and services a manufacturing.
Configuration	An organization's shape, which reflects the division of labor and the means of coordinating the divided tasks is configuration.
Weber	Weber was a German political economist and sociologist who is considered one of the founders of the modern study of sociology and public administration. His major works deal with rationalization in sociology of religion and government, but he also wrote much in the field of economics. His most popular work is his essay The Protestant Ethic and the Spirit of Capitalism.
Standardization	Standardization, in the context related to technologies and industries, is the process of establishing a technical standard among competing entities in a market, where this will bring benefits without hurting competition.
Departmental-	The dividing of organizational functions into separate units is called departmentalization.

Go to **Cram101.com** for the Practice Tests for this Chapter.

zation

Welfare	Welfare refers to the economic well being of an individual, group, or economy. For individuals, it is conceptualized by a utility function. For groups, including countries and the world, it is a tricky philosophical concept, since individuals fare differently.
Service	Service refers to a "non tangible product" that is not embodied in a physical good and that typically effects some change in another product, person, or institution. Contrasts with good.
Administration	Administration refers to the management and direction of the affairs of governments and institutions; a collective term for all policymaking officials of a government; the execution and implementation of public policy.
Marketing	Promoting and selling products or services to customers, or prospective customers, is referred to as marketing.
Functional structure	A type of structure in which units and departments are organized based on the activity or function that they perform is called the functional structure.
Operation	A standardized method or technique that is performed repetitively, often on different materials resulting in different finished goods is called an operation.
Hierarchy	A system of grouping people in an organization according to rank from the top down in which all subordinate managers must report to one person is called a hierarchy.
Consideration	Consideration in contract law, a basic requirement for an enforceable agreement under traditional contract principles, defined in this text as legal value, bargained for and given in exchange for an act or promise. In corporation law, cash or property contributed to a corporation in exchange for shares, or a promise to contribute such cash or property.
Downturn	A decline in a stock market or economic cycle is a downturn.
Basic research	Involves discovering new knowledge rather than solving specific problems is called basic research.
Specialist	A specialist is a trader who makes a market in one or several stocks and holds the limit order book for those stocks.
Alignment	Term that refers to optimal coordination among disparate departments and divisions within a firm is referred to as alignment.
Innovation	Innovation refers to the first commercially successful introduction of a new product, the use of a new method of production, or the creation of a new form of business organization.
Market	A market is, as defined in economics, a social arrangement that allows buyers and sellers to discover information and carry out a voluntary exchange of goods or services.
Deutsche Bank	Deutsche Bank was founded in Germany on January 22, 1870 as a specialist bank for foreign trade. Major projects in its first decades included the Northern Pacific Railroad in the United States (1883) and the Baghdad Railway (1888). It also financed bond offerings of the steel concern Krupp (1885) and introduced the chemical company Bayer on the Berlin stock market.
Investment banker	Investment banker refers to a financial organization that specializes in selling primary offerings of securities. Investment bankers can also perform other financial functions, such as advising clients, negotiating mergers and takeovers, and selling secondary offerings.
Investment	Investment refers to spending for the production and accumulation of capital and additions to inventories. In a financial sense, buying an asset with the expectation of making a return.
Corporate	Corporate strategy is concerned with the firm's choice of business, markets and activities

Strategy	and thus it defines the overall scope and direction of the business.
Enterprise	Enterprise refers to another name for a business organization. Other similar terms are business firm, sometimes simply business, sometimes simply firm, as well as company, and entity.
Corporation	A legal entity chartered by a state or the Federal government that is distinct and separate from the individuals who own it is a corporation. This separation gives the corporation unique powers which other legal entities lack.
DaimlerChrysler	In 2002, the merged company, DaimlerChrysler, appeared to run two independent product lines, with few signs of corporate integration. In 2003, however, it was alleged by the Detroit News that the "merger of equals" was, in fact, a takeover.
Competitiveness	Competitiveness usually refers to characteristics that permit a firm to compete effectively with other firms due to low cost or superior technology, perhaps internationally.
Holding	The holding is a court's determination of a matter of law based on the issue presented in the particular case. In other words: under this law, with these facts, this result.
Organizational structure	Organizational structure is the way in which the interrelated groups of an organization are constructed. From a managerial point of view the main concerns are ensuring effective communication and coordination.
Multinational corporation	An organization that manufactures and markets products in many different countries and has multinational stock ownership and multinational management is referred to as multinational corporation.
Joint venture	Joint venture refers to an undertaking by two parties for a specific purpose and duration, taking any of several legal forms.
Span of control	Span of control refers to the optimum number of subordinates a manager supervises or should supervise.
Supervisor	A Supervisor is an employee of an organization with some of the powers and responsibilities of management, occupying a role between true manager and a regular employee. A Supervisor position is typically the first step towards being promoted into a management role.
Administrative hierarchy	The system of reporting relationships in the organization, from the lowest to the highest managerial levels is referred to as administrative hierarchy.
Production	The creation of finished goods and services using the factors of production: land, labor, capital, entrepreneurship, and knowledge.
Administrator	Administrator refers to the personal representative appointed by a probate court to settle the estate of a deceased person who died.
Personnel	A collective term for all of the employees of an organization. Personnel is also commonly used to refer to the personnel management function or the organizational unit responsible for administering personnel programs.
Complexity	The technical sophistication of the product and hence the amount of understanding required to use it is referred to as complexity. It is the opposite of simplicity.
Dow Chemical	Dow Chemical is the world's largest producer of plastics, including polystyrene, polyurethanes, polyethylene, polypropylene, and synthetic rubbers. It is also a major producer of the chemicals calcium chloride, ethylene oxide, and various acrylates, surfactants, and cellulose resins. It produces many agricultural chemicals.
Downsizing	The process of eliminating managerial and non-managerial positions are called downsizing.
Overhead cost	An expenses of operating a business over and above the direct costs of producing a product is

Go to **Cram101.com** for the Practice Tests for this Chapter.

an overhead cost. They can include utilities (eg, electricity, telephone), advertizing and marketing, and any other costs not billed directly to the client or included in the price of the product.

Productivity	Productivity refers to the total output of goods and services in a given period of time divided by work hours.
Bureaucracy	Bureaucracy refers to an organization with many layers of managers who set rules and regulations and oversee all decisions.
Centralization	A structural policy in which decision-making authority is concentrated at the top of the organizational hierarchy is referred to as centralization.
Policy	Similar to a script in that a policy can be a less than completely rational decision-making method. Involves the use of a pre-existing set of decision steps for any problem that presents itself.
Decentralized organization	An organization in which decision making is spread throughout the organization, rather than confined to a small group of executives is a decentralized organization.
General Motors	General Motors is the world's largest automaker. Founded in 1908, today it employs about 327,000 people around the world. With global headquarters in Detroit, it manufactures its cars and trucks in 33 countries.
Divisional structure	A divisional structure is found in diversified organizations, they contain separate divisions that are based around individual product lines or on the geographic areas of the markets being served.
Committee	A long-lasting, sometimes permanent team in the organization structure created to deal with tasks that recur regularly is the committee.
Compaq	Compaq was founded in February 1982 by Rod Canion, Jim Harris and Bill Murto, three senior managers from semiconductor manufacturer Texas Instruments. Each invested $1,000 to form the company. Their first venture capital came from Ben Rosen and Sevin-Rosen partners. It is often told that the architecture of the original PC was first sketched out on a placemat by the founders while dining in the Houston restaurant, House of Pies.
Decision rule	Decision rule refers to a statement that tells a decision maker which alternative to choose based on the characteristics of the decision situation.
Nonprogrammed decision	Nonprogrammed decision refers to a decision that recurs infrequently and for which there is no previously established decision rule.
Decentralization	Decentralization is the process of redistributing decision-making closer to the point of service or action. This gives freedom to managers at lower levels of the organization to make decisions.
Management system	A management system is the framework of processes and procedures used to ensure that an organization can fulfill all tasks required to achieve its objectives.
Participative management	Participative management or participatory management is the practice of empowering employees to participate in organizational decision making.
Honda	With more than 14 million internal combustion engines built each year, Honda is the largest engine-maker in the world. In 2004, the company began to produce diesel motors, which were both very quiet whilst not requiring particulate filters to pass pollution standards. It is arguable, however, that the foundation of their success is the motorcycle division.
Adoption	In corporation law, a corporation's acceptance of a pre-incorporation contract by action of its board of directors, by which the corporation becomes liable on the contract, is referred to as adoption.

Jack Welch	In 1986, GE acquired NBC. During the 90s, Jack Welch helped to modernize GE by emphasizing a shift from manufacturing to services. He also made hundreds of acquisitions and made a push to dominate markets abroad. Welch adopted the Six Sigma quality program in late 1995.
Consultant	A professional that provides expert advice in a particular field or area in which customers occassionaly require this type of knowledge is a consultant.
General Electric	In 1876, Thomas Alva Edison opened a new laboratory in Menlo Park, New Jersey. Out of the laboratory was to come perhaps the most famous invention of all—a successful development of the incandescent electric lamp. By 1890, Edison had organized his various businesses into the Edison General Electric Company.
Conglomerate	A conglomerate is a large company that consists of divisions of often seemingly unrelated businesses.
International firm	International firm refers to those firms who have responded to stiff competition domestically by expanding their sales abroad. They may start a production facility overseas and send some of their managers, who report to a global division, to that country.
Hearing	A hearing is a proceeding before a court or other decision-making body or officer. A hearing is generally distinguished from a trial in that it is usually shorter and often less formal.
Fraud	Tax fraud falls into two categories: civil and criminal. Under civil fraud, the IRS may impose as a penalty of an amount equal to as much as 75 percent of the underpayment.
Enron	Enron Corportaion's global reputation was undermined by persistent rumours of bribery and political pressure to secure contracts in Central America, South America, Africa, and the Philippines. Especially controversial was its $3 billion contract with the Maharashtra State Electricity Board in India, where it is alleged that Enron officials used political connections within the Clinton and Bush administrations to exert pressure on the board.
Analyst	Analyst refers to a person or tool with a primary function of information analysis, generally with a more limited, practical and short term set of goals than a researcher.
Complaint	The pleading in a civil case in which the plaintiff states his claim and requests relief is called complaint. In the common law, it is a formal legal document that sets out the basic facts and legal reasons that the filing party (the plaintiffs) believes are sufficient to support a claim against another person, persons, entity or entities (the defendants) that entitles the plaintiff(s) to a remedy (either money damages or injunctive relief).
Delegation	Delegation is the handing of a task over to another person, usually a subordinate. It is the assignment of authority and responsibility to another person to carry out specific activities.
Interest	In finance and economics, interest is the price paid by a borrower for the use of a lender's money. In other words, interest is the amount of paid to "rent" money for a period of time.
Universal approach	An approach to organization design where prescriptions or propositions are designed to work in any circumstance is called universal approach.
Conformance	A dimension of quality that refers to the extent to which a product lies within an allowable range of deviation from its specification is called the conformance.
Enabling	Enabling refers to giving workers the education and tools they need to assume their new decision-making powers.
Henri Fayol	Henri Fayol (1841-1925) was a French management theorist whose theories concerning scientific organization of labor were widely influential in the beginning of 20th century. He was the first to identify the four functions of management: planning, organizing, directing, and controlling, although his version was a bit different: plan, organize, command, coordinate,

Go to **Cram101.com** for the Practice Tests for this Chapter.

	and control.
Equity	Equity is the name given to the set of legal principles, in countries following the English common law tradition, which supplement strict rules of law where their application would operate harshly, so as to achieve what is sometimes referred to as "natural justice."
Specificity	The property that a policy measure applies to one or a group of enterprises or industries, as opposed to all industries, is called specificity.
Human organization	Rensis Likert's approach that is based on supportive relationships, participation, and overlapping work groups is called a human organization.
Organization design	The structuring of workers so that they can best accomplish the firm's goals is referred to as organization design.
Leadership	Management merely consists of leadership applied to business situations; or in other words: management forms a sub-set of the broader process of leadership.
Variable	A variable is something measured by a number; it is used to analyze what happens to other things when the size of that number changes.
Context	The effect of the background under which a message often takes on more and richer meaning is a context. Context is especially important in cross-cultural interactions because some cultures are said to be high context or low context.
Ideal bureaucracy	Weber's model that is characterized by a hierarchy of authority and a system of rules and procedures designed to create an optimally effective system for large organizations is an ideal bureaucracy.
Property	Assets defined in the broadest legal sense. Property includes the unrealized receivables of a cash basis taxpayer, but not services rendered.
Role ambiguity	Uncertainty of specifications for a role is role ambiguity. This occurs when duties for a role are not specified. The resolution to role ambiguity may lie in precise role descriptions (job descriptions) or a simplification of the tasks.
Role conflict	Role conflict is a special form of social conflict that takes place when one is forced to take on two different and incompatible roles at the same time.
Trust	An arrangement in which shareholders of independent firms agree to give up their stock in exchange for trust certificates that entitle them to a share of the trust's common profits.
Profit	Profit refers to the return to the resource entrepreneurial ability; total revenue minus total cost.
Charles Schwab	Charles Schwab is the world's second-largest discount broker. Besides discount brokerage, the firm offers mutual funds, annuities, bond trading, and now mortgages through its Charles Schwab Bank.
Verizon	Verizon a Dow 30 company, is a broadband and telecommunications provider. The acquisition of GTE by Bell Atlantic, on June 30, 2000, which formed Verizon, was among the largest mergers in United States business history. Verizon, with MCI, is currently the second largest telecommunications company in the United States.
Insurance	Insurance refers to a system by which individuals can reduce their exposure to risk of large losses by spreading the risks among a large number of persons.
Citibank	In April of 2006, Citibank struck a deal with 7-Eleven to put its ATMs in over 5,500 convenience stores in the U.S. In the same month, it also announced it would sell all of its Buffalo and Rochester New York branches and accounts to M&T Bank.
Corporate	The whole collection of beliefs, values, and behaviors of a firm that send messages to those

culture	within and outside the company about how business is done is the corporate culture.
Boston Consulting Group	The Boston Consulting Group is a management consulting firm founded by Harvard Business School alum Bruce Henderson in 1963. In 1965 Bruce Henderson thought that to survive, much less grow, in a competitive landscape occupied by hundreds of larger and better-known consulting firms, a distinctive identity was needed, and pioneered "Business Strategy" as a special area of expertise.
Organizational Behavior	The study of human behavior in organizational settings, the interface between human behavior and the organization, and the organization itself is called organizational behavior.
Middle management	Middle management refers to the level of management that includes general managers, division managers, and branch and plant managers who are responsible for tactical planning and controlling.
Quality management	Quality management is a method for ensuring that all the activities necessary to design, develop and implement a product or service are effective and efficient with respect to the system and its performance.
Total quality management	The broad set of management and control processes designed to focus an entire organization and all of its employees on providing products or services that do the best possible job of satisfying the customer is called total quality management.
Assignment	A transfer of property or some right or interest is referred to as assignment.
Mistake	In contract law a mistake is incorrect understanding by one or more parties to a contract and may be used as grounds to invalidate the agreement. Common law has identified three different types of mistake in contract: unilateral mistake, mutual mistake, and common mistake.

Go to **Cram101.com** for the Practice Tests for this Chapter.

Organizational goals	Objectives that management seeks to achieve in pursuing the firm's purpose are organizational goals.
Authority	Authority in agency law, refers to an agent's ability to affect his principal's legal relations with third parties. Also used to refer to an actor's legal power or ability to do something. In addition, sometimes used to refer to a statute, case, or other legal source that justifies a particular result.
Subsidiary	A company that is controlled by another company or corporation is a subsidiary.
Antitrust	Government intervention to alter market structure or prevent abuse of market power is called antitrust.
Exchange	The trade of things of value between buyer and seller so that each is better off after the trade is called the exchange.
Monopoly	A monopoly is defined as a persistent market situation where there is only one provider of a kind of product or service.
Holding	The holding is a court's determination of a matter of law based on the issue presented in the particular case. In other words: under this law, with these facts, this result.
Union	A worker association that bargains with employers over wages and working conditions is called a union.
Firm	An organization that employs resources to produce a good or service for profit and owns and operates one or more plants is referred to as a firm.
Analyst	Analyst refers to a person or tool with a primary function of information analysis, generally with a more limited, practical and short term set of goals than a researcher.
Divestiture	In finance and economics, divestiture is the reduction of some kind of asset, for either financial or social goals. A divestment is the opposite of an investment.
Operation	A standardized method or technique that is performed repetitively, often on different materials resulting in different finished goods is called an operation.
Parent company	Parent company refers to the entity that has a controlling influence over another company. It may have its own operations, or it may have been set up solely for the purpose of owning the Subject Company.
Service	Service refers to a "non tangible product" that is not embodied in a physical good and that typically effects some change in another product, person, or institution. Contrasts with good.
Acquisition	A company's purchase of the property and obligations of another company is an acquisition.
Technology	The body of knowledge and techniques that can be used to combine economic resources to produce goods and services is called technology.
Industry	A group of firms that produce identical or similar products is an industry. It is also used specifically to refer to an area of economic production focused on manufacturing which involves large amounts of capital investment before any profit can be realized, also called "heavy industry".
Market	A market is, as defined in economics, a social arrangement that allows buyers and sellers to discover information and carry out a voluntary exchange of goods or services.
Innovation	Innovation refers to the first commercially successful introduction of a new product, the use of a new method of production, or the creation of a new form of business organization.
Regulation	Regulation refers to restrictions state and federal laws place on business with regard to the

conduct of its activities.

Merger	Merger refers to the combination of two firms into a single firm.
Shareholder value	For a publicly traded company, shareholder value is the part of its capitalization that is equity as opposed to long-term debt. In the case of only one type of stock, this would roughly be the number of outstanding shares times current shareprice.
Consolidation	The combination of two or more firms, generally of equal size and market power, to form an entirely new entity is a consolidation.
Shareholder	A shareholder is an individual or company (including a corporation) that legally owns one or more shares of stock in a joined stock company.
Standing	Standing refers to the legal requirement that anyone seeking to challenge a particular action in court must demonstrate that such action substantially affects his legitimate interests before he will be entitled to bring suit.
Productivity	Productivity refers to the total output of goods and services in a given period of time divided by work hours.
Contingency approach	Contingency approach refers to the dominant perspective in organizational behavior, it argues that there's no single best way to manage behavior. What 'works' in any given context depends on the complex interplay between a variety of person and situational factors.
Organization design	The structuring of workers so that they can best accomplish the firm's goals is referred to as organization design.
Bureaucracy	Bureaucracy refers to an organization with many layers of managers who set rules and regulations and oversee all decisions.
Universal approach	An approach to organization design where prescriptions or propositions are designed to work in any circumstance is called universal approach.
Weber	Weber was a German political economist and sociologist who is considered one of the founders of the modern study of sociology and public administration. His major works deal with rationalization in sociology of religion and government, but he also wrote much in the field of economics. His most popular work is his essay The Protestant Ethic and the Spirit of Capitalism.
Management	Management characterizes the process of leading and directing all or part of an organization, often a business, through the deployment and manipulation of resources. Early twentieth-century management writer Mary Parker Follett defined management as "the art of getting things done through people."
Sony	Sony is a multinational corporation and one of the world's largest media conglomerates founded in Tokyo, Japan. One of its divisions Sony Electronics is one of the leading manufacturers of electronics, video, communications, and information technology products for the consumer and professional markets.
Enterprise	Enterprise refers to another name for a business organization. Other similar terms are business firm, sometimes simply business, sometimes simply firm, as well as company, and entity.
Multinational enterprise	Multinational enterprise refers to a firm, usually a corporation, that operates in two or more countries.
Corporation	A legal entity chartered by a state or the Federal government that is distinct and separate from the individuals who own it is a corporation. This separation gives the corporation unique powers which other legal entities lack.

Product differentiation	A strategy in which one firm's product is distinguished from competing products by means of its design, related services, quality, location, or other attributes is called product differentiation.
Market segmentation	The process of dividing the total market into several groups whose members have similar characteristics is market segmentation.
Business strategy	Business strategy, which refers to the aggregated operational strategies of single business firm or that of an SBU in a diversified corporation refers to the way in which a firm competes in its chosen arenas.
Decentralization	Decentralization is the process of redistributing decision-making closer to the point of service or action. This gives freedom to managers at lower levels of the organization to make decisions.
Growth strategy	A strategy based on investing in companies and sectors which are growing faster than their peers is a growth strategy. The benefits are usually in the form of capital gains rather than dividends.
Product line	A group of products that are physically similar or are intended for a similar market are called the product line.
Appeal	Appeal refers to the act of asking an appellate court to overturn a decision after the trial court's final judgment has been entered.
Organization structure	The system of task, reporting, and authority relationships within which the organization does its work is referred to as the organization structure.
Contingency perspective	Contingency perspective suggests that, in most organizations, situations and outcomes are contingent on, or influenced by, other variables.
Structural imperatives	The three structural imperatives, environment, technology, and size, are the three primary determinants of organization structure.
Centralization	A structural policy in which decision-making authority is concentrated at the top of the organizational hierarchy is referred to as centralization.
Labor	People's physical and mental talents and efforts that are used to help produce goods and services are called labor.
Span of control	Span of control refers to the optimum number of subordinates a manager supervises or should supervise.
Economies of scale	In economics, returns to scale and economies of scale are related terms that describe what happens as the scale of production increases. They are different terms and not to be used interchangeably.
Economy	The income, expenditures, and resources that affect the cost of running a business and household are called an economy.
Purchasing	Purchasing refers to the function in a firm that searches for quality material resources, finds the best suppliers, and negotiates the best price for goods and services.
Marketing	Promoting and selling products or services to customers, or prospective customers, is referred to as marketing.
General Electric	In 1876, Thomas Alva Edison opened a new laboratory in Menlo Park, New Jersey. Out of the laboratory was to come perhaps the most famous invention of all—a successful development of the incandescent electric lamp. By 1890, Edison had organized his various businesses into the Edison General Electric Company.
Estate	An estate is the totality of the legal rights, interests, entitlements and obligations

attaching to property. In the context of wills and probate, it refers to the totality of the property which the deceased owned or in which some interest was held.

Manufacturing	Production of goods primarily by the application of labor and capital to raw materials and other intermediate inputs, in contrast to agriculture, mining, forestry, fishing, and services a manufacturing.
Assessment	Collecting information and providing feedback to employees about their behavior, communication style, or skills is an assessment.
Complexity	The technical sophistication of the product and hence the amount of understanding required to use it is referred to as complexity. It is the opposite of simplicity.
Investment	Investment refers to spending for the production and accumulation of capital and additions to inventories. In a financial sense, buying an asset with the expectation of making a return.
Profit	Profit refers to the return to the resource entrepreneurial ability; total revenue minus total cost.
Downsizing	The process of eliminating managerial and non-managerial positions are called downsizing.
Trend	Trend refers to the long-term movement of an economic variable, such as its average rate of increase or decrease over enough years to encompass several business cycles.
Middle management	Middle management refers to the level of management that includes general managers, division managers, and branch and plant managers who are responsible for tactical planning and controlling.
Digital Equipment Corporation	Digital Equipment Corporation was a pioneering company in the American computer industry. Its PDP and VAX products were arguably the most popular mini-computers for the scientific and engineering communities during the 70s and 80s.
Eastman Kodak	Eastman Kodak Company is an American multinational public company producing photographic materials and equipment. Long known for its wide range of photographic film products, it has focused in recent years on three main businesses: digital photography, health imaging, and printing. This company remains the largest supplier of films in the world, both for the amateur and professional markets.
Nabisco	In 2000 Philip Morris Companies acquired Nabisco; that acquisition was approved by the Federal Trade Commission subject to the divestiture of products in five areas: three Jell-O and Royal brands types of products (dry-mix gelatin dessert, dry-mix pudding, no-bake desserts), intense mints (such as Altoids), and baking powder. Kraft later purchased the company.
Customer service	The ability of logistics management to satisfy users in terms of time, dependability, communication, and convenience is called the customer service.
Rebate	Rebate refers to a sales promotion in which money is returned to the consumer based on proof of purchase.
Contract	A contract is a "promise" or an "agreement" that is enforced or recognized by the law. In the civil law, a contract is considered to be part of the general law of obligations.
Compatibility	Compatibility refers to used to describe a product characteristic, it means a good fit with other products used by the consumer or with the consumer's lifestyle. Used in a technical context, it means the ability of systems to work together.
Profit margin	Profit margin is a measure of profitability. It is calculated using a formula and written as a percentage or a number. Profit margin = Net income before tax and interest / Revenue.
Margin	A deposit by a buyer in stocks with a seller or a stockbroker, as security to cover

Go to **Cram101.com** for the Practice Tests for this Chapter.

fluctuations in the market in reference to stocks that the buyer has purchased but for which he has not paid is a margin. Commodities are also traded on margin.

Raw material	Raw material refers to a good that has not been transformed by production; a primary product.
Insurance	Insurance refers to a system by which individuals can reduce their exposure to risk of large losses by spreading the risks among a large number of persons.
Technological change	The introduction of new methods of production or new products intended to increase the productivity of existing inputs or to raise marginal products is a technological change.
Knowledge technology	Knowledge technology refers to technology that adds a layer of intelligence to information technology, to filter appropriate information and deliver it when it is needed.
Continuous process	An uninterrupted production process in which long production runs turn out finished goods over time is called continuous process.
Mass production	The process of making a large number of a limited variety of products at very low cost is referred to as mass production.
Integration	Economic integration refers to reducing barriers among countries to transactions and to movements of goods, capital, and labor, including harmonization of laws, regulations, and standards. Integrated markets theoretically function as a unified market.
Production	The creation of finished goods and services using the factors of production: land, labor, capital, entrepreneurship, and knowledge.
Workflow	Workflow refers to automated systems that electronically route documents to the next person in the process.
Contribution	In business organization law, the cash or property contributed to a business by its owners is referred to as contribution.
Operations technology	The combination of resources, knowledge, and techniques that creates a product or service output for an organization is operations technology.
Consideration	Consideration in contract law, a basic requirement for an enforceable agreement under traditional contract principles, defined in this text as legal value, bargained for and given in exchange for an act or promise. In corporation law, cash or property contributed to a corporation in exchange for shares, or a promise to contribute such cash or property.
Instrument	Instrument refers to an economic variable that is controlled by policy makers and can be used to influence other variables, called targets. Examples are monetary and fiscal policies used to achieve external and internal balance.
Organizational environment	Organizational environment refers to everything outside an organization. It includes all elements, people, other organizations, economic factors, objects, and events that lie outside the boundaries of the organization.
Task environment	Task environment includes specific organizations, groups, and individuals that influence the organization.
Competitor	Other organizations in the same industry or type of business that provide a good or service to the same set of customers is referred to as a competitor.
Unemployment rate	The unemployment rate is the number of unemployed workers divided by the total civilian labor force, which includes both the unemployed and those with jobs (all those willing and able to work for pay).
Interest rate	The rate of return on bonds, loans, or deposits. When one speaks of 'the' interest rate, it is usually in a model where there is only one.

Go to **Cram101.com** for the Practice Tests for this Chapter.

Interest	In finance and economics, interest is the price paid by a borrower for the use of a lender's money. In other words, interest is the amount of paid to "rent" money for a period of time.
New economy	New economy, this term was used in the late 1990's to suggest that globalization and/or innovations in information technology had changed the way that the world economy works.
Dell Computer	Dell Computer, formerly PC's Limited, was founded on the principle that by selling personal computer systems directly to customers, PC's Limited could best understand their needs and provide the most effective computing solutions to meet those needs.
Michael Dell	Michael Dell is the founder of Dell, Inc., the world's largest computer manufacturer which revolutionized the home computer industry.
Sam Walton	I guess in all my years, what I heard more often than anything was: a town of less than 50,000 population cannot support a discount store for very long. Sam Walton was the founder of two American retailers, Wal-Mart and Sam's Club.
Information system	An information system is a system whether automated or manual, that comprises people, machines, and/or methods organized to collect, process, transmit, and disseminate data that represent user information.
Inventory	Tangible property held for sale in the normal course of business or used in producing goods or services for sale is an inventory.
Chief information officer	The chief information officer is a job title for the head of information technology group within an organization. They often report to the chief executive officer or chief financial officer.
Patent	The legal right to the proceeds from and control over the use of an invented product or process, granted for a fixed period of time, usually 20 years. Patent is one form of intellectual property that is subject of the TRIPS agreement.
Business unit	The lowest level of the company which contains the set of functions that carry a product through its life span from concept through manufacture, distribution, sales and service is a business unit.
Disney	Disney is one of the largest media and entertainment corporations in the world. Founded on October 16, 1923 by brothers Walt and Roy Disney as a small animation studio, today it is one of the largest Hollywood studios and also owns nine theme parks and several television networks, including the American Broadcasting Company (ABC).
Preference	The act of a debtor in paying or securing one or more of his creditors in a manner more favorable to them than to other creditors or to the exclusion of such other creditors is a preference. In the absence of statute, a preference is perfectly good, but to be legal it must be bona fide, and not a mere subterfuge of the debtor to secure a future benefit to himself or to prevent the application of his property to his debts.
Disposable income	Disposable income is income minus taxes. More accurately, income minus direct taxes plus transfer payments; that is, the income available to be spent and saved.
Environmental complexity	The number of environmental components that impinge on organizational decision-making is called environmental complexity.
Environmental dynamism	The degree to which environmental components that impinge on organizational decision making change is environmental dynamism.
Brokerage firm	A company that conducts various aspects of securities trading, analysis and advisory services is a brokerage firm.
Deregulation	The lessening or complete removal of government regulations on an industry, especially concerning the price that firms are allowed to charge and leaving price to be determined by

Go to **Cram101.com** for the Practice Tests for this Chapter.

	market forces a deregulation.
Organizational performance	Organizational performance comprises the actual output or results of an organization as measured against its intended outputs (or goals and objectives).
Inputs	The inputs used by a firm or an economy are the labor, raw materials, electricity and other resources it uses to produce its outputs.
Economic system	Economic system refers to a particular set of institutional arrangements and a coordinating mechanism for solving the economizing problem; a method of organizing an economy, of which the market system and the command system are the two general types.
Management philosophy	Management philosophy refers to a philosophy that links key goal-related issues with key collaboration issues to come up with general ways by which the firm will manage its affairs.
Strategic choice	Strategic choice refers to an organization's strategy; the ways an organization will attempt to fulfill its mission and achieve its long-term goals.
Financial transaction	A financial transaction involves a change in the status of the finances of two or more businesses or individuals.
Organization culture	The set of values that helps the organization's employees understand which actions are considered acceptable and which unacceptable is referred to as the organization culture.
Mergers and acquisitions	The phrase mergers and acquisitions refers to the aspect of corporate finance strategy and management dealing with the merging and acquiring of different companies as well as other assets. Usually mergers occur in a friendly setting where executives from the respective companies participate in a due diligence process to ensure a successful combination of all parts.
Economic growth	Economic growth refers to the increase over time in the capacity of an economy to produce goods and services and to improve the well-being of its citizens.
Downturn	A decline in a stock market or economic cycle is a downturn.
Domestic	From or in one's own country. A domestic producer is one that produces inside the home country. A domestic price is the price inside the home country. Opposite of 'foreign' or 'world.'.
Revenue	Revenue is a U.S. business term for the amount of money that a company receives from its activities, mostly from sales of products and/or services to customers.
Value system	A value system refers to how an individual or a group of individuals organize their ethical or ideological values. A well-defined value system is a moral code.
Loyalty	Marketers tend to define customer loyalty as making repeat purchases. Some argue that it should be defined attitudinally as a strongly positive feeling about the brand.
Organic structure	Organic structure refers to an organizational form in which formality is low, power is decentralized and jobs are less specialized and are often broadly defined. Adaptability and flexibility in the face of rapidly changing conditions are usually the primary goals with such structures.
Organic organization	A term created by Tom Burns and G.M. Stalker in the late 1950s, an organic organization is an organization which is flexible and values outside knowledge.
Open system	A system that interacts with its environment is referred to as open system. It is a system that takes in (raw materials, capital, skilled labor) and converts them into goods and services (via machinery, human skills) that are sent back to that environment, where they are bought by customers.
Sociotechnical	Organizational systems that integrate people and technology into high-performance work

Go to **Cram101.com** for the Practice Tests for this Chapter.

systems	settings are referred to as sociotechnical systems.
Management system	A management system is the framework of processes and procedures used to ensure that an organization can fulfill all tasks required to achieve its objectives.
Financial institution	A financial institution acts as an agent that provides financial services for its clients. Financial institutions generally fall under financial regulation from a government authority.
Just In Time	Just In Time is an inventory strategy implemented to improve the return on investment of a business by reducing in-process inventory and its associated costs. The process is driven by a series of signals, or Kanban that tell production processes to make the next part.
Warehouse	Warehouse refers to a location, often decentralized, that a firm uses to store, consolidate, age, or mix stock; house product-recall programs; or ease tax burdens.
Trust	An arrangement in which shareholders of independent firms agree to give up their stock in exchange for trust certificates that entitle them to a share of the trust's common profits.
Stock	In financial terminology, stock is the capital raized by a corporation, through the issuance and sale of shares.
Assignment	A transfer of property or some right or interest is referred to as assignment.
Systems theory	Systems theory refers to a view of an organization as a complex set of dynamically intertwined and interconneci:ed elements, including its inputs, processes, outputs, feedback loops, and the environment in which it operates and with which it continuously interacts.
Systems design	Systems design is the process or art of defining the hardware and software architecture, components, modules, interfaces, and data for a computer system to satisfy specified requirements.
Organizational design	The structuring of workers so that they can best accomplish the firm's goals is referred to as organizational design.
Supervisor	A Supervisor is an employee of an organization with some of the powers and responsibilities of management, occupying a role between true manager and a regular employee. A Supervisor position is typically the first step towards being promoted into a management role.
Standardization	Standardization, in the context related to technologies and industries, is the process of establishing a technical standard among competing entities in a market, where this will bring benefits without hurting competition.
Organizational development	The application of behavioral science knowledge in a longrange effort to improve an organization's ability to cope with change in its external environment and increase its problem-solving capabilities is referred to as organizational development.
Machine bureaucracy	Machine bureaucracy structure is typical of large, well-established organizations. Work is highly specialized and formalized, and decision-making is usually concentrated at the top.
Divisionalized form	Divisionalized form structure is typical of old, very large organizations. Within it, the organization is divided according to the different markets served. Horizontal and vertical specialization exists between divisions and headquarters, decision-making is divided between headquarters and divisions, and outputs are standardized.
Adhocracy	Adhocracy structure is typically found in young organizations in highly technical fields. Within it, decision-making is spread throughout the organization, power resides with the experts, horizontal and vertical specialization exists, and there is little formalization.
Professional bureaucracy	Professional bureaucracy structure is characterized by horizontal specialization by professional area of expertise, little formalization, and decentralized decision-making.
Distribution	Distribution in economics, the manner in which total output and income is distributed among

Go to **Cram101.com** for the Practice Tests for this Chapter.

individuals or factors.

Horizontal specialization	A division of labor through the formation of work units or groups within an organization is a horizontal specialization.
Vertical specialization	Vertical specialization occurs when a country uses imported intermediate parts to create a good it later exports—that is, the country links sequentially with other countries to produce a final good.
Strategic business unit	Strategic business unit is understood as a business unit within the overall corporate identity which is distinguishable from other business because it serves a defined external market where management can conduct strategic planning in relation to products and markets. When companies become really large, they are best thought of as being composed of a number of businesses
General Motors	General Motors is the world's largest automaker. Founded in 1908, today it employs about 327,000 people around the world. With global headquarters in Detroit, it manufactures its cars and trucks in 33 countries.
Reorganization	Reorganization occurs, among other instances, when one corporation acquires another in a merger or acquisition, a single corporation divides into two or more entities, or a corporation makes a substantial change in its capital structure.
Liaison	An individual who serves as a bridge between groups, tying groups together and facilitating the communication flow needed to integrate group activities is a liaison.
Specialist	A specialist is a trader who makes a market in one or several stocks and holds the limit order book for those stocks.
Organizational strategy	The process of positioning the Organization in the competitive environment and implementing actions to compete successfully is an organizational strategy.
Matrix organization	Matrix organization refers to an organization in which specialists from different parts of the organization are brought together to work on specific projects but still remain part of a traditional line-and-staff structure.
Matrix design	Matrix design combines two different designs to gain the benefits of each; typically combined are a product or project departmentalization scheme and a functional structure.
Matrix structure	An organizational structure which typically crosses a functional approach with a product or service-based design, often resulting in employees having two bosses is the matrix structure.
Gain	In finance, gain is a profit or an increase in value of an investment such as a stock or bond. Gain is calculated by fair market value or the proceeds from the sale of the investment minus the sum of the purchase price and all costs associated with it.
Functional structure	A type of structure in which units and departments are organized based on the activity or function that they perform is called the functional structure.
Federal government	Federal government refers to the government of the United States, as distinct from the state and local governments.
Personnel	A collective term for all of the employees of an organization. Personnel is also commonly used to refer to the personnel management function or the organizational unit responsible for administering personnel programs.
Departmental- zation	The dividing of organizational functions into separate units is called departmentalization.
Alpha	Alpha is a risk-adjusted measure of the so-called "excess return" on an investment. It is a common measure of assessing active manager's performance as it is the return in excess of a

benchmark index or "risk-free" investment.

Virtual organization	A temporary alliance between two or more organizations that band together to undertake a specific venture is a virtual organization.
Partnership	In the common law, a partnership is a type of business entity in which partners share with each other the profits or losses of the business undertaking in which they have all invested.
Quick response	An inventory management system designed to reduce the retailer's lead-time, thereby lowering its inventory investment, improving customer service levels, and reducing logistics expense is referred to as quick response.
Electronic mail	Electronic mail refers to electronic written communication between individuals using computers connected to the Internet.
Expense	In accounting, an expense represents an event in which an asset is used up or a liability is incurred. In terms of the accounting equation, expenses reduce owners' equity.
Public relations firm	An organization that develops and implements programs to manage a company's publicity, image, and affairs with consumers and other relevant publics is referred to as a public relations firm.
Public relations	Public relations refers to the management function that evaluates public attitudes, changes policies and procedures in response to the public's requests, and executes a program of action and information to earn public understanding and acceptance.
Advertising	Advertising refers to paid, nonpersonal communication through various media by organizations and individuals who are in some way identified in the advertising message.
Teamwork	That which occurs when group members work together in ways that utilize their skills well to accomplish a purpose is called teamwork.
Intel	Intel Corporation, founded in 1968 and based in Santa Clara, California, USA, is the world's largest semiconductor company. Intel is best known for its PC microprocessors, where it maintains roughly 80% market share.
Global competition	Global competition exists when competitive conditions across national markets are linked strongly enough to form a true international market and when leading competitors compete head to head in many different countries.
Reengineering	The fundamental rethinking and redesign of business processes to achieve improvements in critical measures of performance, such as cost, quality, service, speed, and customer satisfaction is referred to as reengineering.
Restructuring	Restructuring is the corporate management term for the act of partially dismantling and reorganizing a company for the purpose of making it more efficient and therefore more profitable.
Hierarchy	A system of grouping people in an organization according to rank from the top down in which all subordinate managers must report to one person is called a hierarchy.
Microsoft	Microsoft is a multinational computer technology corporation with 2004 global annual sales of US$39.79 billion and 71,553 employees in 102 countries and regions as of July 2006. It develops, manufactures, licenses, and supports a wide range of software products for computing devices.
Classical organization theory	An early approach to management that focused on how organizations can be structured most effectively to meet their goals is a classical organization theory.
Divisional	A divisional structure is found in diversified organizations, they contain separate divisions

structure	that are based around individual product lines or on the geographic areas of the markets being served.
Toyota	Toyota is a Japanese multinational corporation that manufactures automobiles, trucks and buses. Toyota is the world's second largest automaker by sales. Toyota also provides financial services through its subsidiary, Toyota Financial Services, and participates in other lines of business.
Expatriate	Employee sent by his or her company to live and manage operations in a different country is called an expatriate.
DaimlerChrysler	In 2002, the merged company, DaimlerChrysler, appeared to run two independent product lines, with few signs of corporate integration. In 2003, however, it was alleged by the Detroit News that the "merger of equals" was, in fact, a takeover.
International division	Division responsible for a firm's international activities is an international division.
Nestle	Nestle is the world's biggest food and beverage company. In the 1860s, a pharmacist, developed a food for babies who were unable to be breastfed. His first success was a premature infant who could not tolerate his own mother's milk nor any of the usual substitutes. The value of the new product was quickly recognized when his new formula saved the child's life.
Core	A core is the set of feasible allocations in an economy that cannot be improved upon by subset of the set of the economy's consumers (a coalition). In construction, when the force in an element is within a certain center section, the core, the element will only be under compression.
Administrative hierarchy	The system of reporting relationships in the organization, from the lowest to the highest managerial levels is referred to as administrative hierarchy.
Systems view	A management viewpoint that focuses on the interactions between the various components that combine to produce a product or service is called systems view. The systems view focuses management on the system as the cause of quality problems.
Business opportunity	A business opportunity involves the sale or lease of any product, service, equipment, etc. that will enable the purchaser-licensee to begin a business
Organizational Behavior	The study of human behavior in organizational settings, the interface between human behavior and the organization, and the organization itself is called organizational behavior.
Security	Security refers to a claim on the borrower future income that is sold by the borrower to the lender. A security is a type of transferable interest representing financial value.
Customer orientation	Customer orientation is a set of beliefs/ strategy that customer needs and satisfaction are the priority of an organization. It focuses on dynamic interactions between the organization and customers as well as competitors in the market and its internal stakeholders.
Layoff	A layoff is the termination of an employee or (more commonly) a group of employees for business reasons, such as the decision that certain positions are no longer necessary.
Aid	Assistance provided by countries and by international institutions such as the World Bank to developing countries in the form of monetary grants, loans at low interest rates, in kind, or a combination of these is called aid. Aid can also refer to assistance of any type rendered to benefit some group or individual.
Consultant	A professional that provides expert advice in a particular field or area in which customers occassionaly require this type of knowledge is a consultant.
Organization	Organization chart refers to a visual device, which shows the relationship and divides the

Go to **Cram101.com** for the Practice Tests for this Chapter.

267

Go to **Cram101.com** for the Practice Tests for this Chapter.
And, **NEVER** highlight a book again!

chart	organization's work; it shows who is accountable for the completion of specific work and who reports to whom.
Task force	A temporary team or committee formed to solve a specific short-term problem involving several departments is the task force.
Annual report	An annual report is prepared by corporate management that presents financial information including financial statements, footnotes, and the management discussion and analysis.
Organizational structure	Organizational structure is the way in which the interrelated groups of an organization are constructed. From a managerial point of view the main concerns are ensuring effective communication and coordination.

Go to **Cram101.com** for the Practice Tests for this Chapter.

Go to **Cram101.com** for the Practice Tests for this Chapter.
And, **NEVER** highlight a book again!

Boeing	Boeing is the world's largest aircraft manufacturer by revenue. Headquartered in Chicago, Illinois, Boeing is the second-largest defense contractor in the world. In 2005, the company was the world's largest civil aircraft manufacturer in terms of value.
Sony	Sony is a multinational corporation and one of the world's largest media conglomerates founded in Tokyo, Japan. One of its divisions Sony Electronics is one of the leading manufacturers of electronics, video, communications, and information technology products for the consumer and professional markets.
Nike	Because Nike creates goods for a wide range of sports, they have competition from every sports and sports fashion brand there is. Nike has no direct competitors because there is no single brand which can compete directly with their range of sports and non-sports oriented gear, except for Reebok.
Industry	A group of firms that produce identical or similar products is an industry. It is also used specifically to refer to an area of economic production focused on manufacturing which involves large amounts of capital investment before any profit can be realized, also called "heavy industry".
Southwest airlines	Southwest Airlines is a low-fare airline in the United States. It is the third-largest airline in the world, by number of passengers carried, and the largest in the United States by number of passengers carried domestically.
Chief operating officer	A chief operating officer is a corporate officer responsible for managing the day-to-day activities of the corporation. The chief operating officer is one of the highest ranking members of an organization, monitoring the daily operations of the company and reporting to the chief executive officer directly.
Firm	An organization that employs resources to produce a good or service for profit and owns and operates one or more plants is referred to as a firm.
Core	A core is the set of feasible allocations in an economy that cannot be improved upon by subset of the set of the economy's consumers (a coalition). In construction, when the force in an element is within a certain center section, the core, the element will only be under compression.
Assignment	A transfer of property or some right or interest is referred to as assignment.
Operation	A standardized method or technique that is performed repetitively, often on different materials resulting in different finished goods is called an operation.
Service	Service refers to a "non tangible product" that is not embodied in a physical good and that typically effects some change in another product, person, or institution. Contrasts with good.
Marketing management	Marketing management refers to the process of planning and executing the conception, pricing, promotion, and distribution of ideas, goods, and services to create mutually beneficial exchanges.
Management	Management characterizes the process of leading and directing all or part of an organization, often a business, through the deployment and manipulation of resources. Early twentieth-century management writer Mary Parker Follett defined management as "the art of getting things done through people."
Marketing	Promoting and selling products or services to customers, or prospective customers, is referred to as marketing.
Organization culture	The set of values that helps the organization's employees understand which actions are considered acceptable and which unacceptable is referred to as the organization culture.

Go to **Cram101.com** for the Practice Tests for this Chapter.

Organizational Behavior	The study of human behavior in organizational settings, the interface between human behavior and the organization, and the organization itself is called organizational behavior.
Journal	Book of original entry, in which transactions are recorded in a general ledger system, is referred to as a journal.
Interest	In finance and economics, interest is the price paid by a borrower for the use of a lender's money. In other words, interest is the amount of paid to "rent" money for a period of time.
Business Week	Business Week is a business magazine published by McGraw-Hill. It was first published in 1929 under the direction of Malcolm Muir, who was serving as president of the McGraw-Hill Publishing company at the time. It is considered to be the standard both in industry and among students.
Variable	A variable is something measured by a number; it is used to analyze what happens to other things when the size of that number changes.
Organizational performance	Organizational performance comprises the actual output or results of an organization as measured against its intended outputs (or goals and objectives).
Organizational culture	The mindset of employees, including their shared beliefs, values, and goals is called the organizational culture.
Mistake	In contract law a mistake is incorrect understanding by one or more parties to a contract and may be used as grounds to invalidate the agreement. Common law has identified three different types of mistake in contract: unilateral mistake, mutual mistake, and common mistake.
Balance	In banking and accountancy, the outstanding balance is the amount of money owned, (or due), that remains in a deposit account (or a loan account) at a given date, after all past remittances, payments and withdrawal have been accounted for. It can be positive (then, in the balance sheet of a firm, it is an asset) or negative (a liability).
Chief executive officer	A chief executive officer is the highest-ranking corporate officer or executive officer of a corporation, or agency. In closely held corporations, it is general business culture that the office chief executive officer is also the chairman of the board.
Investment	Investment refers to spending for the production and accumulation of capital and additions to inventories. In a financial sense, buying an asset with the expectation of making a return.
Bond	Bond refers to a debt instrument, issued by a borrower and promising a specified stream of payments to the purchaser, usually regular interest payments plus a final repayment of principal.
Foundation	A Foundation is a type of philanthropic organization set up by either individuals or institutions as a legal entity (either as a corporation or trust) with the purpose of distributing grants to support causes in line with the goals of the foundation.
Contribution	In business organization law, the cash or property contributed to a business by its owners is referred to as contribution.
Corporation	A legal entity chartered by a state or the Federal government that is distinct and separate from the individuals who own it is a corporation. This separation gives the corporation unique powers which other legal entities lack.
Complement	A good that is used in conjunction with another good is a complement. For example, cameras and film would complement eachother.
Quantitative research	Quantitative research is the systematic scientific investigation of quantitative properties and phenomena and their relationships. The objective of quantitative research is to develop and employ mathematical models, theories and hypotheses pertaining to natural phenomena. The process of measurement is central to quantitative research because it provides the

fundamental connection between empirical observation and mathematical expression of quantitative relationships.

Corporate culture	The whole collection of beliefs, values, and behaviors of a firm that send messages to those within and outside the company about how business is done is the corporate culture.
Economics	The social science dealing with the use of scarce resources to obtain the maximum satisfaction of society's virtually unlimited economic wants is an economics.
Sam Walton	I guess in all my years, what I heard more often than anything was: a town of less than 50,000 population cannot support a discount store for very long. Sam Walton was the founder of two American retailers, Wal-Mart and Sam's Club.
Equal employment opportunity	The government's attempt to ensure that all individuals have an equal opportunity for employment, regardless of race, color, religion, sex, age, disability, or national origin is equal employment opportunity.
Employment law	Employment law is the body of laws, administrative rulings, and precedents which addresses the legal rights of, and restrictions on, workers and their organizations.
Organization climate	Current situations in an organization and the linkages among work groups, employees, and work performance is called the organization climate.
Context	The effect of the background under which a message often takes on more and richer meaning is a context. Context is especially important in cross-cultural interactions because some cultures are said to be high context or low context.
Entrepreneur	The owner/operator. The person who organizes, manages, and assumes the risks of a firm, taking a new idea or a new product and turning it into a successful business is an entrepreneur.
Cultural values	The values that employees need to have and act on for the organization to act on the strategic values are called cultural values.
Asset	An item of property, such as land, capital, money, a share in ownership, or a claim on others for future payment, such as a bond or a bank deposit is an asset.
Vision statement	The identification of objectives to be achieved in the future is called vision statement.
Organization design	The structuring of workers so that they can best accomplish the firm's goals is referred to as organization design.
Customer service	The ability of logistics management to satisfy users in terms of time, dependability, communication, and convenience is called the customer service.
Innovation	Innovation refers to the first commercially successful introduction of a new product, the use of a new method of production, or the creation of a new form of business organization.
Administration	Administration refers to the management and direction of the affairs of governments and institutions; a collective term for all policymaking officials of a government; the execution and implementation of public policy.
Assessment	Collecting information and providing feedback to employees about their behavior, communication style, or skills is an assessment.
Points	Loan origination fees that may be deductible as interest by a buyer of property. A seller of property who pays points reduces the selling price by the amount of the points paid for the buyer.
Evaluation	The consumer's appraisal of the product or brand on important attributes is called evaluation.

Go to **Cram101.com** for the Practice Tests for this Chapter.

Wells Fargo	Following completion of the First Security acquisition, Wells Fargo had total assets of $263 billion. Its strategy echoed that of the old Norwest: making selective acquisitions and pursuing cross-selling of an ever-wider array of credit and investment products to its vast customer base.
Takeover	A takeover in business refers to one company (the acquirer) purchasing another (the target). Such events resemble mergers, but without the formation of a new company.
Authority	Authority in agency law, refers to an agent's ability to affect his principal's legal relations with third parties. Also used to refer to an actor's legal power or ability to do something. In addition, sometimes used to refer to a statute, case, or other legal source that justifies a particular result.
Organization structure	The system of task, reporting, and authority relationships within which the organization does its work is referred to as the organization structure.
Supervisor	A Supervisor is an employee of an organization with some of the powers and responsibilities of management, occupying a role between true manager and a regular employee. A Supervisor position is typically the first step towards being promoted into a management role.
Collective responsibility	Cabinet collective responsibility is constitutional convention in the states that use the Westminster System. It means that members of the Cabinet must publicly support all governmental decisions made in Cabinet, even if they do not privately agree with them.
Turnover	Turnover in a financial context refers to the rate at which a provider of goods cycles through its average inventory. Turnover in a human resources context refers to the characteristic of a given company or industry, relative to rate at which an employer gains and loses staff.
Manufacturing	Production of goods primarily by the application of labor and capital to raw materials and other intermediate inputs, in contrast to agriculture, mining, forestry, fishing, and services a manufacturing.
Toyota	Toyota is a Japanese multinational corporation that manufactures automobiles, trucks and buses. Toyota is the world's second largest automaker by sales. Toyota also provides financial services through its subsidiary, Toyota Financial Services, and participates in other lines of business.
Entrepreneurship	The assembling of resources to produce new or improved products and technologies is referred to as entrepreneurship.
Bureaucracy	Bureaucracy refers to an organization with many layers of managers who set rules and regulations and oversee all decisions.
Marketing Plan	Marketing plan refers to a road map for the marketing activities of an organization for a specified future period of time, such as one year or five years.
Productivity	Productivity refers to the total output of goods and services in a given period of time divided by work hours.
Research and development	The use of resources for the deliberate discovery of new information and ways of doing things, together with the application of that information in inventing new products or processes is referred to as research and development.
Paradox	As used in economics, paradox means something unexpected, rather than the more extreme normal meaning of something seemingly impossible. Some paradoxes are just theoretical results that go against what one thinks of as normal.
Option	A contract that gives the purchaser the option to buy or sell the underlying financial instrument at a specified price, called the exercise price or strike price, within a specific

Go to **Cram101.com** for the Practice Tests for this Chapter.

	period of time.
Fortune magazine	Fortune magazine is America's longest-running business magazine. Currently owned by media conglomerate Time Warner, it was founded in 1930 by Henry Luce. It is known for its regular features ranking companies by revenue.
Technology	The body of knowledge and techniques that can be used to combine economic resources to produce goods and services is called technology.
Competitor	Other organizations in the same industry or type of business that provide a good or service to the same set of customers is referred to as a competitor.
Enabling	Enabling refers to giving workers the education and tools they need to assume their new decision-making powers.
Market	A market is, as defined in economics, a social arrangement that allows buyers and sellers to discover information and carry out a voluntary exchange of goods or services.
Leadership	Management merely consists of leadership applied to business situations; or in other words: management forms a sub-set of the broader process of leadership.
Motorola	The Six Sigma quality system was developed at Motorola even though it became most well known because of its use by General Electric. It was created by engineer Bill Smith, under the direction of Bob Galvin (son of founder Paul Galvin) when he was running the company.
Radical innovation	Radical innovation refers to a new product, service, or technology, that changes or creates whole industries.
Incremental innovation	Incremental innovation refers to minor changes made over time to sustain the growth of a company without making changes in major product lines, services, or markets which are currently being competed in.
Product life cycle	Product life cycle refers to a series of phases in a product's sales and cash flows over time; these phases, in order of occurrence, are introductory, growth, maturity, and decline.
Profit	Profit refers to the return to the resource entrepreneurial ability; total revenue minus total cost.
Positioning	The art and science of fitting the product or service to one or more segments of the market in such a way as to set it meaningfully apart from competition is called positioning.
Empowerment	Giving employees the authority and responsibility to respond quickly to customer requests is called empowerment.
Employee empowerment	Employee empowerment is a method of improving customer service in which workers have discretion to do what they believe is necessary, but within reason, to satisfy the customer, even if this means bending some company rules.
Driving force	The key external pressure that will shape the future for an organization is a driving force. The driving force in an industry are the main underlying causes of changing industry and competitive conditions.
Merger	Merger refers to the combination of two firms into a single firm.
Security	Security refers to a claim on the borrower future income that is sold by the borrower to the lender. A security is a type of transferable interest representing financial value.
Compaq	Compaq was founded in February 1982 by Rod Canion, Jim Harris and Bill Murto, three senior managers from semiconductor manufacturer Texas Instruments. Each invested $1,000 to form the company. Their first venture capital came from Ben Rosen and Sevin-Rosen partners. It is often told that the architecture of the original PC was first sketched out on a placemat by the founders while dining in the Houston restaurant, House of Pies.

Go to **Cram101.com** for the Practice Tests for this Chapter.

Chief financial officer	Chief financial officer refers to executive responsible for overseeing the financial operations of an organization.
Chief information officer	The chief information officer is a job title for the head of information technology group within an organization. They often report to the chief executive officer or chief financial officer.
Procedural justice	The extent to which the dynamics of an organization's decision-making processes are judged to be fair by those most affected by them is called the procedural justice.
Compliance	A type of influence process where a receiver accepts the position advocated by a source to obtain favorable outcomes or to avoid punishment is the compliance.
Subsidiary	A company that is controlled by another company or corporation is a subsidiary.
Market share	That fraction of an industry's output accounted for by an individual firm or group of firms is called market share.
Advertising	Advertising refers to paid, nonpersonal communication through various media by organizations and individuals who are in some way identified in the advertising message.
Socialization	Socialization is the process by which human beings or animals learn to adopt the behavior patterns of the community in which they live. For both humans and animals, this is typically thought to occur during the early stages of life, during which individuals develop the skills and knowledge necessary to function within their culture and environment.
Credibility	The extent to which a source is perceived as having knowledge, skill, or experience relevant to a communication topic and can be trusted to give an unbiased opinion or present objective information on the issue is called credibility.
Long run	In economic models, the long run time frame assumes no fixed factors of production. Firms can enter or leave the marketplace, and the cost (and availability) of land, labor, raw materials, and capital goods can be assumed to vary.
Bill Gates	Bill Gates is the co-founder, chairman, former chief software architect, and former CEO of Microsoft Corporation. He is one of the best-known entrepreneurs of the personal computer revolution and he is widely respected for his foresight and ambition.
Microsoft	Microsoft is a multinational computer technology corporation with 2004 global annual sales of US$39.79 billion and 71,553 employees in 102 countries and regions as of July 2006. It develops, manufactures, licenses, and supports a wide range of software products for computing devices.
Acquisition	A company's purchase of the property and obligations of another company is an acquisition.
Competitiveness	Competitiveness usually refers to characteristics that permit a firm to compete effectively with other firms due to low cost or superior technology, perhaps internationally.
Analogy	Analogy is either the cognitive process of transferring information from a particular subject to another particular subject (the target), or a linguistic expression corresponding to such a process. In a narrower sense, analogy is an inference or an argument from a particular to another particular, as opposed to deduction, induction, and abduction, where at least one of the premises or the conclusion is general.
Department of Justice	The United States Department of Justice is a Cabinet department in the United States government designed to enforce the law and defend the interests of the United States according to the law and to ensure fair and impartial administration of justice for all Americans. This department is administered by the United States Attorney General, one of the original members of the cabinet.
Speculation	The purchase or sale of an asset in hopes that its price will rise or fall respectively, in

order to make a profit is called speculation.

Antitrust	Government intervention to alter market structure or prevent abuse of market power is called antitrust.
Startup	Any new company can be considered a startup, but the description is usually applied to aggressive young companies that are actively courting private financing from venture capitalists, including wealthy individuals and investment companies.
Public relations	Public relations refers to the management function that evaluates public attitudes, changes policies and procedures in response to the public's requests, and executes a program of action and information to earn public understanding and acceptance.
Configuration	An organization's shape, which reflects the division of labor and the means of coordinating the divided tasks is configuration.
Logistics	Those activities that focus on getting the right amount of the right products to the right place at the right time at the lowest possible cost is referred to as logistics.
Assimilation	Assimilation refers to the process through which a minority group learns the ways of the dominant group. In organizations, this means that when people of different types and backgrounds are hired, the organization attempts to mold them to fit the existing organizational culture.
Brief	Brief refers to a statement of a party's case or legal arguments, usually prepared by an attorney. Also used to make legal arguments before appellate courts.
Graduation	Termination of a country's eligibility for GSP tariff preferences on the grounds that it has progressed sufficiently, in terms of per capita income or another measure, that it is no longer in need to special and differential treatment is graduation.
American Management Association	American Management Association International is the world's largest membership-based management development and executive training organization. Their products include instructor led seminars, workshops, conferences, customized corporate programs, online learning, books, newsletters, research surveys and reports.
Committee	A long-lasting, sometimes permanent team in the organization structure created to deal with tasks that recur regularly is the committee.

Go to **Cram101.com** for the Practice Tests for this Chapter.
And, **NEVER** highlight a book again!

Diversification	Investing in a collection of assets whose returns do not always move together, with the result that overall risk is lower than for individual assets is referred to as diversification.
Reorganization	Reorganization occurs, among other instances, when one corporation acquires another in a merger or acquisition, a single corporation divides into two or more entities, or a corporation makes a substantial change in its capital structure.
Asset	An item of property, such as land, capital, money, a share in ownership, or a claim on others for future payment, such as a bond or a bank deposit is an asset.
Acquisition	A company's purchase of the property and obligations of another company is an acquisition.
Industry	A group of firms that produce identical or similar products is an industry. It is also used specifically to refer to an area of economic production focused on manufacturing which involves large amounts of capital investment before any profit can be realized, also called "heavy industry".
Forming	The first stage of team development, where the team is formed and the objectives for the team are set is referred to as forming.
Conglomerate	A conglomerate is a large company that consists of divisions of often seemingly unrelated businesses.
Enterprise	Enterprise refers to another name for a business organization. Other similar terms are business firm, sometimes simply business, sometimes simply firm, as well as company, and entity.
Production	The creation of finished goods and services using the factors of production: land, labor, capital, entrepreneurship, and knowledge.
Management	Management characterizes the process of leading and directing all or part of an organization, often a business, through the deployment and manipulation of resources. Early twentieth-century management writer Mary Parker Follett defined management as "the art of getting things done through people."
Brand	A name, symbol, or design that identifies the goods or services of one seller or group of sellers and distinguishes them from the goods and services of competitors is a brand.
Synergy	Corporate synergy occurs when corporations interact congruently. A corporate synergy refers to a financial benefit that a corporation expects to realize when it merges with or acquires another corporation.
Licensing	Licensing is a form of strategic alliance which involves the sale of a right to use certain proprietary knowledge (so called intellectual property) in a defined way.
Labor	People's physical and mental talents and efforts that are used to help produce goods and services are called labor.
Regulation	Regulation refers to restrictions state and federal laws place on business with regard to the conduct of its activities.
Privatization	A process in which investment bankers take companies that were previously owned by the government to the public markets is referred to as privatization.
Capitalism	Capitalism refers to an economic system in which capital is mostly owned by private individuals and corporations. Contrasts with communism.
Business Week	Business Week is a business magazine published by McGraw-Hill. It was first published in 1929 under the direction of Malcolm Muir, who was serving as president of the McGraw-Hill Publishing company at the time. It is considered to be the standard both in industry and

Go to **Cram101.com** for the Practice Tests for this Chapter.

among students.

Brief	Brief refers to a statement of a party's case or legal arguments, usually prepared by an attorney. Also used to make legal arguments before appellate courts.
Technology	The body of knowledge and techniques that can be used to combine economic resources to produce goods and services is called technology.
Technological change	The introduction of new methods of production or new products intended to increase the productivity of existing inputs or to raise marginal products is a technological change.
Resource management	Resource management is the efficient and effective deployment of an organization's resources when they are needed. Such resources may include financial resources, inventory, human skills, production resources, or information technology.
Value system	A value system refers to how an individual or a group of individuals organize their ethical or ideological values. A well-defined value system is a moral code.
Purchasing	Purchasing refers to the function in a firm that searches for quality material resources, finds the best suppliers, and negotiates the best price for goods and services.
Innovation	Innovation refers to the first commercially successful introduction of a new product, the use of a new method of production, or the creation of a new form of business organization.
Marketing	Promoting and selling products or services to customers, or prospective customers, is referred to as marketing.
Promotion	Promotion refers to all the techniques sellers use to motivate people to buy products or services. An attempt by marketers to inform people about products and to persuade them to participate in an exchange.
Service	Service refers to a "non tangible product" that is not embodied in a physical good and that typically effects some change in another product, person, or institution. Contrasts with good.
Human resource management	The process of evaluating human resource needs, finding people to fill those needs, and getting the best work from each employee by providing the right incentives and job environment, all with the goal of meeting the needs of the firm are called human resource management.
Market	A market is, as defined in economics, a social arrangement that allows buyers and sellers to discover information and carry out a voluntary exchange of goods or services.
Productivity	Productivity refers to the total output of goods and services in a given period of time divided by work hours.
Assignment	A transfer of property or some right or interest is referred to as assignment.
DuPont	DuPont was the inventor of CFCs (along with General Motors) and the largest producer of these ozone depleting chemicals (used primarily in aerosol sprays and refrigerants) in the world, with a 25% market share in the late 1980s.
Business strategy	Business strategy, which refers to the aggregated operational strategies of single business firm or that of an SBU in a diversified corporation refers to the way in which a firm competes in its chosen arenas.
Business unit	The lowest level of the company which contains the set of functions that carry a product through its life span from concept through manufacture, distribution, sales and service is a business unit.
Information technology	Information technology refers to technology that helps companies change business by allowing them to use new methods.

Go to **Cram101.com** for the Practice Tests for this Chapter.

Avon	Avon is an American cosmetics, perfume and toy seller with markets in over 135 countries across the world and a sales of $7.74 billion worldwide.
Points	Loan origination fees that may be deductible as interest by a buyer of property. A seller of property who pays points reduces the selling price by the amount of the points paid for the buyer.
Leadership	Management merely consists of leadership applied to business situations; or in other words: management forms a sub-set of the broader process of leadership.
Glass ceiling	Glass ceiling refers to a term that refers to the many barriers that can exist to thwart a woman's rise to the top of an organization; one that provides a view of the top, but a ceiling on how far a woman can go.
Firm	An organization that employs resources to produce a good or service for profit and owns and operates one or more plants is referred to as a firm.
Operation	A standardized method or technique that is performed repetitively, often on different materials resulting in different finished goods is called an operation.
Logistics	Those activities that focus on getting the right amount of the right products to the right place at the right time at the lowest possible cost is referred to as logistics.
Artificial intelligence	Computers or computer enhaned machines that can be programmed to think, learn, and make decisions in a manner similar to people is is the subject of artificial intelligence.
Exchange	The trade of things of value between buyer and seller so that each is better off after the trade is called the exchange.
Motorola	The Six Sigma quality system was developed at Motorola even though it became most well known because of its use by General Electric. It was created by engineer Bill Smith, under the direction of Bob Galvin (son of founder Paul Galvin) when he was running the company.
Nokia	Nokia Corporation is the world's largest manufacturer of mobile telephones (as of June 2006), with a global market share of approximately 34% in Q2 of 2006. It produces mobile phones for every major market and protocol, including GSM, CDMA, and W-CDMA (UMTS).
Export	In economics, an export is any good or commodity, shipped or otherwise transported out of a country, province, town to another part of the world in a legitimate fashion, typically for use in trade or sale.
North American Free Trade Agreement	A 1993 agreement establishing, over a 15-year period, a free trade zone composed of Canada, Mexico, and the United States is referred to as the North American Free Trade Agreement.
Free trade	Free trade refers to a situation in which there are no artificial barriers to trade, such as tariffs and quotas. Usually used, often only implicitly, with frictionless trade, so that it implies that there are no barriers to trade of any kind.
Adoption	In corporation law, a corporation's acceptance of a pre-incorporation contract by action of its board of directors, by which the corporation becomes liable on the contract, is referred to as adoption.
E*Trade	E*TRADE is a financial services company based in New York City. It is a holding company primarily known as an online discount stock brokerage serving self-directed investors, many of whom are day traders. As a discount brokerage, it charges a much smaller fee on each trade.
World Trade Organization	The World Trade Organization is an international, multilateral organization, which sets the rules for the global trading system and resolves disputes between its member states, all of whom are signatories to its approximately 30 agreements.

Go to **Cram101.com** for the Practice Tests for this Chapter.

Competitor	Other organizations in the same industry or type of business that provide a good or service to the same set of customers is referred to as a competitor.
Credibility	The extent to which a source is perceived as having knowledge, skill, or experience relevant to a communication topic and can be trusted to give an unbiased opinion or present objective information on the issue is called credibility.
Integration	Economic integration refers to reducing barriers among countries to transactions and to movements of goods, capital, and labor, including harmonization of laws, regulations, and standards. Integrated markets theoretically function as a unified market.
Context	The effect of the background under which a message often takes on more and richer meaning is a context. Context is especially important in cross-cultural interactions because some cultures are said to be high context or low context.
Inventory	Tangible property held for sale in the normal course of business or used in producing goods or services for sale is an inventory.
Users	Users refer to people in the organization who actually use the product or service purchased by the buying center.
Contribution	In business organization law, the cash or property contributed to a business by its owners is referred to as contribution.
Global strategy	Global strategy refers to strategy focusing on increasing profitability by reaping cost reductions from experience curve and location economies.
Holding	The holding is a court's determination of a matter of law based on the issue presented in the particular case. In other words: under this law, with these facts, this result.
Mass marketing	Mass marketing or mass merchandizing refers to developing products and promotions to please large groups of people.
Unfreezing	The process by which people become aware of the need for change is unfreezing.
Performance appraisal	An evaluation in which the performance level of employees is measured against established standards to make decisions about promotions, compenzation, additional training, or firing is referred to as performance appraisal.
Restructuring	Restructuring is the corporate management term for the act of partially dismantling and reorganizing a company for the purpose of making it more efficient and therefore more profitable.
Refreezing	The process of making new behaviors relatively permanent and resistant to further change is refreezing.
Status quo	Status quo is a Latin term meaning the present, current, existing state of affairs.
Reinforcement theory	A motivation theory based on the relationship between a given behavior and its consequences is referred to as the reinforcement theory.
Change agent	A change agent is someone who engages either deliberately or whose behavior results in social, cultural or behavioral change. This can be studied scientifically and effective techniques can be discovered and employed.
Agent	A person who makes economic decisions for another economic actor. A hired manager operates as an agent for a firm's owner.
Consultant	A professional that provides expert advice in a particular field or area in which customers occassionaly require this type of knowledge is a consultant.
Continuous	An uninterrupted production process in which long production runs turn out finished goods

Go to **Cram101.com** for the Practice Tests for this Chapter.

process	over time is called continuous process.
Evaluation	The consumer's appraisal of the product or brand on important attributes is called evaluation.
Control phase	Six-Sigma phase where improved process performance is monitored is referred to as the control phase.
Transition management	The process of systematically planning, organizing, and implementing change is called transition management.
Management team	A management team is directly responsible for managing the day-to-day operations (and profitability) of a company.
Continuity	A media scheduling strategy where a continuous pattern of advertising is used over the time span of the advertising campaign is continuity.
Organization development	The process of planned change and improvement of the organization through application of knowledge of the behavioral sciences is called organization development.
Personnel	A collective term for all of the employees of an organization. Personnel is also commonly used to refer to the personnel management function or the organizational unit responsible for administering personnel programs.
Structural change	Changes in the relative importance of different areas of an economy over time, usually measured in terms of their share of output, employment, or total spending is structural change.
Comprehensive	A comprehensive refers to a layout accurate in size, color, scheme, and other necessary details to show how a final ad will look. For presentation only, never for reproduction.
Authority	Authority in agency law, refers to an agent's ability to affect his principal's legal relations with third parties. Also used to refer to an actor's legal power or ability to do something. In addition, sometimes used to refer to a statute, case, or other legal source that justifies a particular result.
Reengineering	The fundamental rethinking and redesign of business processes to achieve improvements in critical measures of performance, such as cost, quality, service, speed, and customer satisfaction is referred to as reengineering.
Business model	A business model is the instrument by which a business intends to generate revenue and profits. It is a summary of how a company means to serve its employees and customers, and involves both strategy (what an business intends to do) as well as an implementation.
Honeywell	Honeywell is a major American multinational corporation that produces electronic control systems and automation equipment. It is a major supplier of engineering services and avionics for NASA, Boeing and the United States Department of Defense.
Merger	Merger refers to the combination of two firms into a single firm.
Departmental-zation	The dividing of organizational functions into separate units is called departmentalization.
Facilitator	A facilitator is someone who skilfully helps a group of people understand their common objectives and plan to achieve them without personally taking any side of the argument.
Supervisor	A Supervisor is an employee of an organization with some of the powers and responsibilities of management, occupying a role between true manager and a regular employee. A Supervisor position is typically the first step towards being promoted into a management role.
Ford Motor Company	Ford Motor Company introduced methods for large-scale manufacturing of cars, and large-scale management of an industrial workforce, especially elaborately engineered manufacturing

	sequences typified by the moving assembly lines. Henry Ford's combination of highly efficient factories, highly paid workers, and low prices revolutionized manufacturing and came to be known around the world as Fordism by 1914.
Ford	Ford is an American company that manufactures and sells automobiles worldwide. Ford introduced methods for large-scale manufacturing of cars, and large-scale management of an industrial workforce, especially elaborately engineered manufacturing sequences typified by the moving assembly lines.
Market share	That fraction of an industry's output accounted for by an individual firm or group of firms is called market share.
Recession	A significant decline in economic activity. In the U.S., recession is approximately defined as two successive quarters of falling GDP, as judged by NBER.
Inflation	An increase in the overall price level of an economy, usually as measured by the CPI or by the implicit price deflator is called inflation.
Economy	The income, expenditures, and resources that affect the cost of running a business and household are called an economy.
Due process	Due process of law is a legal concept that ensures the government will respect all of a person's legal rights instead of just some or most of those legal rights when the government deprives a person of life, liberty, or property.
Inputs	The inputs used by a firm or an economy are the labor, raw materials, electricity and other resources it uses to produce its outputs.
Organization structure	The system of task, reporting, and authority relationships within which the organization does its work is referred to as the organization structure.
Role ambiguity	Uncertainty of specifications for a role is role ambiguity. This occurs when duties for a role are not specified. The resolution to role ambiguity may lie in precise role descriptions (job descriptions) or a simplification of the tasks.
Role conflict	Role conflict is a special form of social conflict that takes place when one is forced to take on two different and incompatible roles at the same time.
Intervention	Intervention refers to an activity in which a government buys or sells its currency in the foreign exchange market in order to affect its currency's exchange rate.
Leadership grid	A leadership grid evaluates leadership behavior along two dimensions, concern for production and concern for people, and suggests that effective leadership styles include high levels of both behaviors.
Decision tree	In decision theory, a decision tree is a graph of decisions and their possible consequences, (including resource costs and risks) used to create a plan to reach a goal.
Balance	In banking and accountancy, the outstanding balance is the amount of money owned, (or due), that remains in a deposit account (or a loan account) at a given date, after all past remittances, payments and withdrawal have been accounted for. It can be positive (then, in the balance sheet of a firm, it is an asset) or negative (a liability).
Stress management	An active approach to deal with stress that is influencing behavior is stress management.
Case study	A case study is a particular method of qualitative research. Rather than using large samples and following a rigid protocol to examine a limited number of variables, case study methods involve an in-depth, longitudinal examination of a single instance or event: a case. They provide a systematic way of looking at events, collecting data, analyzing information, and reporting the results.

Go to **Cram101.com** for the Practice Tests for this Chapter.

Property	Assets defined in the broadest legal sense. Property includes the unrealized receivables of a cash basis taxpayer, but not services rendered.
Management development	The process of training and educating employees to become good managers and then monitoring the progress of their managerial skills over time is management development.
Contingency planning	The process of preparing alternative courses of action that may be used if the primary plans do not achieve the objectives of the organization is called contingency planning.
Sun Microsystems	Sun Microsystems is most well known for its Unix systems, which have a reputation for system stability and a consistent design philosophy.
Charles Schwab	Charles Schwab is the world's second-largest discount broker. Besides discount brokerage, the firm offers mutual funds, annuities, bond trading, and now mortgages through its Charles Schwab Bank.
Pfizer	Pfizer is the world's largest pharmaceutical company based in New York City. It produces the number-one selling drug Lipitor (atorvastatin, used to lower blood cholesterol).
Strike	The withholding of labor services by an organized group of workers is referred to as a strike.
Team building	A term that describes the process of identifying roles for team members and helping the team members succeed in their roles is called team building.
Utility	Utility refers to the want-satisfying power of a good or service; the satisfaction or pleasure a consumer obtains from the consumption of a good or service.
Foundation	A Foundation is a type of philanthropic organization set up by either individuals or institutions as a legal entity (either as a corporation or trust) with the purpose of distributing grants to support causes in line with the goals of the foundation.
Quality management	Quality management is a method for ensuring that all the activities necessary to design, develop and implement a product or service are effective and efficient with respect to the system and its performance.
Total quality management	The broad set of management and control processes designed to focus an entire organization and all of its employees on providing products or services that do the best possible job of satisfying the customer is called total quality management.
Instrument	Instrument refers to an economic variable that is controlled by policy makers and can be used to influence other variables, called targets. Examples are monetary and fiscal policies used to achieve external and internal balance.
Action plan	Action plan refers to a written document that includes the steps the trainee and manager will take to ensure that training transfers to the job.
Distribution	Distribution in economics, the manner in which total output and income is distributed among individuals or factors.
Raw material	Raw material refers to a good that has not been transformed by production; a primary product.
Control system	A control system is a device or set of devices that manage the behavior of other devices. Some devices or systems are not controllable. A control system is an interconnection of components connected or related in such a manner as to command, direct, or regulate itself or another system.
Resistance to change	Resistance to change refers to an attitude or behavior that shows unwillingness to make or support a change.
Resource allocation	Resource allocation refers to the manner in which an economy distributes its resources among the potential uses so as to produce a particular set of final goods.

Overdetermination	Overdetermination occurs because numerous organizational systems are in place to ensure that employees and systems behave as expected to maintain stability.
Electronic Data Systems	Electronic Data Systems is a global information technology consulting company that defined the outsourcing business when it was established in 1962 by Ross Perot.
Corporation	A legal entity chartered by a state or the Federal government that is distinct and separate from the individuals who own it is a corporation. This separation gives the corporation unique powers which other legal entities lack.
General Motors	General Motors is the world's largest automaker. Founded in 1908, today it employs about 327,000 people around the world. With global headquarters in Detroit, it manufactures its cars and trucks in 33 countries.
Revenue	Revenue is a U.S. business term for the amount of money that a company receives from its activities, mostly from sales of products and/or services to customers.
Profit	Profit refers to the return to the resource entrepreneurial ability; total revenue minus total cost.
Corporate culture	The whole collection of beliefs, values, and behaviors of a firm that send messages to those within and outside the company about how business is done is the corporate culture.
Information system	An information system is a system whether automated or manual, that comprises people, machines, and/or methods organized to collect, process, transmit, and disseminate data that represent user information.
Specialist	A specialist is a trader who makes a market in one or several stocks and holds the limit order book for those stocks.
Security	Security refers to a claim on the borrower future income that is sold by the borrower to the lender. A security is a type of transferable interest representing financial value.
Selective attention	A perceptual process in which consumers choose to attend to some stimuli and not others is referred to as selective attention.
Coalition	An informal alliance among managers who support a specific goal is called coalition.
Complexity	The technical sophistication of the product and hence the amount of understanding required to use it is referred to as complexity. It is the opposite of simplicity.
Domestic	From or in one's own country. A domestic producer is one that produces inside the home country. A domestic price is the price inside the home country. Opposite of 'foreign' or 'world.'.
Environmental complexity	The number of environmental components that impinge on organizational decision-making is called environmental complexity.
Shell	One of the original Seven Sisters, Royal Dutch/Shell is the world's third-largest oil company by revenue, and a major player in the petrochemical industry and the solar energy business. Shell has six core businesses: Exploration and Production, Gas and Power, Downstream, Chemicals, Renewables, and Trading/Shipping, and operates in more than 140 countries.
Complaint	The pleading in a civil case in which the plaintiff states his claim and requests relief is called complaint. In the common law, it is a formal legal document that sets out the basic facts and legal reasons that the filing party (the plaintiffs) believes are sufficient to support a claim against another person, persons, entity or entities (the defendants) that entitles the plaintiff(s) to a remedy (either money damages or injunctive relief).
Gap	In December of 1995, Gap became the first major North American retailer to accept independent monitoring of the working conditions in a contract factory producing its garments. Gap is the

largest specialty retailer in the United States.

Channel	Channel, in communications (sometimes called communications channel), refers to the medium used to convey information from a sender (or transmitter) to a receiver.
Trend	Trend refers to the long-term movement of an economic variable, such as its average rate of increase or decrease over enough years to encompass several business cycles.
Warrant	A warrant is a security that entitles the holder to buy or sell a certain additional quantity of an underlying security at an agreed-upon price, at the holder's discretion.
Investment	Investment refers to spending for the production and accumulation of capital and additions to inventories. In a financial sense, buying an asset with the expectation of making a return.
Organizational Behavior	The study of human behavior in organizational settings, the interface between human behavior and the organization, and the organization itself is called organizational behavior.
Conflict of interest	A conflict that occurs when a corporate officer or director enters into a transaction with the corporation in which he or she has a personal interest is a conflict of interest.
Interest	In finance and economics, interest is the price paid by a borrower for the use of a lender's money. In other words, interest is the amount of paid to "rent" money for a period of time.
Broker	In commerce, a broker is a party that mediates between a buyer and a seller. A broker who also acts as a seller or as a buyer becomes a principal party to the deal.
Bear market	Bear market refers to a falling or lethargic stock market.
Cost structure	The relative proportion of an organization's fixed, variable, and mixed costs is referred to as cost structure.
Stock market	An organized marketplace in which common stocks are traded. In the United States, the largest stock market is the New York Stock Exchange, on which are traded the stocks of the largest U.S. companies.
Stock	In financial terminology, stock is the capital raized by a corporation, through the issuance and sale of shares.
Customer service	The ability of logistics management to satisfy users in terms of time, dependability, communication, and convenience is called the customer service.
Discount	The difference between the face value of a bond and its selling price, when a bond is sold for less than its face value it's referred to as a discount.
Appeal	Appeal refers to the act of asking an appellate court to overturn a decision after the trial court's final judgment has been entered.
Chief information officer	The chief information officer is a job title for the head of information technology group within an organization. They often report to the chief executive officer or chief financial officer.
Enron	Enron Corportaion's global reputation was undermined by persistent rumours of bribery and political pressure to secure contracts in Central America, South America, Africa, and the Philippines. Especially controversial was its $3 billion contract with the Maharashtra State Electricity Board in India, where it is alleged that Enron officials used political connections within the Clinton and Bush administrations to exert pressure on the board.
Accounting	A system that collects and processes financial information about an organization and reports that information to decision makers is referred to as accounting.
Decentralized organization	An organization in which decision making is spread throughout the organization, rather than confined to a small group of executives is a decentralized organization.

Creative destruction	The hypothesis that the creation of new products and production methods simultaneously destroys the market power of existing monopolies is referred to as creative destruction.
Board of directors	The group of individuals elected by the stockholders of a corporation to oversee its operations is a board of directors.
Analyst	Analyst refers to a person or tool with a primary function of information analysis, generally with a more limited, practical and short term set of goals than a researcher.
Bankruptcy	Bankruptcy is a legally declared inability or impairment of ability of an individual or organization to pay their creditors.
Annual report	An annual report is prepared by corporate management that presents financial information including financial statements, footnotes, and the management discussion and analysis.
Economic system	Economic system refers to a particular set of institutional arrangements and a coordinating mechanism for solving the economizing problem; a method of organizing an economy, of which the market system and the command system are the two general types.
Code of ethics	A formal statement of ethical principles and rules of conduct is a code of ethics. Some may have the force of law; these are often promulgated by the (quasi-)governmental agency responsible for licensing a profession. Violations of these codes may be subject to administrative (e.g., loss of license), civil or penal remedies.
EBay	eBay manages an online auction and shopping website, where people buy and sell goods and services worldwide.
Shares	Shares refer to an equity security, representing a shareholder's ownership of a corporation. Shares are one of a finite number of equal portions in the capital of a company, entitling the owner to a proportion of distributed, non-reinvested profits known as dividends and to a portion of the value of the company in case of liquidation.
Fraud	Tax fraud falls into two categories: civil and criminal. Under civil fraud, the IRS may impose as a penalty of an amount equal to as much as 75 percent of the underpayment.
Partnership	In the common law, a partnership is a type of business entity in which partners share with each other the profits or losses of the business undertaking in which they have all invested.
Credit	Credit refers to a recording as positive in the balance of payments, any transaction that gives rise to a payment into the country, such as an export, the sale of an asset, or borrowing from abroad.
Merrill Lynch	Merrill Lynch through its subsidiaries and affiliates, provides capital markets services, investment banking and advisory services, wealth management, asset management, insurance, banking and related products and services on a global basis. It is best known for its Global Private Client services and its strong sales force.
Xerox	Xerox was founded in 1906 as "The Haloid Company" manufacturing photographic paper and equipment. The company came to prominence in 1959 with the introduction of the first plain paper photocopier using the process of xerography (electrophotography) developed by Chester Carlson, the Xerox 914.
Audit	An examination of the financial reports to ensure that they represent what they claim and conform with generally accepted accounting principles is referred to as audit.
Federal Reserve	The Federal Reserve System was created via the Federal Reserve Act of December 23rd, 1913. All national banks were required to join the system and other banks could join. The Reserve Banks opened for business on November 16th, 1914. Federal Reserve Notes were created as part of the legislation, to provide an elastic supply of currency.
Deregulation	The lessening or complete removal of government regulations on an industry, especially

concerning the price that firms are allowed to charge and leaving price to be determined by market forces a deregulation.

Statute	A statute is a formal, written law of a country or state, written and enacted by its legislative authority, perhaps to then be ratified by the highest executive in the government, and finally published.
Supply	Supply is the aggregate amount of any material good that can be called into being at a certain price point; it comprises one half of the equation of supply and demand. In classical economic theory, a curve representing supply is one of the factors that produce price.
Stock option	A stock option is a specific type of option that uses the stock itself as an underlying instrument to determine the option's pay-off and therefore its value.
Budget	Budget refers to an account, usually for a year, of the planned expenditures and the expected receipts of an entity. For a government, the receipts are tax revenues.
Option	A contract that gives the purchaser the option to buy or sell the underlying financial instrument at a specified price, called the exercise price or strike price, within a specific period of time.
Chief financial officer	Chief financial officer refers to executive responsible for overseeing the financial operations of an organization.
Restatement	Restatement refers to collections of legal rules produced by the American Law Institute, covering certain subject matter areas. Although restatements are often persuasive to courts, they are not legally binding unless adopted by the highest court of a particular state.
Fund	Independent accounting entity with a self-balancing set of accounts segregated for the purposes of carrying on specific activities is referred to as a fund.
Capital gain	Capital gain refers to the gain in value that the owner of an asset experiences when the price of the asset rises, including when the currency in which the asset is denominated appreciates.
Portfolio	In finance, a portfolio is a collection of investments held by an institution or a private individual. Holding but not always a portfolio is part of an investment and risk-limiting strategy called diversification. By owning several assets, certain types of risk (in particular specific risk) can be reduced.
Capital	Capital generally refers to financial wealth, especially that used to start or maintain a business. In classical economics, capital is one of four factors of production, the others being land and labor and entrepreneurship.
Gain	In finance, gain is a profit or an increase in value of an investment such as a stock or bond. Gain is calculated by fair market value or the proceeds from the sale of the investment minus the sum of the purchase price and all costs associated with it.
Division of labor	Division of labor is generally speaking the specialization of cooperative labor in specific, circumscribed tasks and roles, intended to increase efficiency of output.
Cultural values	The values that employees need to have and act on for the organization to act on the strategic values are called cultural values.
Policy	Similar to a script in that a policy can be a less than completely rational decision-making method. Involves the use of a pre-existing set of decision steps for any problem that presents itself.

Go to **Cram101.com** for the Practice Tests for this Chapter.

Printed in the United Kingdom
by Lightning Source UK Ltd.
127503UK00001B/5/A